Virtue in Dialogue

Princeton Theological Monograph Series

K. C. Hanson, Charles M. Collier, D. Christopher Spinks,
and Robin Parry, Series Editors

Recent volumes in the series:

Koo Dong Yun
*The Holy Spirit and Ch'i (Qi):
A Chiological Approach to Pneumatology*

Stanley S. MacLean
*Resurrection, Apocalypse, and the Kingdom of Christ:
The Eschatology of Thomas F. Torrance*

Brian Neil Peterson
*Ezekiel in Context: Ezekiel's Message Understood in Its Historical
Setting of Covenant Curses and Ancient Near
Eastern Mythological Motifs*

Amy E. Richter
Enoch and the Gospel of Matthew

Maeve Louise Heaney
Music as Theology: What Music Says about the Word

Eric M. Vail
Creation and Chaos Talk: Charting a Way Forward

David L. Reinhart
*Prayer as Memory: Toward the Comparative Study of Prayer
as Apocalyptic Language and Thought*

Peter D. Neumann
Pentecostal Experience: An Ecumenical Encounter

Ashish J. Naidu
*Transformed in Christ:
Christology and the Christian Life in John Chrysostom*

Virtue in Dialogue

Belief, Religious Diversity, and Women's Interreligious Encounter

MARA BRECHT

☙PICKWICK *Publications* • Eugene, Oregon

VIRTUE IN DIALOGUE
Belief, Religious Diversity, and Women's Interreligious Encounter

Princeton Theological Monograph Series 193

Copyright © 2014 Mara Brecht. All rights reserved. Except for brief quotations in critical publications or reviews, no part of this book may be reproduced in any manner without prior written permission from the publisher. Write: Permissions, Wipf and Stock Publishers, 199 W. 8th Ave., Suite 3, Eugene, OR 97401.

Pickwick Publications
An Imprint of Wipf and Stock Publishers
199 W. 8th Ave., Suite 3
Eugene, OR 97401

www.wipfandstock.com

ISBN 13: 978-1-62032-391-5

Cataloguing-in-Publication data:

Brecht, Mara.

    Virtue in dialogue : belief, religious diversity, and women's interreligious encounter / Mara Brecht ; foreword by Terrence W. Tilley.

    xxii + 268 pp. ; 23 cm. Includes bibliographical references and index.

    Princeton Theological Monograph Series 193

    ISBN 13: 978-1-62032-391-5

    1. Women and Religion. 2. Dialogue—Religious aspects. 3. Religious pluralism. 4. Knowledge, Theory of (Religion). 5. Virtues. I. Tilley, Terrence W. II. Title. III. Series.

BL458 B74 2014

Manufactured in the U.S.A.

For my parents

Contents

Foreword ix
Acknowledgments xiii
Introduction xv

1. Theological "Problems" of Religious Diversity: Shifting from Soteriology to Epistemology   1

2. Epistemological Debates: Past and Present   35

3. "Evoking the Luminous" in Dialogue: A Case Study of a Women's Interreligious Dialogue Group   61

4. Alternative Contemporary Epistemological Models   89

5. Virtues and Virtuous Agents: Resources from the Aristotelian Tradition of Virtue Theory   133

6. The Virtues in Practice and *Prima Facie* Justification   155

7. *Ultima Facie* Justification and Participation through Practice   180

8. Christian Views of Interreligious Dialogue and Forms of Transformation   214

Bibliography 249

Index 263

Foreword

IN THIS IMPORTANT ARGUMENT FOR A NEW WAY OF DOING RELIGIOUS epistemology, Mara Brecht ranges widely and deeply to make her case.

The presenting problem is that a number of contemporary philosophers argue, in effect, that the fact that other good and smart people that I know well do hold fundamental religious beliefs that are opposed to mine ought to undermine my confidence or certainty about my religious beliefs. This position has some initial plausibility. If two good and smart economists disagree about how to fix the economy during a recession, after they have explored and understood each other's theory and recommendations, a certain level of epistemic humility seems in order. Of course, that does not prohibit strong advocacy in the public square. Yet all those in this sort of situation know—or should know—that they are liable to "I told you so" retorts should their views be implemented and fail.

What Brecht shows is that this initial plausibility is misleading. She begins with two important analytical chapters. The first analyzes theories of religious diversity. She shows that initial concerns about whether the "religious other" can be saved have given way to concerns about the disagreements between members of different religious traditions. The discourse has shifted from salvation to religious knowledge. Epistemology has taken center stage. The second chapter sketches the development of epistemology, especially religious epistemology. She shows how recent and contemporary theories have moved away from universal deontological criteria, such as William Clifford's, "It is wrong always, everywhere, and for anyone, to believe anything on insufficient evidence." Clifford's criterion would certainly rule out any sort of warranted religious belief since sufficient evidence for the existence of God or of no God cannot be found. Contemporary theories have moved to a "best practice" approach, a "naturalized" epistemology that looks at what people do when they know. But when the naturalized epistemologists turn to religious belief, they fail to analyze religious practice, but apply norms from science and common sense—and religious faith is neither of these.

Foreword

What is called for is an examination of the epistemic practices of religious people challenged by religious diversity. And Brecht delivers. She analyzes the practices of an intentionally religiously diverse group of women in Philadelphia who gathered—and as of this writing still gather—after 9/11 to sort out their understandings of others' diverse faiths. Finally, a religious epistemologist looks at religious people who continue to believe even when they have internalized the reality of religious diversity through intimate friendships.

To account for what her on-the-ground research has shown, Brecht then turns to contemporary forms of religious epistemology. She finds "reliabilist" epistemologies like Plantinga's interesting, but unable to account for reasonable religious belief formation in the context of real diversity. She then constructs—borrowing ideas from William P. Alston and Linda Zagzebski—a virtue epistemology of religious belief. This argument brings her into dialogue with the proponents of virtue epistemology from Aristotle to the present. She shows how the counter-arguments proffered by the critics of modern virtue epistemology do not undermine her "virtuous doxastic [belief-forming] practice" approach, either with regard to belief formation or justification.

Rather than leaving her theory in the abstract realm, she argues for four cardinal virtues and some necessary "meta-level" dispositions that are required for a virtue epistemology of religious belief in the context of diversity—as exemplified by the group she studied for years.

But Brecht is not merely a philosopher, but a philosophical theologian. Hence, her final chapter answers the "so what" question that epistemological theorists all too often leave unanswered. Using encouraging statements from Catholic and Protestant authorities about interreligious dialogue, Brecht finds that these statements are perplexing. Why encourage dialogue if awareness of diversity through interreligious dialogue weakens or should weaken faith, as a number of epistemologists have argued? This final chapter integrates her research with the Philadelphia women's group to show how dialogue can effect transformation in people—transformation which does not mean abandoning one's religious claims, but seeing them in a new light. Brecht finds three patterns of transformation: a reaffirmation of positive traditional beliefs without negativity or naivete, a form of hybridity in belief (and Christians have often "borrowed" from other traditions), and the possibility of conversion.

Whichever path a participant in interreligious interactions takes, to do so authentically requires the exercise of the virtues expounded in

Foreword

earlier chapters. Her theory, not those that rely on universal criteria for reasonableness and never analyze the formation and reformation of specifically religious beliefs, can account for the churches continuing to support engagement with religious others because her theory shows how diverse believers can and have interacted virtuously and engaged in dialogue that has strengthened and deepened their faiths.

In an era when monographs are narrowly specialized studies of interest to few, this book is both wide-ranging, subtle and clear—and is of real interest to both epistemologists and theologians struggling with problems of religious belief in the context of religious diversity.

Terrence W. Tilley
Avery Cardinal Dulles, SJ, Professor of Catholic Theology
Fordham University

Acknowledgments

THE SCHOLARS AND THEOLOGICAL MENTORS TO WHOM I AM INDEBTED for this book should be clear from the book's contents. I want to take this opportunity to thank another group of people who acted as my theological guides on this project: the members of the Philadelphia women's interreligious dialogue group. I am grateful to each of them for welcoming me into their homes and dialogue community. Their willingness to take time to talk with me individually, their openness in inviting me into the communal conversation, and their interest in my ideas were generous and heartening. It was because of them that I was able to gain traction in places where my wheels had long been turning, and I deeply appreciate the reflections and thoughts they shared with me.

Introduction

RELIGIOUS DIVERSITY IS A LIVED REALITY AND AN EPISTEMOLOGICAL problem. I believe myself to be a thoughtful, honest, and sincere person. I also believe that the family who raised me is full of thoughtful, honest, and sincere people. Each night at dinner we bowed our heads, folded our hands, and prayed a blessing over our food. Every Sunday, we worshipped, prayed, and celebrated together. These are the ways of professing our beliefs. There are innumerable other thoughtful, honest, and sincere persons in the world. They have been raised in families full of thoughtful, honest, and sincere persons just like I have. They say different words of blessing over their evening meals, gather together to worship, pray, and celebrate, and profess their beliefs in different ways. The fact that there are multiple thoughtful, honest, and sincere people who engage in rather different religious practices and hold rather different sets of beliefs raises an important epistemological problem. If people think their beliefs are true and there are multiple, conflicting beliefs, then what does this mean for the justification of their beliefs?

Can we continue to hold to our beliefs as true while having full awareness that others also hold to their different beliefs as true? Religious diversity reveals one key case of epistemic disagreement. Theologians explore religious diversity with Christological, pneumatological, soteriological, and theological-anthropological questions in view. As a discipline, theology has tended to ignore the *epistemological* questions raised by religious diversity. That fact, combined with the existentially and epistemically troubling situation described above, is the impetus for this book. The broad goal of my project is to approach religious diversity as a theologian who foregrounds epistemological questions.

More specifically, this book examines what happens to religious belief as a result of the encounter with the religious other. That is, given one's awareness of other thoughtful, honest, and sincere people and their different religious beliefs, what happens to one's religious beliefs? In what ways are one's beliefs challenged, defeated, or reshaped? Epistemologists examining religious belief in the context of diversity see the encounter with

Introduction

the religious other as a situation that *should* lead believers to doubt their beliefs. However, these epistemological theories are formulated at abstract levels that do not attend carefully enough to the routine experiences of interreligious encounter in practice—experiences that suggest believers come to be strengthened in their beliefs rather than to doubt them.

Interreligious dialogue is the paradigmatic context for the encounter with the religious diversity. That is, participants in interreligious dialogue meet religious others and confront head on different religious beliefs in that context. For this reason, I discuss the epistemological significance of religious diversity at large through the frame of interreligious dialogue. The first two chapters include literature reviews of theologies of religious diversity and religious epistemologies, respectively, so as to situate my discussion within these areas of scholarly inquiry.

My exploration of the epistemological significance of interreligious dialogue works both from the "top-down" and from the "bottom-up." The "top-down" component of my discussion reviews theological and epistemological scholarship on religious diversity to uncover theoretical perspectives on what happens to religious belief given the encounter with religious others. The "bottom-up" component of my discussion is based on a research project to interview participants of a women's interreligious dialogue group. Over the course of two years, I interviewed and talked with members of an interreligious dialogue group in greater Philadelphia about their thoughts on interreligious dialogue. I recorded and transcribed these conversations and cite them throughout the book. (On mutual agreement, I cite my transcriptions of these interviews, but keep the identities of the participants anonymous.)

The "top-down" and "bottom-up" explorations yield competing sets of claims. Theoreticians, and particularly epistemologists, convey the sense that awareness of religious diversity should weaken religious belief. Participants in dialogue, on the other hand, make the case that awareness of religious diversity strengthens their religious beliefs. Because my scholarship is critically informed by feminist theory, I find the evidence of the "bottom-up" set of claims compelling. A guiding principle of feminist theory is to take the real, gritty experiences of people into account when developing abstract theories. Without close attention to the practices and beliefs of ordinary religious people, any discussion about how religious beliefs are formed and held in an interreligious setting would be uninformed by evidence.

Introduction

Given the competing claims of the "top-down" and "bottom-up" approaches, my conviction is that the "top-down" theories have erased the voices of everyday religious believers that would otherwise shed light on how we can think about religious belief theoretically. My principal methodological question is: what can the women's experiences in an interreligious dialogue community tell me, as a theorist, about the shaping of religious beliefs in an interreligious context? The non-theoretical insights which percolate up from conversations with the women from Philadelphia are both the primary resource for the epistemological model I develop and the evidence that warrants or fails to warrant theoretical, epistemological models (including my own).

Project Overview

The book begins by describing the "lay of the land" of Christian theological approaches to religious diversity. Using the traditional tripartite categories of exclusivist, inclusivist, and pluralist, I first introduce the leading voices and major themes within each of these approaches. The driving question for these traditional approaches, I argue, is soteriological and eschatological in nature: in the end, to whom is salvation extended? I next turn to a set of theologians who have begun to inquire into the significance of religious diversity from a somewhat different angle. Paul Griffiths, Harold Netland, and Gavin D'Costa intersect the concern for soteriology with epistemological questions. They see religious diversity as presenting an epistemic quandary for Christian theology and pay attention to the epistemological status of diverse religious beliefs.

Believers assume the religious beliefs they hold are true, even though they may not be able to find justification or warrant for their beliefs. When diverse religious believers make diverse claims, a problem for their beliefs as claims to truth arises. By approaching religious diversity from this perspective, Griffiths, Netland, and D'Costa re-inscribe the boundaries of the Christian theological debate on religious pluralism. While they raise important epistemological *questions* about religious diversity, they do not posit epistemological solutions. At the conclusion of the chapter, I propose to examine religious diversity as an epistemological issue that begins "on the ground"—from the position of religious believers—and works toward constructing an epistemological model that makes sense of religious belief in the context of diversity.

Introduction

In the next chapter, I explore two critical debates in the history of epistemology as well as discussions about religious diversity in contemporary epistemology. Reviewing the historical debates, between W. K. Clifford and William James in the second half of the nineteenth century and among Anthony Flew, R. M. Hare, and Basil Mitchell in the mid-twentieth century, allows me to introduce and explain key epistemological concepts. These concepts concern the conditions for belief formation, the criteria for belief justification, and the extent to which believers grasp the grounds for their beliefs. These concepts are also foundational for future developments in epistemology.

Contemporary epistemologists Robert McKim and Richard Feldman view religious diversity as an instance of epistemic disagreement. Given epistemic conflict generated by religious diversity, these contemporary epistemologists argue that believers must either suspend or hold their religious beliefs tentatively. I invoke the concepts drawn out of the historical debates to characterize the nature of McKim and Feldman's respective proposals. I refute their proposals on the grounds that they mistakenly abstract religious belief from religious practice and do not attend to actual accounts of what happens to a person's belief given her awareness of diversity. The theoretical "lessons" of chapter 2 are that an adequate epistemological model must conceptually hold belief and practice together and must take seriously actual accounts of religious belief in the situation of diversity as evidence for constructing epistemological models.

Accounts of what happens to religious belief in the context of interreligious dialogue occupy the majority of chapter 3. I first briefly describe the origins and history of the Philadelphia women's interreligious dialogue group with which I conducted this research. I then move to share the women's comments on their experiences of the interreligious dialogue group and their reflections on the role it has played in their religious lives. In recounting these comments and reflections, I use resources from feminist epistemology to build my own theoretical ideas around their words so as to point out the epistemological significance of interreligious dialogue.

The most epistemologically salient ideas suggested by their experiences are that, through listening to the stories of each other, the women learn new ways of conceiving religious beliefs; that there is a deep interplay between beliefs and practices; and that interreligious dialogue creates a unique epistemic community that complements—rather than stands in competition with—the home religious communities of the participants. The voices of the women from Philadelphia provide the substance for my

Introduction

challenge to the assumptions of McKim and Feldman and compel me to find alternative resources in contemporary epistemology for exploring the epistemological significance of interreligious dialogue.

The fourth chapter describes and analyzes alternative contemporary epistemological models through the work of Alvin Plantinga, William Alston, and Linda Zagzebski. Plantinga and Alston develop religious epistemologies and offer some reflections on the question of religious diversity. Zagzebski constructs a general epistemological theory and, although she does not comment on religious diversity, she briefly discusses religious beliefs. As a whole, their theories incorporate a broader range of factors for belief formation and justification, including the processes and methods involved in cognition, than do the theories of McKim or Feldman, which focus primarily on evidential standards for belief. In the end, Plantinga's theory promotes a circular, autonomous theory of belief formation and standard for justification that cannot hold up in the context of diversity. Alston identifies criteria for reliable practices by which beliefs are formed and justified and Zagzebski anchors her understanding of belief formation and justification in the intellectual character of agents. Taken together, Alston and Zagzebski's projects supply resources for constructing an epistemological theory that is adequate to the situation of religious diversity and that I construct in this book. I call this theory the virtuous doxastic practice epistemological model.

The goal of the fifth and sixth chapters is to add texture and depth to the framework for the Alstonion-Zagzebskian hybrid, virtuous doxastic practice epistemological model, which holds that people form and justify beliefs through the exercise of intellectual virtues that are socially instilled and regulated, suggested at the conclusion of chapter 4. Questions of how people develop their intellectual character and how people learn the practices by which they form beliefs guide these two chapters. In chapter 5, I focus on theoretical resources from the Aristotelian tradition of virtue theory for making sense of intellectual virtue. I posit that intellectual virtues are the excellences of human persons that provide us with orientation for good epistemic functioning in the world. Exercising epistemic virtues leads both to good or justified beliefs as well as to the flourishing of our epistemic communities.

We acquire virtues in the context of communities and through habituation. Chapter 6 focuses on this aspect of the virtuous doxastic practices model. I combine Alasdair MacIntyre's theory of practice with the Alstonian notion of doxastic practice to explain the interdependence

Introduction

between agent and community in virtuous development and the exercise of virtue, and, thereby, belief formation and justification. In this chapter, I also identify four cardinal epistemic virtues (steadfastness, judiciousness, prudence, and creativity) and two "meta-level" epistemic virtues (integrity and wisdom) and use the literature of American Jewish author Chaim Potok to provide examples of these virtues in (fictive) practice. By the conclusion of this pair of chapters, I apply the virtuous doxastic practice model to religious beliefs to demonstrate how religious beliefs are formed and justified *within* religious traditions.

If beliefs are formed and justified by being the outcome of virtuous doxastic practices, which are learned in the context of specific religious communities (the position argued for in chapters 5 and 6), it may look as though the VDP theory promotes relativism. Chapter 7 shifts to consider the way religious beliefs are formed and justified *across* religious traditions, so as to rebut the charge of relativism. The position I take in this chapter is that believers may gain a higher level of justification for their beliefs precisely in the situation of interreligious dialogue, rather than in spite of it. Philosophical-ethical comparative theorists Lee Yearley and comparative theologian Francis X. Clooney along with philosopher Jürgen Habermas and theologian James Wm. McClendon provide resources for developing an account of how interreligious dialogue can be understood as the setting where both diverse religious beliefs and diverse virtuous doxastic practices are productively compared and where the practice of participating in dialogical encounter forms a contextual standard of epistemological justification.

The final chapter examines the way interreligious dialogue is construed in mainstream Christian churches according to a central document from the Pontifical Council for Interreligious Dialogue (*Dialogue and Proclamation*) and various documents on interreligious dialogue from the World Council of Churches. Both the Roman Catholic Church and the World Council of Churches see interreligious dialogue as possibly transformative—and positively so—for Christians who engage in it. Beginning from this positive appraisal of dialogue, I explore three forms of transformation (the transformation of "returning home," the transformation of double religious belonging, and the transformation of conversion) and consider their epistemological and theological significance.

The first form of transformation—the transformation of "returning home"—is what the Christian church hopes for, and it is the form of transformation for which I draw out concrete theological and epistemological

Introduction

implications: through interreligious dialogue, Christians reform their religious beliefs, convictions, and attitudes and come to hold to the Christian tradition in a new way *because* interreligious dialogue offers a level of epistemological justification for religious beliefs not available from within the Christian tradition alone. While the other forms of transformation—that of double religious belonging and conversion—are not explicitly rejected by the church in these documents, neither are they embraced. I explain the epistemological and theological significance of these forms of transformation by being in conversation with Perry Schmidt-Leukel's vision for transformation through integration and conclude that these others types of transformation may contribute also to the development of Christian belief practices, albeit in an unusual, "back door" type of way.

The contributions of the book are intended to be both theoretical and practical in nature and are addressed to both to theological and philosophical (especially religious epistemological) audiences. I call for recognizing the significance of the theological shift from soteriological to epistemological issues and, therefore, draw attention to the need to integrate religious epistemology more systematically into theological discourse on diversity. I establish the inadequacies of various epistemological positions regarding religious belief in the context of religious diversity and constructively build a new approach to religious epistemology that accepts the insights and overcomes the oversights of previous epistemological work. The distinctive proposal of the virtuous doxastic practices model is intended to be useful both to individual believers and religious traditions, and particularly Christians, for understanding how religious beliefs are formed and maintained in the context of religious diversity. I demonstrate how my approach not only fits with but also helps to resolve a potential problem in interreligious dialogue as advocated by the Roman Catholic Church and World Council of Churches.

There is also no evidence of any major projects or books to date that explore the epistemological significance of religious diversity through the frame of interreligious dialogue. This book makes a unique contribution by offering a distinctive proposal, useful for both individual believers and religious traditions, for understanding how religious belief formation and justification in our religiously diverse world. While theological discourse, up to this point, might realize the depth of the encounter with the religious other (this can be seen through theologian's attention to religious diversity), it has been unable to integrate the encounter with diversity into its epistemological framework.

Introduction

With a well-formulated epistemological theory in place, academic theological discourse on the significance of religious diversity can move forward beyond some of the impasses it currently faces. Theological discourse in the context of the Christian church can embrace interreligious dialogue as an important accompaniment to Christian formation and reconsider the role dialogue can play in the life of the Christian community. And, finally, those who find themselves—through dialogue—with a deep appreciation for the beliefs of religious others and, at the same time, a renewed strength in their own beliefs may be vindicated in this experience.

1

Theological "Problems" of Religious Diversity[1]
Shifting from Soteriology to Epistemology

THE STORY OF CHRISTIANS FACING RELIGIOUS DIVERSITY AS A CHAL-lenging issue for Christian faith has been recounted many times in many different ways. For some, Paul Knitter points out, the story of Christians wrestling with diversity shares its starting point with the Christian story itself. The New Testament gives witness to this, for example, in Acts: "There is no salvation through anyone else, nor is there any other name under heaven given to the human race by which we are saved" (4:12).[2] Gavin D'Costa posits a much later beginning to the story, arguing that religious plurality can only be properly understood as a Christian theological issue since the invention of "religion" by Cambridge Platonists in the sixteenth century. Prior to the sixteenth century, religions did not exist as we now think of them. D'Costa argues that the concept of "religion" became reified with the rise of the Western nation-state and thus can only be considered in light of this historical evolution.[3]

Jacques Dupuis tells another version of the story by beginning, most significantly, with St. Cyprian's third-century dictum *extra ecclesia nulla salus*, "outside of the Church there is no salvation."[4] Cyprian's pithy statement initiated a legacy of Christians dealing with diversity by adhering to a blanket assessment for all non-Christian salvation—it was a non-possibility.[5] Phillip Quinn claims that although Christians have never

---

1. Parts of this chapter first appeared as "What's the Use of Exclusivism?" *Theological Studies* 73:1 (March 2012).

2. Knitter, *Introducing Theologies of Religions*, 3.

3. D'Costa, *Christianity and the World Religions*, 57–58.

4. Dupuis, *Toward a Christian Theology of Religious Pluralism*, 87–88. See also Sullivan, *Salvation Outside the Church?*

5. Although Cyprian's statement initiated a particular legacy of exclusionary practices, Cyprian did not create his dictum for these purposes. As Francis Sullivan

been ignorant of religious diversity, it holds a special place in Christian theological thinking today given pluralistic democracies and an increase in sophisticated scholarship on multiple religious traditions.[6] What is significant for this book is not *where* this narrative begins or *how* it unfolds, but rather *what questions* underlie the ways theologians construct the storyline. What specific problems do they identify with religious pluralism? What answer or solution do they offer to that problem? In short, how do Christian theologians account for the fact of religious diversity?

This chapter engages three major points of discussion, which are organized into three corresponding sections. The first two sections trace the scope of the theological discussion on religious diversity and the third section sets up the constructive work I endeavor to do in the rest of the book. In the first section, I introduce the tripartite paradigm (exclusivist, inclusivist, pluralist) that is classically used to describe types of Christian theological responses to religious diversity. I provide a general sketch of each category and briefly summarize the theories of a few key theologians representing the exclusivist, inclusivist, and pluralist positions. These three ways of addressing diversity are "top-down" in approach. That is to say, they begin with *theological* questions—and, most significantly, questions about salvation—and analyze religious diversity from there. I will demonstrate that, as a result of this top-down approach and of a focus centered on the question of the final salvific efficacy (or lack thereof) of religions other than Christianity, theologians operating within the three classic categories both limit the force of their theological claims and distort the issue of religious diversity.

Second, I discuss the work of Paul Griffiths, Harold Netland, and Gavin D'Costa on religious diversity. These theologians are informed by principles from studies in philosophy of religion; they employ a "middle-down" approach by placing greater emphasis on religious belief and practice.[7] As a result, Griffiths, Netland, and D'Costa shift the emphasis of the

---

demonstrates in *Salvation Outside the Church?*, addressing religious diversity was not the real target of Cyprian's aim. Rather, Cyprian's statement was intended as a rhetorical device to sway Christians who left the church to return to it.

6. Quinn, "Towards Thinner Theologies," 145.

7. While definitely less "top-down" than the classic approaches, these approaches still do not warrant the label "bottom-up" (a term characteristically applied to liberation theology, for example, which takes as its methodological starting point the suffering of the communities in which it is grounded) in that they do not pull from actual "on-the-ground" accounts of religious belief and practice. However, because these approaches at least begin from hypothetical, generalized accounts of belief and practice, rather than abstract theological or philosophical questions, I assign them the distinctive label of "middle-down."

discussion and widen the possibilities for theological engagement with diverse religious traditions, particularly with their focus on religious believers' ways of knowing truth and religious beliefs as expressive of truth. While these efforts are exciting and often fruitful, there are a few important ways in which they falter. In general, although Griffiths, Netland, and D'Costa note key epistemological problems generated by religious diversity, they fail to develop adequate epistemological accounts that respond to these problems.

Finally, in the third section, I weave together positions offered by philosophically- or epistemologically-minded theologians to complement the positive achievements of Griffiths, Netland, and D'Costa, and, more specifically, to adumbrate a "stance" toward religious diversity that: (1) recognizes religions as being in the business of making claims to truth, and (2) regards religious believers as sincere and serious agents of religious beliefs.

Old Wine, Old Wineskins

There are three basic categories—exclusivist, inclusivist, and pluralist—into which theologies of religious pluralism are said to fit. Recently, the tripartite classification has been challenged as overly simplistic and, consequently, responsible for hindering the debate, but for the purposes of this chapter it will be useful for drawing out the main issues and stakes of the Christian theological discussion on religious pluralism.[8] A top-down approach and nearly myopic focus on the eschatological salvific significance of religious traditions are the "red threads" running through and connecting together each type of approach to religious diversity—exclusivism, inclusivism, and pluralism.

Exclusivism

Exclusivists typically begin and complete their inquiry into religious pluralism with reflection grounded in a methodologically literalist reading of

8. D'Costa is one example of a theologian who sees the classic exclusivism-inclusivism-pluralism paradigm as frustrating rather than advancing the conversation. D'Costa rejects the threefold typology on the grounds that it "fails to deliver on the question of the unbeliever in precise enough ways" and that "the terminology conceals the fact that all the different positions are exclusive in a very proper technical sense." He offers instead a sevenfold paradigm with which to classify responses to religious diversity (D'Costa, *Christianity and the World Religions*, 34–35).

the bible and "fundamentalist" (literalist) appropriation of the tradition, using Cyprian's dictum as a "proof text." While exclusivist theologians may assiduously study other religious traditions and engage with other religious people, they also always emphasize the uniqueness of the Christian message, the particularity of Jesus Christ, and the finality of God's offer of salvation through Jesus Christ revealed to us in the bible. Exclusivist theologians take the position that, as Knitter writes, "they are simply holding to the clear message of the New Testament" and that "one of the most evident and central messages [of the New Testament] is that Jesus is the means, the only means . . . that God has given to humans [for salvation]."[9] Christian belief and practice alone constitute the one, true religion.

Griffiths claims that exclusivism follows naturally from religious conviction.[10] If Christians *really* believe Jesus' message that salvation comes only through him and believes in the necessity of discipleship, then how could Christians also affirm the salvific significance of other religious traditions? Such an affirmation would be at least in tension with and at most incompatible with their central convictions.

While this characterization of exclusivism seems severe, it is not as though exclusivists, and particularly contemporary exclusivist scholars, are not aware of the contentiousness of their position. Netland, for example, states that exclusivism is ". . . especially difficult to maintain once [exclusivists] are exposed to the great religious figures in other traditions."[11] Exclusivists acknowledge the compelling power of other religious beliefs, practices, and leaders. Indeed, exclusivists may even be compelled *themselves* by such things. Yet, they maintain the position that salvation comes only in and through Christ because, as D'Costa writes, they believe the exclusivist position "best advance[s] the authenticity of the Christian tradition."[12] Thus, while exclusivists acknowledge the richness in other religious traditions and perhaps see their ethical values, cultural beauty, and even meaning for adherents, they cannot take these traditions seriously as having the truth to be soteriologically efficacious for the eschaton. Christianity is the only option for salvation; all those who are beyond the pale of Christianity are outside the possibility of salvation. Soteriological exclusivism has been the dominant position throughout almost all of

---

9. Knitter, *Introducing Theologies of Religions*, 27.
10. Griffiths, *Problems of Religious Diversity*, 154.
11. Netland, *Dissonant Voice and the Question of Truth*, 28.
12. D'Costa, *Christianity and the World Religions*, 32.

Christian history.[13] While particular exclusivist theologians emphasize different issues, they have not been noted in this brief sketch.[14]

13. Knitter, *Introducing Theologies of Religions*, 19.

14. Two twentieth- and twenty-first century theological positions, one characteristically Protestant (developed by Karl Barth), and the other Roman Catholic (put forward by the Congregation for the Doctrine of the Faith), represent exclusivist theological positions. These provide helpful illustrations of the general position. Paul Griffiths provides a useful description of Barth's Protestant version. (It is important to note that Barth's exclusivist position softened or was reformulated in his later writings on Christianity's relationship to the world religions.) For Barth, and the early Barth in particular, because human experience and knowledge is distorted by sin, the only proper way to begin any theological discourse is not with what humans do or say but with what God does and says. Revelation, which is God's word, must provide both the starting point for theology and the standard by which any evaluation of religions is done or by which any theological discourse is judged. Griffiths writes, "Christianity is not, for Barth, intrinsically superior to any other religion; instead it is on par with them as being opposed to and contradicted by revelation. But . . . Christianity [in Barth's view] has been chosen by God as the locus of revelation, the place in human history where God chooses (has chosen and will continue to choose) to reveal himself to us." Thus, because God reveals Godself in Christianity, and because that revelation entails the offer of salvation, it follows that Christianity is not "*a* true religion" but "*the* true religion" (Griffiths, *Problems of Religious Diversity*, 152–53). The Congregation for the Doctrine of Faith (CDF) offers the Catholic version of exclusivism in the document *Dominus Iesus* (*DI*). Drawing on the Second Vatican Council Dogmatic Constitution on Divine Revelation, *Dei Verbum*, the CDF states the following in *DI*: "The proper response to God's revelation is 'the obedience of faith (Rom. 16:26; cf. Rom. 1:5; 2 Cor. 10:5–6) by which man freely entrusts his entire self to God, offering 'the full submission of intellect and will to God who reveals' and freely assenting to the revelation given by him'" (*Declaration "Dominus Iesus"* [2000]). Jesus Christ offers revelation to us; the purpose of discipleship and assent to belief in Christ is salvation. In the CDF's view, Jesus Christ is the perfection of revelation and is also the condition for the possibility of human salvation. *DI* states, "Jesus perfected revelation by fulfilling it through his whole work of making himself present and manifesting himself: through his words and deeds, his signs and wonders, but especially through his death and glorious resurrection from the dead and finally with the sending of the Spirit, he completed and perfected revelation and confirmed it with divine testimony" (§5). *DI* stresses the role of Jesus Christ as the one, who, in his words and deeds, offers the definitive model for Christian behavior and who, in his death and resurrection, offers the possibility of our salvation: "The universal salvific will of the One and Triune God is offered and accomplished once for all in the mystery of the incarnation, death, and resurrection of the Son of God" (§14). Jesus Christ offers revelation to us; Christian assent thus entails both belief in and discipleship of Christ—that is, practically modeling one's life on the words and deeds of Jesus Christ. Although Christ manifests the truth and provides Christians with a discipleship model, God's salvific power, enacted through the Trinity, transcends and extends beyond Christianity. For example, *DI* states, "Whatever the Spirit brings about in the human hearts and in the history of peoples, in cultures and in religions, serves as a preparation for the Gospel and can

Inclusivism

Where "exclusivism" ordinarily indicates salvation comes exclusively through Jesus Christ, the moniker inclusivism points to the idea that non-Christians may be included in Christian salvation.[15] Inclusivist theologies are characterized by a fundamental tension: they stress the necessity of Christ while also affirming the possibility of salvation for those who are not Christian.[16] Inclusivist theologians achieve their goal in a variety of ways; one of the most famous inclusivist theories is put forth by Karl Rahner in his notion of the "anonymous Christian." Rahner's theory represents the kinds of theoretical moves inclusivists make in their effort to hold tension between the value of other traditions and the absolute offer of salvation in Christianity.

Rahner's anonymous Christian is any person who "has been taken hold of" by the grace of God's love.[17] This person could be an avowed Hindu or Muslim or Buddhist, yet as an anonymous Christian, Christian salvation is available to her. Rahner explains this seemingly paradoxical theory on the basis of two theological foundations. First, all grace—no matter what religious tradition it manifests itself in and at what time it makes itself present—is ultimately the grace God made available through Christ.[18] Second, Christ is not the *efficient* cause of salvation but rather the *final* cause, which is to say that Christ is most properly understood as being the goal of salvation rather than as the person or being who produces salvation. These two theological premises allow Rahner to explain how non-Christians "become" Christians through the Christian grace that is implicitly present in their home traditions and how salvation is available to them.[19]

---

only be understood in reference to Christ, the Word who took flesh by the power of the Spirit "so that as perfectly human he would save all human beings and sum up all things" (§12). In other words, while Christian discipleship is extremely important, the CDF concedes in *DI* that Christian discipleship is not *absolutely* necessary insofar as God's offer of salvation cannot be spatially or temporally constrained by an earthly instantiation. Although *DI* represents an exclusivist position, it is often inclusivist in tone or intention (Hill Fletcher, *Monopoly on Salvation?*, 54).

15. The "new" exclusivists (e.g., Gavin D'Costa, J. A. DiNoia, Harold Netland) are not soteriological exclusivists.

16. Netland, *Dissonant Voices*, 24.

17. Rahner, *Later Writings*, 394–95.

18. Rahner, *Foundations of Christian Faith*, 313–18.

19. In an interview about Karl Rahner's influence, Harvey Egan tells a story about

An inclusivist position like Rahner's intends to honor diverse religious traditions and encourage religious others in their home practices. And, at the same time, such an inclusivist position maintains the centrality and necessity of Christianity because salvation—though available through God—is only available as a real possibility through Christ. Inclusivism is typically criticized for not achieving its own goal; while inclusivists may think they maintain a healthy tension between respecting other religious traditions and upholding the necessity of Christ for salvation, in fact the tension actually collapses. Griffiths criticizes inclusivism on logical grounds; he argues that when inclusivism is pushed to its limits, it is in fact exclusivism.[20] Inclusivists ultimately privilege Christian salvation and this means that other religious traditions—no matter in what clothes they are dressed by inclusivists—will always be ancillary or inferior to Christianity. The subtly domineering attitude assumed—albeit inadvertently—by inclusivists leads Knitter to the conclusion that inclusivism can easily slip into imperialism.[21]

Pluralism

Pluralist theologians maintain the position that the great religious traditions are truly diverse (that is, they cannot be accommodated to "fit" into a Christian scheme as inclusivists suggest) and are equal (that is, Christianity does not have a privileged position as the exclusivists hold and inclusivists imply) as such. Pluralism is frequently expressed in colloquial metaphors such as "all religions are different paths up one mountain" or "all religions are many streams flowing into one river." The idea captured with such imagery is that religious traditions are individually distinctive and unique, but they also all contribute or are a part of something larger than themselves. S. Mark Heim summarizes the classic pluralist position: "Pluralists stress a common goal or process present in the various faiths

---

a conversation between Rahner and the Japanese Zen master Nishitani. Nishitani challenged Rahner's phrase "anonymous Christian" as imperious. He asked Rahner how he would feel to be called an "anonymous Buddhist." Rahner told Nishitani, in earnest, that he would be honored to bear the name. Rahner's comment conveys the sense that it is perfectly acceptable and even encouraged on theological grounds to find positive value in other religious traditions, fitting their beliefs and practices into one's own religious horizon, even while remaining situated in the Christian tradition (Egan, "Centenary of Catholic Theologian Karl Rahner").

20. Griffiths, *Problems of Religious Diversity*, 159.
21. Knitter, *Introducing Theologies of Religions*, 215.

beneath their specific accounts of their own ends."²² The uniqueness of Christian salvation that inclusivists and exclusivists are intent on preserving is, for pluralists, really just one culturally-instantiated permutation of a universally salvific process.

Whereas exclusivist theologians work to advance authentic Christianity (as D'Costa nicely phrases it) and inclusivists try to hold tension between the value of religious diversity and the uniqueness of Christianity, the pluralist tack typically involves appealing to philosophical principles to handle religious diversity. Wilfred Cantwell Smith and John Hick develop two of the most widely recognized and important pluralist position. Cantwell Smith begins with the presupposition that everything humans can know—particularly in the case of what humans can know about God—is necessarily partial.²³ The way a person knows, both religiously and in mundane matters, is never just objective, but rather always involves how she knows it *for* herself. Thus, according to Cantwell Smith, we cannot make sense of any religious proposition without considering how it is applied to the personal life of the believer.²⁴ Christians, then, do not believe in the doctrine of Christian salvation as an objective truth, but believe it rather according to how it is experienced in and applied to their lives. Because knowledge is deeply subjective²⁵ and is also always partial, Cantwell Smith posits a "unity of knowledge" that stands behind the various representations of it in diverse religious traditions.²⁶

Cantwell Smith's pluralist position is governed by the ontological assumption, D'Costa notes, that there are two levels of reality and two levels of truth corresponding to that reality: ordinary and transcendent.²⁷ Hick takes a similar position and appeals to Kant to illuminate his theory: there is one transcendent reality that is differently experienced by the followers of diverse religious traditions.²⁸ According to a Kantian epistemology of perception, there is a distinction between *noumenon*, the thing in itself

22. Heim, "Salvations," 342.
23. Smith, *Wilfred Cantwell Smith*, 19.
24. Netland, *Dissonant Voices*, 120.
25. Cantwell Smith recoils from the use of the word "subjective" because of its pejorative connotations (i.e., "subjective" is taken less seriously than "objective"). Netland explains that, for Smith, something is true to the extent that it is internalized and appropriated in someone's life. This definition should indicate why subjective is appropriate here (Netland, *Dissonant Voices*, 130).
26. Smith, *Wilfred Cantwell Smith*, 39.
27. Netland, *Dissonant Voices*, 147.
28. Hick, *Disputed Questions*, 7.

(the object as it is in its transcendent existence), and *phenomenon*, the thing as we experience it (the object we experience in ordinary existence).[29] To know or experience an object is always to experience *as* or to know *as*.

The implications for theologians, and particularly for theologians of religious diversity, is that they can only proceed negatively. Practically, this means that theologians are able to make concrete claims only about what God is *not*. Theologians and believers must surrender the impulse to describe, explain, portray, or express who or what God *really* is in any positive or attributive terms. For Hick, there is an inordinate imbalance between what "the Real" (God/the ultimate) is and what we can know about "the Real." Thus, we cannot determine whether one formulation of "the Real" is more adequate than any other formulation. Knitter illuminates this point by summarizing the tenets of Hick's position in the following way: "that the Divine is as real as it is mysterious, that what religions know and proclaim about the Divine is true, but the Truth is infinitely more than what is known."[30] Both Cantwell Smith and Hick draw the conclusion that salvation parallels truth: because no religion is more capable than any other in making a claim about the absolute end for humanity, salvation, like truth, must be universal and uniform.[31]

Common Tenets of the Classic Approaches

For most theologians reflecting on religious diversity as a significant theological issue—from the New Testament writers to third century bishops to citizens of today's democracies—the central question driving the inquiry is soteriological and eschatological: are non-Christians saved in the end? If so, how is this the case? And if not, why not? Salvation is the central issue in classic theologies of religious diversity and, consequently, these theologians generally ignore what diverse believers actually believe.

Salvation is a central question in the Christian tradition and so it is unsurprising that it plays a dominant role in the Christian imagination about the religious other. The logic of this soteriological orientation runs as follows: membership to the Christian church entails a commitment to Jesus Christ who—both biblically and traditionally—offers his disciples salvation. How must Christians think about this offer for salvation when it

---

29. Netland, *Dissonant Voices*, 204.
30. Knitter, *Introducing Theologies of Religions*, 116.
31. There are other pluralist options available besides assuming one universal salvation. S. Mark Heim argues for multiple salvations. See Heim, *Salvations*.

comes to non-Christians? To whom is salvation extended? While exclusivists, inclusivists, and pluralists alike may tolerate, learn from, accept, and/or embrace the followers of other traditions, Christians find themselves needing to reckon with the question of who is saved and who is not.

The salvation of religious others is both the motivating reason for the inquiry and the goal of inquiry itself in the classic approaches. That is, theologians taking classic approaches begin with the concern for non-Christian salvation and conclude with a judgment about it. Classic exclusivists and inclusivists see religious diversity as a *soteriological* problem that is fundamentally about the manner in which diverse religious traditions function in the (Christian) eschatological scheme for humankind. This virtually unilateral focus obscures other important issues raised by religious diversity. Terrence W. Tilley notes that the "problem" of religious diversity is properly understood as a situated problem, because it is as embodied people that we encounter religious others.[32] Approaching religious diversity from primarily a *soteriological* point of view and with a *soteriological* warrant misses the situated and embodied factors that affect one's experience with and understanding of religious diversity.

While salvation plays a role in the pluralist positions discussed above, it plays a less prominent one—or better, one that is balanced by other concerns—than it does for exclusivists and inclusivists. For Cantwell Smith and Hick, religious diversity raises ontological, epistemological, and philosophical issues as well as soteriological ones.[33] They examine diversity primarily in terms of *universal* truth and religious believers' apprehension of that truth. Although pluralists should be commended for widening the focus of the theological discussion on religious diversity beyond salvation, their theories are not the final word on the matter. They attend to other issues besides eschatological salvation—such as truth—but because they privilege the "inescapable relativity of all human consciousness,"[34] their

32. Tilley, *The Wisdom of Religious Commitment*, 26.

33. This is not to say that there is not an important existential or experiential dimension to their concern for religious pluralism. In fact, in the case of Hick, he began to develop his pluralist position as a result of his experience as a pastor ministering to immigrants from India and Pakistan whom he could not accept as being necessarily consigned to hell (see Hick, *John Hick*). My point here is that Cantwell Smith and Hick see philosophy and philosophical theology as the best possible means for intellectually dealing with the issue of religious diversity.

34. Burkle, "Jesus Christ and Religious Pluralism," 459. Moreover, the claim that religious truth is specially incomprehensible is problematic because, as Gary Gutting points out, incomplete knowledge of a subject is not unique to religion (Gutting, *Religious Belief and Religious Skepticism*, 52).

focus is less on religious beliefs as claims to truth and more on people's capacity (or lack thereof) to grasp universal truth.[35] The outcome is that while "truth" is explicitly on the table in the pluralist discussion, no evaluative statements are made about it nor is it explored in a way that is recognizable to the practical, situated experiences of religious believers. That is, while pluralists address the philosophical and epistemological issues around religious diversity, they portray these issues in abstract and conceptual terms, rather than as they are witnessed to in the lives of religious people. Thus, the conceptual terms in which these thinkers describe religious truth is connected to a view of "reason" that is linear, logical, and abstractive, which overlooks alternative facets of reason or ways of thinking (specifically, those facets/ways that are embodied, sensorial, and imaginative).

New Wine, Old Wineskins

If one looks at religious diversity as principally an eschatological, soteriological problem, there are three common possible responses.[36] These are (1) to claim that non-Christians do not have access to salvation; (2) to develop a theological principle (like Rahner's anonymous Christian) that explains how non-Christians can be granted Christian salvation; (3) to argue that all religions have equal access to a universal form of salvation. These responses to diversity are *externally* oriented, top-down, and theological in nature. They are primarily concerned with the religious other in theory—that is, in the abstract—and with her soteriological status. Focusing on the soteriological problem of diversity not only obscures from view the actual religious beliefs of the diverse believers in question, but also makes diversity into a "future"—rather than present or imminent—issue. In the following section, I introduce the work of three theologians who explore different layers of religious diversity. These theologians reveal alternative patterns of orientation and offer ways to consider truth as a necessary part of the situated and embodied encounter with religious diversity.

---

35. Ibid., 460.

36. A fourth, less common possibility is available in Heim's "multiple salvations," which holds that religions access different ultimate ends.

Virtue in Dialogue

Paul Griffiths and the Uneasiness Conditions

In *Problems of Religious Diversity* Paul Griffiths poses the epistemological questions generated by diversity self-reflectively. What about *one's own* religious beliefs and commitments given religious diversity? Should the awareness of religious diversity reduce a person's epistemic confidence in her own beliefs?[37] Griffiths' work focuses on the possible epistemological responses—many of which are *internally* directed—to the awareness of diversity.

In order to deal with these epistemological responses, Griffiths must make a case for why religious diversity is an epistemological problem at all. He begins this explanation by offering a theory of religion. Griffiths takes religion to be a form of life that is both comprehensive and of central importance in the life of the believer.[38] If this is the case, then the statements made by religious people about their religious beliefs ought to be taken seriously as truth claims. Making a religious claim, Griffiths continues, involves accepting or assenting to a particular form of life.[39] Thus, in the face of diversity, there are important questions to be raised not just about salvation but, even prior to that, there are questions about the actual truth of one's own and others' religious claims.[40]

The underlying purpose of Griffiths' work is to establish a problem (or, better, set of problems) of religious diversity *beyond* the soteriological ones introduced in the preceding section of this chapter. He discusses the epistemological implications of diversity and offers three ways in which religious claims conflict or are discordant. Religious claims may be contradictory, contrary, or non-compossible. Those that are contradictory both make a claim to truth where only one can be true. (A lesser or modified version of contradictoriness is approximate contradictoriness. This is when religious claims are not *formally* contradictory.) For example, Muslims believe the universe is created and guided by a powerful

---

37. Griffiths, *Problems of Religious Diversity*, 70. Robert McKim wrestles with this very question (of whether one's confidence in her belief should be reduced given religious diversity), as I will demonstrate in the following chapters. He concludes that indeed it should. In the following chapter, I discuss McKim's position as well as that of Richard Feldman (who more radically states that one should actually suspend belief, rather than just hold it tentatively) and argue against both of their conclusions. While Griffiths addresses the types of positions propounded by McKim and Feldman, he does not engage with either directly.

38. Griffiths, *Problems of Religious Diversity*, 9.

39. Ibid., 21.

40. Ibid., 17.

and active God. Buddhists believe the universe is non-theistically guided. These beliefs about the way the universe is governed are contradictory. *Either* the universe is theistically governed *or* it is not. Religious claims that are contrary both make a claim to truth but neither "need" be true.[41] For example, Christianity maintains a view of "Jesus of Nazareth as supreme among human beings" while other religions (Judaism and Islam, for example) do not. The belief that Jesus is supreme and the belief that Jesus is an important prophet but is by no means supreme (in the case of Islam, for example) exclude one another viz. truth, but it is also possible that neither claim is true. Finally, claims that are non-compossible are those that prescribe courses of action (for the persons subject to the claims) that are mutually exclusive. This is to say that no one person can take both courses of action. Griffiths gives the example of a Christian claim—"read the Bible as if it were the most the important book in the world"—and a Muslim claim—"read the Qur'an as if it were the most important book in the world"—to show how these would make competing claims to guide the life of any one person.[42]

In the encounter with religious others, people have the opportunity to become aware of the contradictoriness, contrariety, and/or non-compossibility of their beliefs. It is precisely in the context of interreligious conversation—to draw on an earlier example—that a Muslim can learn about the Buddhist belief in a non-theistically guided universe and recognize it as a contradiction of her own belief. Realizations such as these generate what Griffiths calls "epistemic uneasiness."[43] What Griffiths captures with the notion of epistemic uneasiness is that contradictory, contrary, and non-compossible beliefs present not just logical problems, but religious and existential ones as well. Our religious beliefs both make claims to truth and prescribe right actions. Thus, the epistemic uneasiness brought about by the fact of opposing beliefs should lead us to question the validity of both that truth and guideline for right action.

Specifically, Griffiths sees three situations that generate epistemic uneasiness. As shorthand, these can be called Griffiths' "uneasiness conditions." A person should be uneasy in the following cases: (1) if the dissenting religious claims are authoritative and come from trustworthy sources; (2) if one had little confidence in one's beliefs to begin with;[44] (3) if one's

---

41. Ibid., 32–34.
42. Ibid., 34.
43. Ibid., 97.
44. Ibid., 73.

religious beliefs lack a "rider" or "codicil" for successfully explaining the existence of diverse (and dissenting) religious beliefs.[45] If any of these conditions are met, then Griffiths recommends that believers should be troubled or reduce confidence in the truthfulness of their beliefs. Religious diversity does not, for Griffiths, undercut religious beliefs. Rather, it presents religious believers with an opportunity to be more thoughtful about and more present to diversity's deep implications. Griffiths writes, "Epistemic uneasiness often (and properly) produced by increasing Christian awareness of deep diversity should be acknowledged as a neuralgic point of creative conceptual growth for Christian thought."[46]

Griffiths' primary intention is to reframe the approach to religious diversity in terms of truth, epistemology, and philosophical coherence, rather than in terms of soteriology. The classic ways of dealing with diversity—exclusivism, inclusivism, and pluralism—can be related to Griffiths' uneasiness conditions in such a way that illuminates how his epistemological approach works. For exclusivists, Griffiths states, religious diversity is a problem because it challenges coherence. An exclusivist would see her home religious tradition as uniquely privileged with respect to truth. The claims made by her tradition are *necessarily* true and the fact of contradictory, contrary, and non-compossible claims raise only logical problems.[47] In terms of Griffiths' uneasiness conditions, the exclusivist can "write off" the problem of dissent by arguing that alien religious claims cannot ever come from trustworthy or authoritative sources (authoritative and trustworthy on the matter of religious truth) because alien religious traditions are intrinsically non-trustworthy and non-authoritative (on the matter of religious truth). The premise is flawed and so too are the propositions that follow.

---

45. Ibid., 74–75.

46. Ibid., 97. This passage represents a significant internal tension in Griffiths' work. He writes in two distinctive genres and for two distinctive audiences. On one hand, he discusses diversity from a generically religious standpoint and writes for a "disinterested" scholarly community. On the other hand, Griffiths comes at diversity as a believer in Christianity's truths and writes for a community that, like him, makes sense of diversity by thinking of it in the service of Christian theology. These genres and corresponding audiences overlap at times, as this passage shows. The kinds of perspective that Griffiths develops in the latter genre (i.e., the position that diversity is in the service of Christian theology) necessarily informs his conclusions about religious diversity. This becomes especially clear in Griffiths' theory of restrictivism, which is discussed in more detail in the following footnotes.

47. Ibid., 56.

Theological "Problems" of Religious Diversity

Griffiths states that inclusivists see alien claims as possibly true. Inclusivists might recognize that contradictory, contrary, or non-compossible religious claims come from authoritative and trustworthy sources. This could lead to epistemic uneasiness. However, the inclusivist can appeal to a theological codicil to explain how it is the case that other traditions represent some truth in their claims. For example, a Christian inclusivist can say that while other religious traditions make some true claims, they only do so because an element (such as the Holy Spirit) of the home tradition is implicitly operative in the alien tradition. It will be the case, then, that the home religion makes a higher or greater proportion of true claims than do the alien traditions.[48]

In the case of pluralists, religious diversity does not create a real epistemological problem. It is not that pluralists ignore its *epistemological* implications, it is just that they do not see these implications as *problematic*. Differing religious claims "[raise] no special problem" with respect to truth because all religions make equally valid claims to truth.[49] In terms of the uneasiness conditions, it will be the case that opposing claims are recognized to come from authoritative and trustworthy sources. However, one's confidence in her belief need not be troubled because all religions can appeal to the general codicil that diverse religious traditions are individual particular representations of universal truth and that no one has any greater access or any more validity than any other.

Griffiths does not offer a highly developed solution to the problem of religious diversity.[50] In fact, he only heightens the issue by showing that

---

48. Ibid., 57.

49. Ibid., 48. This applies to pluralists who are grounded by both Kantian and Wittgensteinian principles. Earlier in this chapter and for reasons of brevity, I depicted pluralists of the Kantian-stripe (Hick and Cantwell Smith) and left aside those pluralists who draw on Wittgenstein. It is important here to note that all types of pluralists can arrive at this conclusion—that religious diversity raises no special problem with respect to truth—although by different means. Kantian-influenced pluralists can argue that conflicting claims raise no special problem because ultimate truth stands behind every tradition's individual rendition. Wittgensteinian-influenced pluralists can explain that conflicting claims raise no special problems because "truth" is really just a linguistically-specific depiction of reality that is no more or no less valid than any other. (Moreover, on Wittgenstein's view, there is no place outside or beyond a form of life from which to judge those depictions of reality.) The difference in reasoning, while important, is not actually relevant here.

50. In fact, Griffiths does present a constructive solution to the problem of diversity, although it is not as developed as it might be (he writes that it is a "bare-bones account" [ibid., 166]). He calls his position "restrictivism" and explains that it is a form of universalism (universal salvation). Restrictivism holds that belonging to Christianity

it is an epistemological problem rather than only a soteriological one. His goal is to offer a presentation of what precise epistemological issues religious diversity raises and to suggest ways in which theologians have (or have not) dealt with these epistemological issues.

At the heart of Griffiths' work lies his firm conviction that appealing to the privatization of religious belief as an explanation for diversity is not an option. On a privatized account of religious belief, each religious believer can have confidence in her belief (thus dismissing all three uneasiness conditions) because she has confidence in her pattern of belief formation. While privatization provides an "epistemic haven," Griffiths states, this does not make it an accurate explanation or an epistemologically good response.[51] Alvin Plantinga formulates one of the most developed and noteworthy of these privatization strategies in his theory of basic beliefs, which—in broad terms—posits that a religious belief is epistemologically sound if it is properly basic for a believer. In chapters 4 and 5, I will use Griffiths' critique of the privatization argument to help dismantle Plantinga's theory and to develop an epistemologically (and theologically) adequate response to religious diversity.

Harold Netland and Logical Criteria for Evaluation

Harold Netland states that the theological discussion on religious diversity has been a debate predominantly about the extent to which God is operative in other religious traditions.[52] Construed in this way, the discussion of religious diversity has been essentially non-epistemological. Focusing on God's presence and action shows what Netland claims to be a functionalist or pragmatist interpretation of religion itself. The guiding question, on such a functionalist account of religion, is about what God does, revealing an underlying assumption that what is most important about religion—its very essence—is its function. If religions are characterized primarily by what they *do*, then they will be judged according to how well they do it.[53]

Netland finds fault with this because, he claims, the function of religion is not the central issue: "the most important question is not what a religion does for society, but rather whether what it affirms about the

---

is necessary for salvation. Griffiths leaves the definition of "belonging to" sufficiently open so that it is not clear who does and does not belong (ibid., 164–65).

51. Ibid., 83–84.

52. Netland, *Dissonant Voices*, 20.

53. Ibid., 156–57.

Theological "Problems" of Religious Diversity

nature of reality is in fact the case."[54] In other words, what is most significant about religious traditions is the truth to which they attest. Functionalist views of religion—in their attention to what religions do above what they claim—are misguided and ultimately disregard the issue of truth. By disregarding the issue of truth, functionalist views of religion lead to "vacuous relativism [wherein] all beliefs are granted equal status and no one perspective is allowed to have priority over or rule out competing alternatives."[55] That is, if religions are not judged on the basis of what they claim, then they are all equally "true." Religious diversity, by functionalist lights, does not generate conflict.

Taking a functionalist view of religion is one strategy for "solving" the problem of diversity. There are alternative strategies—strategies that attend to the truth claims of religions—taken by theologians and philosophers to "solve" the problem of diversity that Netland believes also lead to vacuous relativism (Cantwell Smith and Hick represent these strategies for Netland). These approaches begin by suggesting that truth comes in both propositional and non-propositional forms. They hold that, first, truth in "the logically basic sense" is "a quality or property of propositions." In short, truth, logically, is something that can be stated in linguistic form.[56] In terms of religious traditions, truth is represented in the belief claims made by religious believers.

The second way philosophers and theologians understand truth, Netland claims, is that it is "not a static property of propositions or doctrines but rather a dynamic product of human involvement with what is said to be true."[57] Truth is a *dynamic product* of human involvement. There is no truth apart from how a person absorbs it in her life and assents to it in action. In other words, truth is expressed through dynamic action and behavior. In terms of religion, and particularly the issue of religious diversity, this means that statements of belief, professions of faith, or systematic truth claims are not the *only* or even the most important objects of evaluation. Rather, ritual actions, patterns of behavior, and the forms of life engaged in by religious believers should also be seen as expressive of truth.

According to Netland's assessment, this strategy heightens the second view of truth at the expense of the first: they hold that religions are

54. Netland, "Exclusivism, Tolerance, and Truth," 92.
55. Netland, *Dissonant Voices*, 30.
56. Ibid., 114.
57. Ibid., 119.

evaluated by the truth they express, but this truth is most significantly manifested by what religious people do or how they function. Thus, what "counts" for thinkers like Cantwell Smith and Hick when it comes to evaluating religions given religious diversity is the non-propositional kind of truth. Netland calls this a "powerful and influential" strategy because, by redefining the terms of truth, it *looks as if* truth claims are taken into account, but ultimately it promotes a disguised form of functionalism that thereby leads to relativism. To Netland's mind, it is a convenient or expedient response to religious diversity. He states that when one is "disquieted" by religious plurality—when one confronts alternative, deeply and sincerely held religious beliefs and is arrested by that fact—relativism is an "easy option."[58]

To repeat, Netland's fundamental claim is that "the most important basis on which to evaluate various religions is the question of truth."[59] The question of truth is inescapable and, no matter what strategy one takes to avoid it, it will ultimately percolate to the surface. Insofar as dynamic human action is expressive of a religion's truth, even truth-oriented functionalist interpretations of religion (such as those of Cantwell Smith and Hick) must reckon with the question of truth eventually precisely *because* non-propositional truth is human dynamic engagement with propositional truth.[60] Netland does not disagree with a strategy that points out two forms of truth—propositional and non-propositional. In fact, he takes up the basic insight that non-propositional truth is dynamic and important for evaluating religious traditions. However, he argues that propositional truth and non-propositional truth are *inextricably* related. Thus, *contra* Cantwell Smith, "personal truth which is [a type of non-propositional truth] should not be regarded as an alternative to propositional truth."[61]

---

58. Ibid., 29.

59. Ibid., 166.

60. The phrase "product of human involvement" marks another underlying meaning to Netland's claim. Human involvement or participation in truth suggests the idea that truth precedes or pre-exists human expression of it and it is human involvement in—not creation of—truth that allows for truth to manifest itself in the world. Since he is a Christian, I take Netland to be bringing Christian grace into the equation; grace allows humans to become involved with God's truth and to "profess" that truth through religious actions and statements of belief. While this meaning is likely as significant (if not more significant) for Netland as the claim that truth is expressed in other ways besides statements, I mention it here in the footnote rather than the text because it is less important for my methodologically oriented discussion.

61. Netland, "Exclusivism, Tolerance, and Truth," 91.

Theological "Problems" of Religious Diversity

Scholarly evaluation of religions should go beyond statements, but should do so without also losing sight of the non-propositional truth claims that are entailed by action. To illuminate how this scholarly evaluation works in practice, Netland presents summaries of four religious traditions (Hinduism, Islam, Shintoism, Buddhism) according to three basic questions: what is the religion's understanding of the human condition, of the nature of the ultimate, and of the nature of salvation? The answers Netland gives to these three questions for each of the four traditions assume his definition of dynamic, non-propositional truth.

Netland reaches three conclusions from this method of evaluation. First, he claims it *is* the case that religions make genuinely incompatible truth claims. He writes, "[While] mere difference in perspective in and of itself does not entail opposition of beliefs, there are instances in which the various religious clearly do seem to be making mutually incompatible claims about the nature of reality." Both Netland's view of the nature of truth and his understanding of the relationship between propositional and non-propositional truth lead him to this deduction that religions make genuinely incompatible claims.

Second, Netland claims that these incompatibilities occur at both doctrinal (belief) and ethical (action) levels. As an example of a doctrinal incompatibility, Netland points to the conception of Jesus as the "Son of God" in Islam and Christianity. The Qur'an mentions Jesus in "fifteen surahs and ninety-three verses" and "depicts Jesus as explicitly disclaiming deity." Islam rejects as blasphemous the Christian belief that Jesus was begotten of God and is divine as such.[62] These beliefs express truth propositionally (i.e., "Jesus is the 'Son of God' *v.* Jesus is not the 'Son of God'") and their mutual incompatibility is apparent.

An example of incompatibility at the level of action can be extrapolated from Netland's discussion of ritual purification in various traditions. Netland details the Shinto rites of purification and notes the underlying metaphysical reasons for these rites, "Humankind is basically pure and good; it is contact with what is impure (blood, sickness, death), the action of evil spirits, or failure to cultivate the inherit goodness within which results in disharmony and requires ritual purification." In Islam, washing oneself, or performing ablution, is required before one offers daily prayer or *salat*. Shinto ritual cleansing requires the believer to rinse out her mouth and pour clean water over her hands.[63] Islamic ritual cleansing engages in

---

62. Netland, *Dissonant Voices*, 90–91.
63. Ibid., 104.

similar actions, but not with the same rules (i.e., Islamic ablutions require believers to wash various body parts—hands, mouth, nose, face, arms, and so on—in a particular order) or for the same reasons (i.e., Islamic ablutions are performed to prepare oneself for prayer). Netland's point is that although there is nothing about the actions of Shinto ritual cleansing that seem incompatible with Islamic cleansing (for example, both use clean water; both require cleansing mouth and hands), they are incompatible because the religious truths expressed by engaging in these actions are incompatible. If using Griffiths' system of classification (contradictory, contrary, and non-compossible), Netland would argue that Shinto ritual cleansing and Islamic cleansing are non-compossible *because* these actions as dynamic expressions of Shinto and Islamic beliefs about the religious significance of cleansing are contrary.

Finally, Netland states that, given the data of diverse traditions, it is "prima facie untenable" to argue that religions are all just culturally conditioned responses to one ultimate reality.[64] Both Netland's theory of the relationship between propositional and non-propositional truth and his textured descriptions of various religious traditions contribute toward this final judgment. In sum, his position is as follows: when considering religious diversity, truth is at stake, "truths" do conflict, and positing an abstract theory of universal truth to handle these conflicts is unacceptable. Stated another way, Netland's conviction is that there is but one real and particular truth, with which other particular "truths" necessarily conflict. As a scholar, it is his task to set up a system through which "truths" can be evaluated.

Whether Netland's project is convincing hinges on his ability to demonstrate that his proposal for evaluating religious traditions is not only *not* problematic but is in fact the very way to do justice to religious traditions.[65] His understanding of truth as both propositional and non-propositional or dynamic contributes toward the end of doing justice to religions. He states: "If we are to have a comprehensive understanding of the religious

---

64. Ibid., 110–14.

65. Netland here reveals his commitment to a general epistemic principle that undergirds his entire project. He writes, "Irrespective of whether one adopts a favorable, unfavorable, or even an indifferent attitude toward religions, one cannot escape at least implicitly making some judgments about the desirability or propriety of belonging to particular religious traditions" (ibid., 155). This statement reveals Netland's view of knowledge as necessarily involving judgment—without the step of judgment, knowing is incomplete and impotent. This reflects a theory of knowledge developed by theologian Bernard Lonergan in *Insight*. This view of knowledge sees it not as just "taking a look" but rather as fundamentally a task of judgment.

traditions of humankind that takes seriously both the varied data of the religions and is epistemologically sound, it is very difficult to escape the conclusion that at least some of the central claims of some religions must be false."[66] In short, religious people take themselves seriously as positing truth claims, so too should scholars who evaluate those claims.[67] If scholars take the conflict of religious truth claims seriously, this means that they must make judgments about these truth claims—some will be true and some will be false.

Netland must identify how or by what standards it is possible to make these evaluations or judgments. He argues "some non-arbitrary criteria exist"[68] that can be "legitimately" applied to evaluate competing religious worldviews.[69] Specifically, Netland identifies five categories of ostensibly non-arbitrary criteria for evaluating the truth claims expressed both propositionally and dynamically by religious believers. Competing claims can be judged according to (1) basic logical principles such as the principle of identity, non-contradiction, and the excluded middle. According to the principle of identity, Netland writes, "when [it is] applied to statements . . . if a statement is true, then it is true." The principle of non-contradiction builds on this idea and holds that the same thing cannot be one thing and another thing at the same time. In terms of propositional statements, this means that a statement cannot be true and false at the same time. Finally, the principle of the excluded middle maintains that any statement must be true or false (there is no "middle" state into which it can fall). If a claim violates any of these principles, it cannot be judged to be true. Claims can also be tested for (2) self-defeat. If a religious claim "provides the grounds for its own refutation" (i.e., defeats itself), then that claim cannot be true. A religious claim must also be tested for its (3) coherence of worldview; (4) explanatory adequacy within a relevant range; and (5) consistency with knowledge in other fields.[70] If a religious claim fails on any of these counts, Netland argues that the religious claim is not true and, possibly, that the religion itself can be rejected as false.

Netland's discussion is, overall, a defense of the legitimacy of exclusivism both theoretically and in concrete form. Exclusivism, Netland contends, need not be only *Christian* exclusivism. Because Netland sees

66. Ibid., 233.
67. Ibid., 228.
68. Ibid., 152.
69. Ibid., 183.
70. Ibid., 184–88.

his standards for evaluation as "non-arbitrary" as well as logical and philosophical in nature (rather than, say, theological or cultural), exclusivism can come in any form. Thus, Hindu exclusivism or Muslim exclusivism are also possibilities. Exclusivism also does not entail the positions that all claims of other religions are necessarily false or that all other practices are vicious, that exclusivists cannot learn from other religions, or that there is no value in other religions.[71]

Concretely, Netland defends a Christian exclusivist position. For him, Christian beliefs "pass" the necessary tests; in other words, when analyzed in terms of Netland's putative non-arbitrary criteria, Christian claims succeed. If Christian claims meet these standards and the claims of other religious traditions do not, it follows that Christian beliefs are true and opposing beliefs are false. He states,

> If indeed one is justified in accepting the Christian faith as true—as I'm convinced is the case—then one is also justified in making judgments about other religious traditions on the basis of Christian teaching, and in rejecting as false those beliefs from other traditions that are incompatible with the Christian faith.[72]

While Netland does not argue that Christianity has, as he puts it, a "monopoly on truth," he still makes a strong claim about the status of other religious traditions viz. truth.[73] He writes,

> To be sure, the follower of another religion is not yet in a saving relationship with God, and indeed, like all persons who have not responded to God's grace in Jesus, lives in a state of rebellion and disobedience. But this should not obscure the fact that even here there is a fundamental relationship of the creator to the creation, the human creature being made in the image of the creator.[74]

Netland concludes with a statement on the theological status of non-Christian religious people—namely that, while in a state of rebellion and disobedience (not to mention the fact that they are in the habit of professing falsehoods), they still are closely related to God.

From Netland's perspective, his hands are tied; given his beliefs as a Christian and the evaluative criteria he develops for adjudicating

71. Ibid., 35.
72. Ibid., 195.
73. Ibid., 294.
74. Ibid., 298.

conflicting beliefs, he reaches the only possible conclusion to be reached about non-Christians religions. Netland's position is problematic less for its conclusion than it is for the "non-arbitrary" evaluative standards by which he reaches his conclusion. For example, Netland draws on the Western philosophical tradition to develop his criteria and yet leaves aside the fact of historical collusion between Western philosophy and religious traditions in the West (most particularly, Christianity). He misses the point that the religious traditions that have developed in a close—and even indivisible—relationship with the Western philosophical tradition will be more likely to meet the "non-arbitrary" standards than those traditions that have not. Nevertheless, the salient lesson to be taken away from Netland's proposal is *that* objective criteria might be developed for evaluating religious beliefs, even if it is not the particular criteria that Netland himself develops.

Gavin D'Costa and Reading Diversity Theologically

The discussion on religious diversity, Gavin D'Costa alleges, is a stunted one. Theological theories about the world religions are given short shrift in scholarly discourse today because they are seen as having biased rather than disinterested foundations. The "outsider" or rejected status assigned to theology by contemporary academia can be traced to the construction of the concept of religion itself. According to D'Costa the concept of "religion" was invented in the sixteenth century by Platonist philosophers at Cambridge University.[75] Leaving aside the details of D'Costa's account of how "religions" came to exist as they do today, it is sufficient to note one highly relevant point that D'Costa makes about the construction of religion: religion became privatized as a result of the rise of the Western nation-state, and the notion of privatized religion has since been "exported" to the world.[76]

D'Costa's crucial claim is that religions, and so religious diversity, are understood today according to the privatized account. A primary tenet of a privatized view of religion is that because religions are closed, private systems, they must be translated to those who are outside of them if they are to be explained and understood. D'Costa firmly opposes this. As he argues, the idea that religion can and must be put in terms of public, "secular" reason does not consider that the distinctive qualities of religious

75. D'Costa, *Christianity and the World Religions*, 57–58.
76. Ibid., 99.

traditions may be lost or damaged in the process of translation. Moreover, this expectation for "clean translation," which conjectures that religion can be studied and explored only through the use of unbiased, secular reason does not acknowledge the inherent biases of even an "unbiased" account.[77]

For D'Costa, these problematic assumptions—that religion can be translated and that secular reason, as unbiased and pure, is in the unique position to do the translating—lead to a hegemonic dominance of secularist interpretations on religious traditions. The upshot of the privatized account is that it ultimately bars theological readings, which are thought to be *in principle* at odds with secular reason, from entering the conversation on religious diversity. It is worth quoting D'Costa at length to illuminate this point:

> As with the entire industry of criticism of colonial culture, there sometimes lurks an assumption that either a neutral secular description of Hinduism [for example] or alternatively a self-description of Hinduism (including its persecuted minorities) is the only acceptable form of description. While Marxists and feminists constitute a large number of colonial critics, ironically they cannot conform to these strictures, for they obviously introduce new biases. This highlights my point that theological interpretation *per se* does not necessarily reduce the value of a descriptive account, for all accounts are interpretive.[78]

All readings are interpretative and all readings are biased. Theological readings are no different than secular readings of religion in that they are interested.[79] And, in fact, theological readings are better than what D'Costa calls ideological secular readings (ideological secular readings are those that are guided by political or social commitments) because they (theological readings) acknowledge their commitments forthrightly.

D'Costa's goal is to route the discussion on religious pluralism back into theological territory. He writes, "theology's reading of the world religions, in their particularity and complexity, is the most truthful reading available."[80] Like Griffiths and Netland, D'Costa is clear about the types of theological perspectives that are useful and adequate for understanding religious pluralism. D'Costa appeals to a helpful distinction drawn by Stephen Duffy between two types of theological discourse—*a priori*

77. Ibid., 113–15.
78. Ibid., 70.
79. Ibid., 94–95.
80. Ibid., 101.

theologies and *a posteriori* theologies—on religious diversity in order to show which he (D'Costa) sees as useful and adequate. These two ways of reading of religious pluralism do different things, answer different questions for different audiences, and they should not be confused as trying to do the same thing.[81] (D'Costa makes the point that even "secular" readings of diversity will employ one of these ways of reading.)

Comparative theologies—a type of theological discourse not yet discussed in this chapter—are the foremost representative of *a posteriori* theologies. Comparative theologies, as Duffy puts it, "demand detailed knowledge of other traditions."[82] James L. Fredericks and Francis X. Clooney provide two prominent examples of comparative theologians. Fredericks articulates the comparative method: those doing comparative theology must be theologians in their own traditions as well as have "competence in the traditions, texts, languages, symbols, etc. of a religion other than Christianity." He goes on to explain that the work of comparative theology "is achieved as a carefully limited constructive act of the imagination. Of necessity, therefore, comparative theology will proceed slowly and tentatively."[83] As an advocate of comparative theology, Clooney argues for "a theology that proceeds by examples and dwells in particularity." This work—work that Clooney himself pioneers—"creates a new theological environment in which to rethink what we are doing as Christians and theologians in a world that is richly, amazingly diverse."[84]

While D'Costa appreciates the highly textured and careful work of scholars such as Fredericks and Clooney, he is critical of the comparative theological movement for shying away from the issue of truth and for being tentative in making truth claims.[85] Comparativists focus entirely—and intentionally—on "inculturation" but do so in such a way, D'Costa continues, that is "out of relation with mission and dogmatics."[86] D'Costa ex-

---

81. Ibid., 41.

82. Duffy, "A Theology of the Religions and/or a Comparative Theology?" 109.

83. Fredericks, "A Universal Religious Experience?" 87.

84. Clooney, "The Study of Non-Christian Religions in the Post-Vatican II Roman Catholic Church," 493.

85. Schmidt-Leukel raises a parallel criticism of comparative theology. He writes, "If proponents of comparative theology exclude, at the outset, the possibility of revision and significant transformation as a potential result of their comparative work, or it they denounces such transformation as distortion, then the seriousness of their endeavors as a pursuit of truth is questionable" (Schmidt-Leukel, *Transformation by Integration*, 103).

86. D'Costa, *Christianity and the World Religions*, 40. Clooney's new book

presses concern over comparative theologians' avoidance of "the process of judgment and the issue of truth." D'Costa perhaps exaggerates the extent to which comparative theologians suspend a concern for truth in the process of comparison. What one should take away from D'Costa, here, is that the primary goal of comparative theologians is to engage in careful comparative work rather than theological explanation. Clooney frames a similar insight more positively by drawing out the sense that theology only truly *follows* from comparison. He writes, "Comparative theology . . . is a theology deeply changed by its attention to the details of multiple religious and theological traditions; it is a theology that occurs truly only *after* comparison."[87]

D'Costa also criticizes *a priori* theologies. Duffy writes that *a priori* theologies are those that "[are addressed] solely to the faith commitments and the theological positions held within a Christian community."[88] Exclusivists, inclusivists, and even some pluralists fall into this category. Like Griffiths, D'Costa finds fault with the barely ancillary status *a priori* theologies grant to truth. While religious diversity may call for Christian theologians to take a position on the soteriological status of non-Christians, D'Costa asserts that this cannot be done without an epistemological framework and a notion of how religious people know or claim truth. He writes, "final salvation requires not only an ontological and causal, but also an epistemological relationship to Christ."[89]

D'Costa's position is, in short, as follows. Religious diversity demands a response. This response can be properly generated from only a theological perspective and *must* make a statement on truth in at least some sense. The real question of religious pluralism for theologians is about the *way* in which Christian grace actually brings about salvation for non-Christians.[90] D'Costa states that no developed answer to this question exists and he sees his project as meeting this need. He defines his position, "universal access exclusivism," in four tenets. First, all people will have an opportunity (either in this life or the afterlife) to hear the gospel. Second, God always reveals the gospel, even to those who do not hear it. Third, we must

---

(discussed in chapter 7) goes a long way toward overturning this kind of reading (represented here by D'Costa) of the method and aims of comparative theology.

87. Clooney, "Comparative Theology," 522. In *The Truth, the Way, the Life*, Clooney puts his theory of comparative theology into practice by examining three holy mantras from a Christian theological perspective.

88. Duffy, "A Theology of the Religions and/or a Comparative Theology?" 107.

89. D'Costa, *Christianity and the World Religions*, 24.

90. Ibid., 210.

accept it as a legitimate theological mystery as to how God reaches the unevangelized. Fourth, while Christian faith and baptism are the normal means for salvation, there are other ways people can prepare themselves for salvation.[91]

His position is exclusivist in the sense that it is *only* through Christian means that people are offered salvation. However, the universal access component follows the inclusivist or pluralist lead in that it works to construct a "way in" for non-Christians (and D'Costa creates this "way in" epistemologically). Even though D'Costa can find no immediate answer to the question of how non-Christians are *actually* saved, he looks within the tradition for resources to answer this question. Christ's descent into hell provides D'Costa with a model for his universal access exclusivist "postmortem solution." This solution posits that it is in the afterlife that non-Christians can gain access to salvation because it is there that knowledge of the truth comes to fruition.[92] For D'Costa, knowledge and salvation are necessarily tied together. One cannot be saved by Christ without knowing the truth offered in Christ (otherwise, D'Costa would end up with a type of Rahnerian anonymous Christian explanation). D'Costa chooses Christ's descent into hell, because, as he states, it is "only in the event of the 'descent' does the unity of the epistemological and ontological take place."[93] The principal message D'Costa conveys is that any theological response to religious diversity must involve a robust epistemological component if it is to be adequate.

Contributions and Limitations

One of the central, though understated, ways in which Griffiths, Netland, and D'Costa advance the theological discussion on religious pluralism is in how they construct religion conceptually and, by extension, religious beliefs and believers. Recall that both Griffiths and D'Costa make statements against the privatization of religious beliefs and Netland takes a stand against the functionalist interpretation of religion. Griffiths discusses privatization as it pertains to the belief forming process; he rejects the idea that beliefs are formed by the individual alone and thus are not subject to any outside criticism or evaluation. D'Costa similarly is concerned with privatization. In his case, the concern for privatization is

---

91. Ibid., 31.
92. Ibid., 162.
93. Ibid., 167.

as it applies to a whole religious tradition; he rejects the notion that, as privatized, religions are sequestered off from one another and thus can only be understood through the lens of "objective" secular reason and so cannot rightly be challenged by claims internal to other (private) religious traditions. Netland makes a case against the functionalist interpretation of religion as fundamentally reductionistic and, as an alternative, offers a more robust understanding of the "essence" of religion and the religious truth expressed therein.

Taking these three points together and phrasing them in positive terms, I maintain that "religion" admits of the following features: (1) one can critically evaluate religious traditions both in what claims they make as well as by what they do (particularly as actions/behaviors are dynamic expressions of truth); (2) one can stand in any religious tradition to evaluate another religious tradition; and (3) individuals belonging to their religious traditions are responsible to standards for their beliefs that are *at least* external to their personal belief-forming processes. That is, believers having well-formed beliefs are creditable to their traditions and/or their religious guides, rather than to just their personal (individual) processes for forming beliefs. While none of the philosophers and theologians mentioned in this chapter have explicitly claimed that believers may be also responsible to standards external to the traditions in which they formed their beliefs, this is the theory that I will be venturing and testing in the following chapters of this book.

Griffiths, Netland, and D'Costa also make invaluable contributions to the theological discussion on religious diversity by foregrounding truth (and, by extension, epistemology insofar as epistemology is a method for discussing religious truth expressed through belief). Although "truth" is central to their discussions, it is not always clear just what *about* truth is at issue. While they—unlike the theologians and philosophers representing classic approaches to diversity—do not simply *assume* the place of truth, what Griffiths, Netland, and D'Costa assert about truth are bound up in other concepts (such as salvation) in such a way as to obscure their concepts of the conditions and criteria for truth. Neither is it clear that Griffiths, Netland, and D'Costa (as well as other theologians who raise epistemological concerns) share the same concerns with each other about truth and religious diversity. As a consequence of this, theologians end up talking past each other when it comes to this topic. Are they theorizing about the conditions for true belief? Are they developing criteria by which we evaluate religious beliefs as true? And can they address how the conditions for true belief and criteria for evaluating belief fit together?

Theological "Problems" of Religious Diversity

In all three cases, the strength of the insights they provide on epistemology also call attention to their weaknesses or, at least the ways in which they fail to clearly address with which categories they are working (that is, whether their discussions are defining conditions for truth or criteria for judging beliefs). Griffiths neatly clarifies the way in which religious beliefs function as truth claims and come into conflict as such. He offers a theory of the conditions for true belief by making a case for how religious beliefs involve assent to a form of life. By giving a way for believers to think through their own beliefs given diversity, Griffiths' uneasiness conditions function as preliminary criteria for evaluating belief. While Griffiths suggests that it is the task of the theologian to recognize and deal with epistemological conflicts (the uneasiness conditions make this possible), his culminating statements on the matter of truth are soteriologically- rather than epistemologically oriented. Thus, in the end, Griffiths does not make use of the conditions or criteria he lays out to a particularly full extent.

Netland convincingly argues that, if religious beliefs make claims to truth (rather than just lead to particular actions) and if these claims conflict, then they must be judged according to some independent standards. The evaluative criteria for judging belief that Netland lays out turn out to be less neutral or less objective than he thinks. Furthermore, Netland conflates Christian truth with a theory of the conditions for truth (that is, what makes something true is that it is Christian), thus undermining the objectivity of his account. Finally, D'Costa, for his part, claims that whatever the answer is—to the problem of religious diversity—it needs to be both epistemological and theological in nature. This connects with his notion of the criteria for evaluating religious belief—those criteria must be theological in nature. Like Griffiths, however, D'Costa does not quite get around to developing an epistemological theory and, like, Netland, his understanding of the conditions for true belief are putatively Christian.

New Wine, New Wineskins

The classic approaches to religious diversity—exclusivism, inclusivism, and pluralism—are focused on salvation. This focus is paired with an eschatological concern. The key part of salvation that exclusivists, inclusivists, and pluralists lay stress on its future aspect: they are interested in how religions will prove eventually salvific for their followers. On the classic model, religious diversity is most pressing as an eschatological-soteriological issue. This does not mean theologians taking the classic approaches are unconcerned with truth; it is rather that they *assume* the truth of

Christianity. Proponents of these approaches assume an inextricable relationship between salvation and truth (i.e., Christianity is a "saving truth") and they are able maintain this assumption because, given the cultural hegemony of Christianity in the contexts in which they write, there is little to challenge this assumption.

The approaches of Griffiths, Netland, and D'Costa are also concerned with salvation. However, their soteriological focus is intersected with epistemological concerns rather than eschatological ones: they are interested in how religious claims are epistemologically formulated and how those claims function with respect to the salvific efficacy of the religious traditions. To a certain extent, Griffiths, Netland, and D'Costa focus on truth because, given a shift in the cultural situation from their preceding generation (simply, an increase in diversity across the globe and in their particular locales), they can no longer *assume* the truth of Christianity but instead must *assert* the truth of Christianity. The issue of truth, particularly as it is expressed in statements of belief by believers, is thus foregrounded in these new approaches and developed through the inquiry into believers' epistemic access to and understanding of truth. On the new models, religious diversity is most pressing as an epistemological-soteriological issue.

In a passage assessing the investigative goals of comparative theology, Perry Schmidt-Leukel notes two fields of inquiry for the study of religions: "the hermeneutical range of [a religion's] possible meaning" and "the epistemological range of [religion's] possible truth."[94] These categories are heuristically helpful for this discussion. While the hermeneutical and epistemological ranges may overlap in certain ways, they are elementally *distinctive* ranges; for it is possible to talk about the meaning of a religious belief without raising the question of the belief's truth. Philosopher Gary Gutting offers an example of discussing religious belief in terms of its hermeneutical range: "Since religious language is essentially talk about God, our question [about religious diversity] amounts to that of the meaning of talk about God."[95] When religious beliefs are construed as expressive of meaning rather than truth, opposition and conflict recede into the background and it is irrelevant to try to apply criteria for evaluating the truth of belief.

Take the following statement by theologian Gordon Kaufman in an essay on religious diversity as exemplary of this strategy. Kaufman writes that all religious claims are articulated in symbolic language. Symbolic

---

94. Schmidt-Leukel, *Transformation by Integration*, 101.
95. Gutting, *Religious Belief and Religious Skepticism*, 44.

language is a form of language whose "primary function," Kaufman states, "is not so much to articulate 'truths' about the world and the human . . . as it is to present a framework within which basic orientation and meaning for the whole of human life can be formed."[96] Beliefs for Kaufman are primarily statements expressing "meaning" rather than statements making claims to truth. Kaufman abstracts meaning from truth to preserve the sense that all religious claims are valuable, even if they possibly conflict. Kaufman takes what Fredericks calls an "apologetic stance." He affirms the notion that people have ineffable religious experience in multiple traditions,[97] and, at the same time, looks at religious beliefs in such a way so that their primary function is to express meaning rather than claim truth.

Opposition and conflict come to the foreground when the discussion is focused on a religion's epistemological range of possible truth. The inquiry into a religion's hermeneutical range and its epistemological range are distinctive investigations—each with its own warrants and outcomes. Each kind of investigation has a role to play in the theological discussion on religious diversity. However, it is a mistake to collapse them together without conceptual clarity about which investigation (into the hermeneutical range of possible meaning or the epistemological range of possible truth) holds priority or takes precedence.[98] Theologians can mislead their readers by not articulating whether they are interested primarily in the hermeneutical range of meaning or the epistemological range of truth. What may seem to be a successful strategy for handling the philosophically and theologically thorny issues associated with religious diversity may be "successful" simply because it investigates only into the hermeneutical range, and does not acknowledge that it ignores or does not address the epistemological range. This book is an investigation into the epistemological range of religious beliefs' "truth" or, more accurately, justification.

If we take beliefs seriously as statements of truth as Griffiths, Netland, and D'Costa maintain we should (precisely because believers do so), then opposing religious beliefs will be problematic or challenging for our own beliefs. In short, as Erik Baldwin and Michael Thule write, we must acknowledge that "religious belief can be defeated by an awareness of

---

96. Kaufman, "'Evidentialism,'" 41.
97. James Fredericks, "A Universal Religious Experience?" 75.
98. This is not to say that these investigations do not bear on each other in important ways, but rather just that they are rightly understood as distinctive tasks.

religious pluralism."⁹⁹ "Defeated" here means just as it sounds; one's belief can be undermined, undercut, or damaged because one has become aware of other, conflicting religious beliefs. My awareness of the different prayers and rituals in which others engage make me wonder about my own prayers and rituals. Acknowledging the possibility of defeat for one's own religious beliefs is not fatalistic or defeatist. Rather, this acknowledgment cultivates a particular kind of stance toward religious diversity that takes oneself and other believers seriously as professing beliefs which make truth claims. This stance is necessary if the theological discussion on religious diversity is to rise to the kinds of challenges posed by Griffiths, Netland, and D'Costa. The following and final section shifts away from discussing the methodological commitments of theologians dealing with religious diversity (Griffiths, Netland, and D'Costa all make a case, in some sense, for how theology should go about its business) toward developing a sketch of the "taking belief seriously" stance.

Lessons from Philosophy of Religion

Gary Gutting exhibits a variety of the "taking belief seriously" stance. Gutting begins with an expressivist characterization of religion and then moves to discuss the role beliefs play therein: "A religious form of life provides the training that enables the believer to have [experiences of God], to appropriately express them in religious language, and to respond to the truths so expressed with appropriate actions."¹⁰⁰ Religious forms of life provoke and enable people to come into contact with God and to make statements about that experience. However, Gutting is wary of defining religion only in terms of religious experience; to do so "would be to abandon any real commitment to religious *beliefs*, which must be assertions of what is true, not merely devices for triggering certain experiences."¹⁰¹ Religious beliefs thus have a stake in truth.

Gutting rejects theologians and philosophers who avoid the issue of truth. Those who argue beliefs cannot really make a claim to truth because religious beliefs are not "testable hypotheses" ignore the reality that factual data are relevant to believers.¹⁰² Just because religious beliefs may not be able to be empirically verified does not mean that empirical facts do not

---

99. Baldwin and Thune, "The Epistemological Limits," 445.
100. Gutting, *Religious Belief and Religious Skepticism*, 64.
101. Ibid., 54.
102. Ibid., 34–36.

Theological "Problems" of Religious Diversity

play a role in how one understands her beliefs. Gutting also rejects those theories that suggest "religious beliefs fall outside the category defined by the reasonable/unreasonable distinction and so cannot be properly subjected to the process of [epistemic] justification (giving reasons)."[103] If it is the case that religious believers state beliefs as expressions of what they see as true (about the universe, reality, God, etc.), then religious beliefs should be subjected to critical, epistemological evaluation just as any other type of belief would.

Gutting thus defends an "epistemic need for continuing discussion of [religious beliefs'] truth status."[104] If religions are forms of life that are both meaningful and make claims to truth, if religious believers arrive at their beliefs not privately and not only for pragmatic reasons and, finally, if religious believers come into contact with conflicting religious beliefs that can possibly defeat their own, then it may be the case that believers make what J. L. Schellenberg calls "comparative assessments" as a result of the encounter with religious diversity. Practically, this means that reflective Christians will "consider their beliefs to be as *probable* as alternatives from within their own tradition, *somewhat more probable than* the relevant alternatives from within Judaism and *considerably more probable than* Buddhist alternatives."[105] In other words, believers will weigh their beliefs against other beliefs.

In this "weighing" process, it is incumbent upon believers to make sense of religious beliefs. The normative proposal—raised by Griffiths, Netland, and D'Costa—that religious believers *should* think critically about the truth status of their beliefs implicitly rejects what Gutting calls "methodological conservatism." Methodological conservatism is the position that the fact of one's holding a belief justifies holding that belief.[106] In other words, just because a believer claims *x* does not mean that she *should* claim *x*—that she is justified, rational, ethical, or reasonable in claiming *x*. The following chapters will examine this notion of justification in detail and clarify its meaning. For present purposes it is sufficient to note that this "taking belief seriously" stance toward diversity proposed here maintains that it is incumbent upon believers to make sense of their beliefs,

---

103. Ibid., 25.
104. Ibid., 174.
105. Schellenberg, "Pluralism and Probability," 146.
106. Gutting, *Religious Belief and Religious Skepticism*, 102. Gutting notes the point that what is justified here is not the truth of the belief but of the act of holding the belief.

33

given the reality of religious diversity, rather than just take their beliefs for granted or accept them at face value. This stance requires believers to look more closely at what they believe, since what they believe is an assertion of truth.

A central consequence of this stance, which views beliefs as claims to truth—and considers the conditions and criteria through which truth is understood and evaluated—and begins from the perspective of the situated, embodied believers who encounter religious diversity is that believers are responsible epistemic agents. Being an epistemic agent is not about choosing what to believe or in which religious tradition to claim membership. Rather, being an agent is about having agency or being invested in what beliefs one professes and lives out. This book proposes to start the discussion on the theological significance of religious diversity from the position of the situated and embodied believer who encounters diversity as an *epistemic* agent.

Because this project insists upon a stance toward diversity that entails "taking belief seriously" and argues that—as an outcome of such a stance—it will be the case that believers weigh their beliefs against others' beliefs, it is necessary (1) to explain how religious beliefs can be understood and analyzed epistemologically and (2) to suggest ways in which religious beliefs can be systematically evaluated by believers. The following chapter begins working toward these ends through, first, an exploration of past developments in philosophical and epistemological scholarship viz. religious beliefs and, in the latter section, delving into contemporary epistemological discussions on religious diversity wherein diversity is viewed as an instance of epistemic disagreement.

2

Epistemological Debates
Past and Present

THE FOCAL CLAIMS OF THE PREVIOUS CHAPTER WERE THAT RELIGIOUS diversity has been wrongly construed as only a soteriological issue and that there is a need for seeing religious beliefs as epistemologically contestable. The chapter concludes by recommending a "taking-belief-seriously" stance. Ideally this stance will lead to questions about the epistemological status of one's own and others' beliefs in the context of religious diversity: How can we be sure our beliefs are the right beliefs if so many good, smart, and honest people disagree? How can we properly respond to the challenges raised by religious diversity? The aim of this chapter is to demonstrate how questions arising from contrasting and contradictory religious beliefs are intimately connected to questions about the general nature and foundation of religious belief itself.

In many ways, the encounter with the religious other is not the only experience that pushes one to question the justifiability—that is to say, the rightness, reasonability, epistemic soundness, or epistemological defensibility—of her belief.[1] Certainly these types of questions become increasingly complicated as more layers (more religious traditions, more complex types of beliefs) are considered, but the heart of the question is constant: How do we think about the justification of our own religious beliefs given that others hold conflicting beliefs?

---

1. It may not take an encounter with a Hindu for a Muslim to wonder about her belief in a radically monotheistic God and it does not take an encounter with a Buddhist for a Christian to wonder about her belief in God-incarnate. Awareness of even minor discrepancies between beliefs can be enough to push a person to question her beliefs. That is, a Catholic might question her belief that the Eucharist transubstantiates when she learns that her Episcopalian friend believes instead that Eucharist symbolically transforms.

Virtue in Dialogue

This chapter begins by analyzing two key debates: the ethics of belief debates of the second half of the nineteenth century and the "Theology and Falsification" debate of the mid-twentieth century.[2] In the following histories, I trace the scope and details of these debates in order to illustrate important differences regarding the impetuses and methods for philosophers doing epistemology.[3] These sections provide "snapshots" of the way significant concepts arise and function in epistemology so as to provide readers with a background matrix of concepts and terminology helpful for understanding the later discussion.

This chapter, secondly, turns to examine two contemporary epistemologists, Robert McKim and Richard Feldman, who are interested in the very same question that motivates this project; namely, what is to be said about religious belief given the reality of religious diversity and, thus, conflicting belief? In this part of the chapter, I refer to the "snapshots" taken in the preceding section in order to evaluate McKim and Feldman's epistemologies along three key lines: their method or approach to epistemology, their standards for belief justification, and their understanding of the subject's role in belief justification. This rubric of evaluation allows me to argue that the epistemological theories of McKim and Feldman are, in the end, inadequate: they develop their respective positions by using non-religious examples; depend upon an artificial split between religious practice and belief; and, finally, take internalist epistemic criteria for granted in a field in which the internalist approach is in dispute. The movement of this chapter—from historical epistemological context to contemporary discussions in the epistemology of religious disagreement—is meant to lay the groundwork for developing a new epistemological model that will be presented in the following chapters.

---

2. The "ethics of belief" debates include a "debate" staged by William James against William Kingdon Clifford in a lecture to the philosophical clubs of Yale and Brown Universities. In James'ss lecture (1896), called "The Will to Believe," James takes up Clifford's position as he (Clifford) delivered it twenty years earlier in a lecture titled "The Ethics of Belief" presented to the London Metaphysical Society (1876). See James, *The Will to Believe*. The "Theology and Falsification" debate, as I will also later discuss, is an actual debate among philosophers that is conducted and recorded in the book *New Essays in Philosophical Theology* (1955).

3. Religious epistemology has concerned philosophers at least since the ancient Greeks. I choose to begin with the modern debates, rather than with ancient, medieval, or Enlightenment epistemological discussions because I see the modern one as a clear historic example of philosophers grappling with epistemological concerns pertinent to religious diversity.

Tracing the History of Religious Epistemology

Ethics of Belief Debates

Normative and Non-normative Approaches

The monikers normative and descriptive distinguish ways of doing epistemology and note truly epistemo*logical*, rather than epistemic, categories. These terms indicate analytical categories for scholarly investigation of belief rather than categories intrinsic to knowledge itself. How an epistemologist answers the question, "What is the purpose or role of epistemology?" will determine whether her epistemology can be called normative or non-normative in approach. In chapter 1 I alluded to these categories through the use of the related—though less technical—concepts of "criteria for belief" and "conditions of belief."

Normative epistemologies make deontological and regulative claims about belief formation and justification, work deductively, and are concerned primarily with the criteria for beliefs. They develop definite requirements that are analytically applied to belief-forming situations in order to determine the status of belief. Normative epistemologists gauge how well formed beliefs are in order to discriminate between beliefs being justified or unjustified. For example, a normative epistemologist would begin with an epistemological rule such as "a person must be awake to form a good belief" and then would use this rule to evaluate particular instances of belief formation. If Alice awakes in the morning and exclaims, "I believe Jack is making breakfast," a normative epistemologist will apply the "awake rule" to Alice's claim to determine whether her belief is good according to that rule. If the normative epistemologist finds that Alice formed the belief about Jack making breakfast while sleeping, the epistemologist would disqualify Alice's claim as good.

Non-normative epistemologists, by contrast, use a descriptive and inductive method. They simply point out or describe the way in which beliefs have come to be formed and held. Their focus is on the general or ordinary conditions that give rise to belief. Like normative epistemologists, these epistemologists also analytically apply categories of justification. However, they do not do so to the end of discriminating between what *should* count as a warranted or justifiable belief, but rather they point out what *does* count as a justified or warranted belief. To continue with the previous example, a non-normative epistemologist might be interested in how beliefs about breakfast are formed. If the epistemologist determines that people, like Alice, form good beliefs about breakfast being made while sleeping (that is, it turns out that the Jacks of the world are in fact making breakfast), the epistemologist will develop an epistemological framework to explain how it is that such good beliefs about breakfast are formed during sleep (perhaps Alice smells the bacon and eggs cooking while she is asleep, expects Jack to make breakfast, and forms the belief).

Foundationalist and Non-foundationalist Justificatory Standards

How an epistemologist answers the question, "What are the factors or conditions that lead a belief to justification?" will indicate whether an epistemology is foundationalist or non-foundationalist. Foundationalist epistemologists assert that it is possible to trace back every belief to some foundation. Beliefs are justified according to their foundations. A foundation may come in the form of a "basic belief" or a piece of evidence that provides the basis from which all other beliefs are properly derived. In nineteenth- and twentieth-century epistemology, evidential foundationalism holds precedence. As the name suggests, evidential-foundationalists focus on evidence as *the* justifying condition for holding that belief (that is, evidence forms a foundation on which all other beliefs are constructed).[4] Epistemologists who appeal to evidence as the justifying standard for beliefs require a particular quality or quantity of evidence (upon which a belief rests) for a belief to be justified.

Non-foundationalism is a "catchall" term and non-foundationalist epistemologies come in various stripes. Weakly, it can be said that non-foundationalists appeal to other factors beyond evidence and "basic beliefs" in order to justify belief. Such factors include (but are not limited to) the contexts and situations in which beliefs are formed and the extent to which one belief coheres with the rest of the believer's beliefs. More strongly, non-foundationalists reject even the very search for foundations (in evidence or otherwise) as sufficient or necessary for justifying beliefs.[5]

---

4. This paragraph notes that foundationalists count "basic beliefs" and evidence as foundations. For the purpose of simplicity and relevance, I only discuss evidence and evidential foundationalism in any detail and leave the topic of "basic beliefs" untouched for the moment. In chapter 4, I pick up the idea of a "basic belief" and a type of foundationalism predicated on the notion of basic beliefs in my discussion of Alvin Plantinga.

5. These are not clean categories. Any epistemologist can straddle the boundary between a normative and descriptive approach or sometimes seem to appeal to solid

Epistemological Debates

One historically significant engagement regarding epistemological foundationalism occurred in the nineteenth-century "ethics of belief" debates over the epistemic-ethical requirement of what constitutes sufficient evidence for a belief. In the following sections, I review that debate through the language of these epistemological terms (normative/descriptive and foundational/non-foundational).

William Kingdon Clifford and the "Sufficiency of Evidence" Maxim

William Kingdon Clifford and William James are two of the principal voices representing opposing positions in the ethics of belief debates. In 1876, Clifford delivered a lecture titled "The Ethics of Belief" to the London Metaphysical Society, there articulating his position unapologetically: "It is wrong always, everywhere, and for anyone, to believe anything on insufficient evidence."[6] This epistemological stance has extremely stringent requirements for all types of belief. A belief may be justified only if it is based on a sufficiency of evidence and, in Clifford's estimation, there is an ethical problem if a person believes something without such evidence.

In order to make his case for why this is so, Clifford offers the example of a shipowner who is about to send people off to sail on a dilapidated vessel. The outward appearance of the vessel, the shipowner's awareness of the ship's history ("she had seen many seas and climes, and often had needed repairs"), and concerns raised by the shipowner's fellow sailors all suggest the vessel is not in any condition to sail. Even given all of this, the shipowner continues to believe otherwise. He set his ship out to sail regardless of its poor condition. At the end of his epistemological parable, Clifford writes that the shipowner "got his insurance money when [the ship] went down in midocean and told no tales."[7]

The shipowner did not have sufficient evidence to believe his vessel was seaworthy. Because he stubbornly carried through with his belief regardless of the fact that he lacked sufficient evidential grounds, the ship

---

foundations and other times reject them entirely. Further, it is not clear that being normative in approach means one must be a foundationalist about justifying standards or that being descriptive in approach leads one to be a non-foundationalist. The epistemologists discussed here rarely, if ever, categorize themselves in these terms, but I use the categories in order to gain conceptual traction on the various historical options when it comes to the question of justified belief.

6. Clifford, *The Ethics of Belief and Other Essays*, 96.
7. Ibid., 70.

and crew were unprepared to weather a storm. They sank. In this example, the ethical problem brought about as a result of the shipowner's faulty belief is clear. But Clifford thinks that he can tell the story another way, where the consequences of his belief are not so destructive (the ship sets sail and returns safely), and the ethical problems remain the same. For Clifford, the fact of a better outcome matters "not one jot."[8] The circumstances that are created as a result of one's belief are merely accidental and neither support nor detract from the legitimacy or justification of that belief. Beliefs are justified by the evidence for them, not the consequences that may be the result of holding those beliefs.

Clifford establishes a law ("sufficiency of evidence") and tests various cases according to that law. He is interested in regulating what may or may not count as justified belief and accomplishes this by setting a standard for the kinds of foundations that would allow for belief justification. He thus uses a normative epistemological method with an evidential-foundationalist justificatory requirement. In the original parable, the shipowner sets his ship to sail and essentially hopes for the best. The shipowner's dream is about as good as "hoping for the best," evidentially speaking. Neither the dream nor hope for a good outcome count as real evidence and, thus, neither can properly justify this belief.

The upshot of Clifford's argument is that beliefs must be based on evidence in all cases and not on the expected or imagined outcomes of the beliefs.[9] The implication for religious belief is that, on Clifford's view, religious beliefs need sufficiency of evidence to be held and/or acted upon; without sufficiency of evidence, religious beliefs cannot be justified. It is significant to note that it is not merely beliefs, but also actions taken on the basis of these beliefs that are being evaluated. Clifford takes beliefs to be dispositions to act; he draws a close link between belief and action. This Cliffordian insight—that a belief is a disposition to act—will offer an

---

8. Ibid.

9. There is an extremely important value to Clifford's stringent justificatory standards that needs to be acknowledged. The kind of standard that Clifford outlines is the very same standard that we ordinarily apply, for example, in our expectations for public infrastructure. Take for example the dikes around New Orleans or the bridge spanning the Mississippi River in Minnesota; we expect the Army Corps of Engineers or the National Transportation Authority to abide by the kind of evidentialist, normative epistemological justification that Clifford recommends. Without such an expectation in place for the engineers who "know" how to build the dikes, bridges, roadways, dams, and so on, it is likely that we would have more catastrophes like the New Orleans and Minnesota bridge example than could be noted here. The question becomes if and how this applies to religious beliefs in the situation of religious diversity.

important alternative to later epistemologists who drive a wedge between belief and action.

William James and the "genuine option situation"

Two decades after Clifford's lecture, James contested Clifford's basic claim in his address to the philosophical clubs of Yale and Brown Universities. In this famous lecture, titled "The Will to Believe," James develops his epistemological stance in sharp contrast to Clifford's by working out a special circumstance called the "genuine option situation." Options, James explains, can be parsed in three ways. Options can be, according to James, "living or dead; forced or avoidable; momentous or trivial." When an option is living, the choice for its alternative is equally compelling as the choice for it. Living options (as opposed to dead ones) have an existential value: they are living because they are alive or real for us. A dead option is dead because it has no compelling power.

When an option is forced, there is "no possibility of not choosing." In other words, forced options are like forks in the road; if we are traveling along a road and we come to a fork, we have no choice *but* to choose the high or low road. And, finally, when an option is momentous, it provides a person with a unique, irreplaceable opportunity. Unlike its antithesis, a trivial option, a momentous option has a "once in a lifetime" quality. When an option is living, forced, and momentous all at once and it is not clearly decidable on the basis of evidence (either because the evidence is not available or because we cannot wait for the evidence to appear), it constitutes what James called a "genuine option situation."[10]

The genuine option situation, is essentially, for James, the situation we find ourselves in with regard to religious belief. In fact, it is the *sine qua non* of James's genuine option situation. As noted, James thinks that whenever an option before us has the three characteristics of being living, forced, and momentous, a belief *must be* claimed—that is to say, a person must believe one of the options—regardless of the evidence or lack of evidence at hand.[11] James gives the following mundane example to illuminate the the genuine option situation: if a man is waiting to ask a woman to marry him (waiting until he has enough evidence, James writes,

---

10. James, *The Will to Believe*, 3–4.

11. This is not to say that religious belief is chosen *without regard to* evidence, but rather that belief, if chosen, is chosen because of the circumstance and not because of the amount or quality of evidence.

to be "perfectly sure that she would prove an angel after he brought her home"), he is not simply abstaining from the choice for the time being or avoiding the option to choose. Rather, that man is making a choice for a "certain particular kind of risk."[12] Similarly, in the case of religious belief, the choice to be agnostic is not *avoiding* the choice to believe in God but is, rather, choosing a less risky belief about God.

Because we are inescapably presented with the choice to believe, it would be a misunderstanding of the nature of that choice to slowly deliberate upon it until a preponderance of evidence would make one belief stand out more clearly over and against another. James asks where the "objective certitude and evidence" of which Clifford speaks are to be found on this "moonlit and dreamvisited planet."[13] He does not expect that people can achieve certitude for religious beliefs: given the living, forced, and momentous nature of the option for religious belief, we are in such a position where evidence is obscured from view (hence the world of moonlight and dreaminess), and yet a choice must be made. Because we have neither an "infallible intellect" nor "objective certitude," it would be wrong to wait, James explains, for the "bell in us to toll" to signal whether religious belief be true.[14]

Since the choice cannot be decided on the basis of evidence alone and is a matter of how to live, act, and be in the world, it necessarily involves one's emotion and will. James is calling into question Clifford's assertion that we need a sufficient base of evidence in all cases in order to achieve justified belief.[15] What, James might ask, can really count as "sufficient" in this circumstance? How can we be sure that we have enough evidence to actually believe? James defends the justifiability of religious belief on contextual grounds; if the context or circumstance in which we find ourselves constitutes the genuine option situation, then that contributes to the justification of those beliefs that are formed in the genuine option situation.[16]

If believers are "forced" to decide (either to live with or without the belief, for example), then it follows that people can be justified in holding

12. Ibid., 26.

13. Ibid., 14.

14. Ibid., 30. And indeed we cannot wait if the option is forced.

15. James's point is not to dismiss Clifford's evidentialist justificatory requirement entirely. Rather, his point is that the shipowner is not in the same position with regard to the question of sailing as the potential believer is with regard to religious belief. As such, James argues that they should not be held to the same standards.

16. James discusses all of this in terms of rationality, which, for the purposes of clarity, I am equating with justifiability or justification.

religious beliefs (or in not holding religious beliefs, as the case may be). The implication of James's point for religious belief here are a paradigmatically non-foundationalist. Some beliefs simply cannot be determined on the foundational grounds of evidence or argument. In James's estimation, it is "better and wiser to yield to our hope that it may be true."[17] James does not argue, however, that it is "better and wiser" to suppose a religious belief as true simply because it is as likely that it is true, based on the evidence, as it is not. It is *not* the case that religious belief must be chosen because it is like Pascal's wager (e.g., "it is better to bet for it than against it"), but rather because we *must* choose it or lose it.

On one level, James makes his case by pointing out Clifford's weakness. He shows that Clifford does not (and indeed cannot) articulate just what is sufficient evidence or how we can know to recognize it. If we follow Clifford, epistemologically, we will find ourselves on a slippery slope. When do we know we have sufficient evidence? This is not to say, however, that James contests the role evidence can play in belief formation and justification. James does not deny a relationship between evidence and belief, but he does rethink what the various standards of justification for some beliefs may be. In Clifford's framework, beliefs are justified *if and only if* they have solid evidential ground to support them. In James's framework, some beliefs can be justified for reasons besides evidence given certain situations (and the situation itself constitutes that reason).[18]

This takes us to another, and more significant dimension, of James's argument. For James, Clifford fails to understand the nature of how we arrive at our beliefs. It is not the case that a person simply chooses to believe

---

17. Ibid., 27.

18. James does not advocate for people to form beliefs willy-nilly. Rather, he observes that belief formation is constrained by time and context; if we had to wait until all the necessary evidence was gathered together to form a belief, we would be stuck with never having any beliefs at all. If it is a choice *between* forming beliefs without a "sufficiency" of evidence so that we can live according to those beliefs *and* forming beliefs with a "sufficiency" of evidence, but being unable to act while waiting for those beliefs to form, James takes the insufficient evidence/genuine option situation alternative. On another note, according to James's logic, if a situation meets the criteria to fall under the genuine option situation category, then the belief that is formed out of that situation is *de facto* justified. The fact of the particular context (the genuine option situation) allows for justification of the belief arising in that context. Like Clifford, James takes a deontological or normative approach toward justification: namely, x situation calls for justification of belief. What differentiates James from Clifford is his recognition that different situations shape our epistemic duties differently. And in the case of the genuine option situation, our epistemic duty is different than it is in another non-genuine option type of situation.

or not to believe according to what she knows intellectually or rationally or by the evidence that is before her. Rather, a religious belief can be understood as something that may be arrived at because it is alive as an issue, is forced as an option, and is of unique significance for our lives. Here, James develops a justificatory principle: *in some cases* beliefs cannot be based on evidence alone and cannot be separated from why or in what context they are formed (in this case, as a living, forced, momentous option). James—characteristically non-foundationalist—points out a special circumstance or context to justify certain beliefs.

People form religious beliefs in an immense variety of ways. For Clifford, unless those ways add up to a sufficiency of evidence for a particular belief, that belief is not only unjustified but also it is immoral for the person holding the belief. Clifford's requirement is arrived at through a normative approach and is foundationalist in character. James, by contrast, seeks to describe situations in which we form beliefs and show they can be taken as justified, given certain contextual requirements. Because James's mode of doing epistemology involves both a descriptive (in that he observes and describes a certain belief-forming situation that holds weight) and a normative dimension (in that he makes claims about what can and cannot be considered a justified belief), he creates a normative epistemological model through a descriptive approach. In other words, James gives a descriptive account of what happens when people form beliefs—and particularly religious beliefs—but, at the end of the day, he wants to make normative judgments about the justifiability of those beliefs. Thus, his normative standards are based not on an *a priori* view of what *should* count for justified religious beliefs but rather on a description of what *does* count as justification. This makes James's an *a posteriori* epistemology in that it follows from examples of religious belief formation.

The "Theology and Falsification" Debate

More than half a century after Clifford and James, another religious epistemological debate emerged that is helpful for setting the stage for the contemporary epistemological discussion. Where Clifford and James debate about what evidence or situations that can justify belief, the participants in the "Theology and Falsification" discussion argue over what makes a belief meaningful. In one sense, meaningfulness is an epistemically prior question to the ethics of belief debates. Clifford and James just assume the meaningfulness of the beliefs and raise questions about their justifiability or justification. The "Theology and Falsification" debate questions that assumption. In order to understand the significance of the "Theology and Falsification" debate on the issue of meaningfulness, and the way that debate unfolds, it will be necessary to first introduce one more pairing of epistemological categories (internalist and externalist) about which epistemologists today must make a choice.

Internalism and Externalism

Clifford and James both strove to identify universal standards for belief justification. Clifford wrote about the standard of evidence and James created the concept of a genuine option situation. Importantly, their epistemological projects were method-oriented rather than person-relative. Clifford and James did not worry about what the shipowner and the believer in the genuine option situation thought about their own beliefs; they worried about what their beliefs were and whether what the believer believed was justified, according to an objective, independent justificatory standard.[19] They think about epistemology at a generic, universal level and evaluate beliefs rather than believers. To accommodate the shift in focus from method-centered to person-centered epistemology, epistemologists complicate the paradigm for epistemological justification.

In a person-centered approach, epistemologists consider whether any individual person is justified in what she believes. Since epistemologists no longer just talk abstractly and universally, epistemological language moves away from "belief" and "justification" and toward language more familiar to the persons themselves, such as "knowledge" and "know." In order to understand how internalism and externalism fit with this person-centered shift in focus onto knowing, it is worthwhile first to give a brief account of the standard epistemological definition of "knowledge." This account is captured by the acronym JTB, which is the abbreviated form of "justified true belief." According to this JTB definition, a belief is knowledge if it is both justified and true. In an ideal situation, a justified belief happens also to be true, but justification cannot *make* a belief true: truth is independent

---

19. James comes closer to reflecting on these questions about the believer's involvement in belief than does Clifford. It is not that James and Clifford are entirely unconcerned with questions about the *process* of belief formation; it is rather just that the loci of their epistemological evaluations were beliefs themselves. James takes a more holistic view of the larger process of belief formation, but he does so toward the end of evaluating the belief itself as justified and not in the interest of making a claim about the subject's or process's justification.

of justification. Knowledge exists when justified belief and truth coincide and is thus always dependent on both.

Contemporary epistemologists, unlike Clifford and James, question the extent to which the believer grasps her grounds or reasons for her belief.[20] In other words, they consider the extent to which persons are responsible for belief formation and justification and, because knowledge is inextricably tied to justification, to what extent persons actually *know* what they think they know. These questions move the contemporary discussion forward and introduce the vocabulary of "internalism" and "externalism." The way that an epistemologist handles issues about the extent to which a person understands her reasons for belief—and can provide justifying grounds for that belief—will reveal the epistemologist to be either an internalist or externalist.

An internalist epistemologist demands that the reason for a believer's belief must be within the believer's cognitive grasp in order for that belief to be justified (and thus to be on the road to becoming knowledge). Internalism is sometimes talked about, idiomatically, as the rule stating that a person has "to know how she knows" in order for her belief to gain justification. In other words, a believer should only have a belief if she can understand how she has come to that belief and on what grounds she can defend that belief. She must be able to articulate why and how she believes what she does. An internalist epistemologist would require Alice to account for her belief that Jack is downstairs making breakfast; she must be able to state, for example, whether she was awake or asleep when forming this belief and what kinds of factors (e.g., the smell of bacon wafting through the air or her background knowledge that Jack makes breakfast daily) influenced her belief.

An externalist account holds that it is *not* necessary for the subject to grasp the reason for her belief in order for it to be justified or warranted. The term warrant is significant here. Warrant and warranting do the same work that justify and justifying do: both are alleged to be the "special ingredient" that has to be added to true belief in order to amount to knowledge (JTB). Colloquial uses of justify and warrant point to the differences in connotation that carry over into the epistemological uses of the terms. Externalists tend to use "warrant" rather than "justify" because it involves a less legalistic or adversarial connotation. Justifying one's belief suggests

---

20. "Grounds" and "reasons" here refers to any of the various foundational reasons (e.g., evidence; basic belief) or non-foundational reasons (e.g., one' context; coherence with other beliefs; one's mechanisms for belief formation such as sense perception; one's virtue of aptness in belief formation) that can be given for justification.

standing before a tribunal and making an argument for it; warranting one's belief suggests having a permit for its existence. For externalists, a person does not need "to know how she knows" a belief in order to be said to be warranted in believing it.[21] The externalist epistemologist may see Alice's belief as warranted even if Alice cannot explain why she believes Jack is making breakfast (e.g., "I *just* know he is").[22]

ANTHONY FLEW AND THE PRINCIPLE OF FALSIFICATION

In the 1955 watershed book *New Essays in Philosophical Theology*, Anthony Flew develops the principle of falsification, which tests the extent to which a statement can be falsified.[23] Flew uses the principle to make an argument against the putative meaningfulness of religious assertions. Statements that can be falsified—that is, those that are compatible with only a *particular* state of affairs—are meaningful; statements that cannot

---

21. Externalist epistemologies hold that the epistemic requirements made by internalism are not only impractical but also untenable. For example, externalist epistemologists point out that internalist requirements make it impossible for any child to have knowledge because children have beliefs without understanding how or in what way they arrived at those beliefs. In fact, children *do* know some things, and internalists do not account for this fact.

22. There is a natural tendency to see internalism aligned with foundationalism because both are more rigorous or "hard" and externalism and non-foundationalism paired together because both are more open or "soft." However, it is important to see that foundationalism/non-foundationalism and internalism/externalism make different kinds of demands on belief justification or belief warrant. What is important for foundationalists and non-foundationalists is the debate over *what* justifies belief. What is important for internalists and externalists is whether the believer must know *how and why* she holds her belief.

23. The historical antecedent to Flew's principle of falsification is verificationism, a philosophical theory propagated by the Vienna Circle. As empiricists, Vienna Circle philosophers began from the premise that only what can be seen, heard, or felt—those things that are literally from the "data of our experience"—have epistemic worth (Misak, *Verificationism*, 59). According to this theory, unless a statement can be verified as either true or false, it is, in effect, a meaningless statement. The criterion of verification is impossibly stringent and technically rules out all metaphysical, theological, mathematical, and even logical claims as meaningful. Because the foundational claim of verificationism—that all statements must be empirically verified to be "real"—could not itself be empirically verified, the theory collapsed under its own weight. While verificationists ultimately failed, it laid the groundwork for Karl Popper to construct the principle of falsification. Whereas verificationism look for evidence to show that a statement can be verified, and thus true, Popper's principle of falsification looks for possible evidence to show how a statement could be falsified. Flew's principle riffs on this theme.

be falsified—that is, those that are compatible with *any* state of affairs—are meaningless.[24] For if nothing (no evidence, no possible state of affairs) can count against a statement or belief—if the belief is unfalsifiable—then what could it mean? For Flew, religious beliefs tend to fall in the category of statements that are compatible with any state of affairs.

Like W. K. Clifford, Flew offers a parable to illustrate his principle. This parable, an adaption of John Wisdom's story in the article "Gods," is about coming across a clearing in a jungle growing many flowers and weeds.[25] A religious believer and a skeptic debate whether a gardener attends the plot. The believer claims the plot must be maintained by a gardener. The skeptic questions the believers evidence for this claim. In responding to the skeptic's objections, the believer finally argues that it is an invisible gardener, who can be neither seen nor heard, who clandestinely comes to lovingly tend his garden. The skeptic asks how this differs from an imaginary gardener or even from no gardener at all.

The believer's initial statement that it is a loving gardener who trims the leaves and nurtures the plants must be amended to accommodate the skeptic's objections. In Flew's estimation, it is amended so greatly (i.e., at first it is a belief about an average gardener tending the garden and it later turns into an invisible, smell-less, silent gardener who tends) that it obtains "an altogether different status." This process of amending statements to accommodate objections is what Flew calls "death by a thousand qualifications."[26]

Flew states that religious claims tend to follow the pattern of the invisible-gardener assertion, which was, he explains, "so eroded by qualification that it was no longer an assertion at all."[27] The belief about the gardener tending the garden lost its value proportional to the qualifications made about the gardener. *Meaning* is at issue for Flew. What value can a

24. In the essays by Hare and Mitchell that Flew discusses in his portion of "Theology and Falsification" (in Flew and MacIntyre, *New Essays in Philosophical Theology*), "assertions" and "utterances" are at issue. Flew, Hare, and Mitchell debate what distinguishes utterances from assertions. An utterance, according to Flew especially, is something like a plain or general statement that would be meaningless if there were no grounds or reasons that could count against it. An assertion, on the other hand, carries more weight; it is meaningful because it can be falsified. "Utterance" is the genus and "assertion" is a species of the utterance-genus, of which there are many others including exclamations, questions, requests, et cetera.

25. Wisdom, "Gods," 185–206.

26. Flew, "Theology and Falsification," in Flew and MacIntyre, *New Essays in Philosophical Theology*, 97.

27. Ibid., 98.

statement have if we do not know what it asserts and denies, and hence what it means? And if we do not know what it means, we cannot claim it as true or false.

The logic that undergirds Flew's question is that a statement has meaning only if it is connected to the data of experience. Flew writes, "If an utterance is an assertion, it will be equivalent to a denial of the negation of that assertion."[28] The principle of falsification tests for counterexamples. In simpler terms, an assertion is a statement that claims that "things stand thus and thus; *and not otherwise.*"[29] If any utterance is to be an assertion, it must have a potential counterexample. Since the believer's alleged statement about the gardener does not really make a claim (because of its innumerable qualifications), it is meaningless.

In the ethics of belief debate, Clifford uses a normative method to sort out what counts as a justified belief. He argues that beliefs are justified if they are based on good evidence, regardless of the consequences of the belief. Flew, like Clifford, takes a strongly normative approach. His goal is to arbitrate between an utterance being meaningful and meaningless. He does this by drawing on the principle of falsification as a criterion for evaluation. Flew does not look for a certain amount of evidence that would allow a statement to be verified as true but rather for any evidence that would show it to be false. If a statement is, hypothetically, able to be falsified, then the utterance can be called an assertion. (If, however, the falsifying evidence is overwhelming, then the assertion cannot be maintained.[30]) Said another way, an assertion must be falsifiable in principle or structurally.

R. M. Hare and *Bliks*

In response to Flew's use of the falsification principle, R. M. Hare introduces the concept of *blik*. *Bliks* are something like a worldview, which is not explanatory (that is, it does not explain our beliefs) but provides the mechanism by which we decide what counts as an explanation (for our beliefs).[31] *Bliks* are both *what* we see about the world and, at the same

---

28. Ibid.
29. Ibid., 106.
30. Stephen T. Davis called my attention to this point about Flew's use of an "evidential limit" (Davis, "Theology, Verification, and Falsification," 25–26).
31. Hare, "Theology and Falsification," in Flew and MacIntyre, *New Essays in Philosophical Theology*, 101. Horsburgh, "Mr. Hare on Theology and Falsification," 256–59, offers resources for putting this definition together.

time, the *way* we see it. The "thousand qualifications" that Flew sees as deadly are necessarily, for Hare, an inexorable part of making statements at all. Hare uses the concept of *blik* to show that while *bliks* are not falsifiable ("for my *blik* is compatible with any finite number of such [empirical] tests"[32]), they are still tremendously meaningful. This directly challenges Flew's claim that the only statements that are meaningful are those that are falsifiable.

Hare's concept of *blik* acts similarly (though more radically) to the way a non-foundationalist justificatory standard does. Take, for example, the comparison between Hare's *blik* and James's genuine option situation. James describes a particular situation that allows for belief justification even if evidence is lacking. Hare describes a pervasive, ubiquitous situation (created by the presence of one's *blik*) that allows for statements to be meaningful regardless of evidence or falsifiability. Hare's point is that all beliefs are developed and evaluated in the context of a believer's *blik*. Therefore when epistemologists go about their work to question the meaningfulness of statements or justifiability of beliefs, the standards for meaning or justification must be context- and subject-specific (in other words, *blik*-specific).

Hare might say that if a belief fits in or is in accord with one's overall *blik*, then a statement of that belief is meaningful. If a belief is out of line with or directly contradicts any of the beliefs that make up one's *blik*, then it naturally follows that one would find it (the belief in question) false or meaningless. Rather than evidence (Clifford), the genuine option situation (James), or the falsification principle (Flew), it is one's *blik* that provides the standard by which statements/beliefs can be judged. His *blik* model suggests a kind of self-regulating internal mechanism for meaningfulness: if a statement does not cohere with one's *blik*, then it could not survive as a meaningful statement.

Hare's challenge to Flew is externalist in nature; because a *blik* is by itself a mechanism for sorting out incoherent statements/beliefs, one need not (and, indeed, cannot) grasp the precise way in which one comes to make those statements of belief. Hare's descriptive approach and externalist standard draw attention to the subjective nature of belief formation and statement-making and helpfully throws doubt on the neatness of Flew's falsification principle. The *blik* model is troubling, however, in that virtually all utterances are meaningful because there is no way to conclusively

---

32. Hare, "Theology and Falsification," in Flew and MacIntyre, *New Essays in Philosophical Theology*, 101.

falsify any statement as an assertion, given the close connection beliefs have to the *blik* out of which they grow. Hare's *bliks* concept open an epistemological Pandora's box wherein it becomes impossible to adjudicate among statements/beliefs because it is impossible to adjudicate among *bliks*.

Basil Mitchell and Non-conclusive Falsifiablity

Basil Mitchell follows Hare on the point of conclusive falsifiability but disagrees with him about *bliks*. Mitchell points out that Hare's notion of *bliks* forecloses on the possibility that a person can recognize that something can really "count against" her belief. For Mitchell, things can indeed count against one's belief and can be admitted as such. However, Mitchell points out, nothing will count *conclusively* against that belief.[33] For once a person commits herself to a belief, Mitchell explains, statements about that belief cannot be conclusively falsified and it is "precisely this situation which constitutes the trial of . . . faith."[34] In other words, things counting against one's beliefs will be perceived as challenges to be endured rather than defeaters to be accepted. However, this fact does not diminish the significance of assertions.

Mitchell writes, "I agree with Flew that theological utterances must be assertions."[35] Mitchell provides a *via media* between Flew, who holds that statements are only meaningful if they can be falsified, and Hare, who holds that statements can be meaningful even if they are not falsifiable. Mitchell makes a move similar to James, descriptively formulating a non-foundationalist type of exception to a normative, foundationalist justificatory standard. He defends, *contra* Hare, that evidence can and does count against one's belief but points out, *à la* Hare, that evidence will not count conclusively against one's faith.[36] Mitchell thus maintains Flew's

---

33. Mitchell, "Theology and Falsification," in Flew and MacIntyre, *New Essays in Philosophical Theology*, 105. "Things" is the word used by Mitchell himself and is, I think, meant to be as broad as it sounds. Examples of "things" that can count against beliefs would include, but not be limited to, empirical observations, utterances, facts, competing worldviews, etc.

34. Mitchell, "Theology and Falsification," in Flew and MacIntyre, *New Essays in Philosophical Theology*, 104.

35. Ibid., 105.

36. Mitchell does not use the word *blik*; instead he discusses "articles of faith" to describe those conceptual things that evidence will not count against (i.e., perspective, worldview, central idea).

principle that statements must be falsifiable if they are to be meaningful but reorients the principle to take account of what is practically possible with regard to conclusive falsification.[37]

The real value of this falsification "snapshot" surfaces here, in Mitchell's insight: evidence is relevant though not necessarily foundational for accepting or rejecting a belief. Mitchell's argument is descriptive in its attention to the importance of how beliefs practically function—namely, as commitments. However, he raises the point only in order to mitigate, but not dismiss, a type of foundationalist standard for the meaningfulness of statements. The differences among Flew, Hare, and Mitchell may be as much hermeneutical as they are epistemological. In the last chapter, I inquired into the aims of theologies of religious pluralism. Did they intend to investigate into the range of a religion's possible meaning (hermeneutical)? Or were they after the religion's range of possible truth (epistemological)? These questions can likewise be applied to the "Theology and Falsification" debate. Flew pursues the epistemological question and Hare pursues the hermeneutical one. Mitchell, while recognizing the significance of a religion's *meaning* in the life of the believer, runs his argument along epistemological lines.

To summarize all the various positions briefly: Clifford and Flew approach epistemology normatively and argue for rigorous foundational standards for, respectively, justification and meaningfulness. James, Hare, and Mitchell work descriptively (at least at some points) to pull apart the normative, foundationalist cloth at its seams. They recognize nonfoundational factors that contribute to belief justification or statement meaningfulness. These three thinkers point toward, but do not develop fully, naturalized epistemology, which is a category of non-normative contemporary epistemology that will be discussed in chapter 4. Flew and Mitchell presuppose that a person is able to understand the grounds or reasons for her belief, reflecting internalist-like standards. Hare advances an externalist-like constraint on statements of belief and contends that

---

37. Flew responds to Mitchell, it should be noted, by stating that he is unsatisfied by the *bliks* qualification. He rejects *bliks* by way of making two points. First, he states that *bliks* are basically unorthodox. Hare proposes *bliks* to obviate the problem of falsification; in so doing, he allows for anything to "count" as a theological assertion. If all is permissible, there can be no orthodoxy. Second, he states that *bliks* cannot really even function in the way that they are intended to, which is to allow for a broadened spectrum of what can be an assertion. Flew writes, "If they were not even intended as assertions then many religious activities would become fraudulent, or merely silly" (Flew, "Theology and Falsification," in Flew and MacIntyre, *New Essays in Philosophical Theology*, 108).

persons should not be held accountable for the grounds of their beliefs because they *cannot* be—*bliks* just do not work that way. With the exception of James, all of these thinkers develop *a priori* epistemologies for religious belief. Their epistemologies are *a priori* on the issue of religion in the sense that they do not draw from instances of actual religious belief but rather, draw from other (prior) epistemic circumstances that are then applied to the religious situation.

Contemporary Discussions

In chapter 1, Paul Griffiths laid out the epistemological challenge of religious diversity as follows: if an opposing religious claim is deemed to be from a trustworthy source and if there is no good way to explain away the opposing claim, it follows that one's own religious belief will be epistemically troubled.[38] This is exactly the situation that concerns contemporary epistemologists of religious disagreement. Robert McKim and Richard Feldman develop two epistemological principles, the T-Principle and S-Principle, to guide the religious believer who is aware of conflicting claims. When religious believers apply these principles, they are left with only tentative religious belief with religious practice (McKim) or suspended religious belief with religious practice (Feldman). In both cases, believers can practice their religions even if they are not justified in their beliefs. Because the T- and S-Principles are predicated on evidential-foundationalist and internalist assumptions, as this section will show, and because these assumptions are drawn from everyday situations rather than specifically religious situations (thus, their epistemologies are developed *a priori* on the issue of religious belief), McKim and Feldman fail to adequately address the full range of possible epistemological outcomes of interreligious encounter.

Epistemologies of Religious Disagreement

ROBERT MCKIM AND THE PRINCIPLE OF TENTATIVITY

Epistemologist Robert McKim claims and defends the following normative principle—the Tentativety Principle (T-Principle)—for what should happen when a religious believer meets the sort of challenges stated by Griffiths. He writes, "Disagreement (of the sort under discussion

---

38. Griffiths, *Problems of Religious Diversity*, 73–75.

[religious]) about an issue or area of inquiry provides reason for whatever beliefs we hold about that issue or area of inquiry to be tentative."[39] According to this principle, the awareness of opposing religious claims should lead one to have less confidence in the epistemic soundness of the belief, but not to suspend belief or practices.

An example from ordinary life will be helpful here for understanding the meaning of how McKim's T-Principle applies to Griffith's situation. Perhaps my mother believes the flowers in the garden are crocuses. My father believes they are tulips. My mother has known my father for thirty-five years, is aware of his knowledge of landscaping and *flora* around their home, and generally trusts his judgment. While my mother feels confident in her belief that the flowers are crocuses, she knows my father to be trustworthy (in this matter and others) and cannot think of any good explanation for why he would not recognize the flowers as crocuses (she is sure they are talking about the same patch of flowers, is aware that he has never had a problem distinguishing crocuses and tulips in the past, and knows that he is not in any way cognitively impaired). Given these circumstances, my mother is left to wonder about her belief that the flowers in the garden are crocuses. What should people do when they find themselves in this type of situation when it is with regard to religious beliefs?

McKim's argument for the T-Principle is two-pronged. He first wisely makes the case that people should approach religious others with humility about their own beliefs.[40] Secondly, he looks to carve out a place for the justifiability of being faithful to one's own religious tradition, so that beliefs should be held tentatively, but not dropped. Given one's tentatively held beliefs, McKim recommends a "sort of perseverance, or attempt to keep one's faith." This involves, McKim continues, "an attempt to make as much of it as possible important to [the believer]: this may take the form of an effort to live as if the beliefs in question are true."[41] Because McKim wants to respect the epistemic challenge that religious diversity poses—a challenge the first chapter called for acknowledging—and do so without being hostile to religious traditions or to religious believers' fidelity to those traditions, he concludes that the best one can do is hold belief tentatively and continue to practice one's religion.

---

39. McKim, *Religious Ambiguity and Religious Diversity*, 143.

40. This may happen precisely by recognizing the religious other as trustworthy and by avoiding the temptation to explain away the religious other's beliefs.

41. Ibid., 171.

Epistemological Debates

McKim tries to walk the line between evidential-foundationalist internalism and a kind of non-foundationalist internalism. Because he argues that, upon close evaluation, we cannot *really* hold beliefs without sufficient evidence in the face of disagreement, he finally insists on evidence-based internalist criteria for justifying belief. He assumes that it is within the believer's cognitive grasp to know how and why she acquired and holds her belief. But because some beliefs are the keystone around which people build their lives, they should be justified at least in remaining in their religious traditions. The piece about the keystone is the non-foundationalist element of McKim's theory. It might be called a contextual non-foundational reason for belief.

McKim ends up calling for tentatively-held belief. Because he recognizes a greater context and a wide range of factors influencing belief formation and belief maintenance (such as involvement in community and commitment to a way of life), he develops a pragmatic non-foundational criterion to justify religious practice. It is because he deems it possible to divorce belief from practice that McKim is able to do this, thus minimally satisfying the non-foundationalist conviction that the grounds for belief may lie outside of foundations such as evidence.[42] The wedge McKim drives between belief and actions arising from belief (namely, religious practices) is particularly open to criticism from the perspective of Clifford, who closely connects belief and action.

RICHARD FELDMAN AND THE PRINCIPLE OF SUSPENSION

The S-Principle is as follows: in the face of diverse religious beliefs, a person's contested religious belief should be suspended. With this principle, Richard Feldman draws an even stronger conclusion than McKim about the situation created by religious diversity. His is achieved through a normative method and is evidential-foundationalist and internalist in orientation. According to Feldman, if religious belief is like other types of complex belief such as political and ethical belief—and he argues that it is—then the fact of religious diversity poses an insurmountable challenge for religious believers.

If one critically reflects upon her own belief in light of opposing beliefs presented by religious diversity (again, a move lauded in chapter 1),

---

42. While McKim does create space for "rational" tentatively held belief and "rational" religious practice, it seems he does this only as a concession to his externalist conscience.

Feldman points out that it will be difficult, even impossible, for her to find good reasons to support the claim that her belief is "true" and thus justified. Considering that no one can be certain that her belief is *the* true belief and that everyone has access to knowing how and why they believe what they do (an internalist assumption), Feldman takes the position that the most epistemically responsible thing to do is to suspend belief altogether.

For Feldman, it is appropriate to continue religious practice while suspending religious belief. What is to be suspended is the expectation that one's religious tradition has the exclusive claim to truth; this need not involve renouncing involvement in the religious tradition or religious practice itself. In order to carve out a space (one that is even smaller than McKim's) for the justifiability of religious practice, Feldman also drives a wedge between religious practice and belief.[43] Feldman writes:

> It is possible that the choice about being religious or not, or the choice among the various religions, is in some ways like the fork in the road example. This is an extremely important choice we must make, and our information about the matter is limited. No one is to be criticized for making a choice. If this is right, it may show that our religious choices have a kind of practical rationality. However, it does not show that our religious beliefs are epistemically rational.[44]

The choice to hold religious beliefs cannot be justified, for Feldman, but the choice to maintain religious practice is granted a sort of pragmatic justification.[45]

---

43. Terrence W. Tilley deals with one example of the kind of fissure between belief and practice that Feldman discusses. In analyzing prayer as a linguistic practice, Tilley argues that prayer need not be understood as a practice that presumes belief in God. Rather, hope is sufficient grounds for belief. He concludes with the suggestion that prayer may in fact be the "practice *through which* these beliefs become as justified as they can be" (Tilley, "'Lord Help My Unbelief,'" 239–47). Tilley does not, however, separate practice from proposition. There is a distinction to be drawn between the epistemic attitude of believing and the proposition that is believed.

44. Feldman, "Reasonable Religious Disagreements."

45. In the end, Feldman construes religious practice as the ugly step-sister to religious belief—the ugly step-sister who is allowed to attend the ball not because anyone genuinely desires her presence, but rather because everyone would feel too guilty if she were excluded.

Assessing the Contemporary Approaches

To demonstrate the nuance of the contemporary discussion, it will be beneficial to relate these contemporary epistemologies back to the historical debates. The epistemologists discussed here take their cues from Clifford and Flew much more than they do James, Hare, and Mitchell. McKim and Feldman develop a normative epistemological approach, create evidential-foundationalist justificatory requirements for religious belief, and set an internalist constraint on belief.

Clifford argues that a believer is epistemically and morally justified in holding a belief only if it is based on sufficient evidence. To express Clifford's model in the language of contemporary epistemology, then, if S knows that p, p is justified only if p is supported by E. For Clifford, if E exists in support of p, then S meets the normative, evidentialist requirement for belief that p.

The situation of religious diversity, however, raises the following, more complex situation: S_1 knows that p_1 on the basis of E_1 where S_2 knows that p_2 on the basis of E_2. Using Clifford alone, p_1 and p_2 both may be epistemically good if the evidence for them is sufficient. If p_1 and p_2 are contradictory, however, Clifford has a problem. How can both S_1 and S_2 be justified in believing their conflicting beliefs? Clifford's version of justification deals with the fact that conflicting belief (S_1 knows that p_1 on the basis of E_1 and S_2 knows that p_2 on the basis of E_2) by stating that either S_1 or S_2 or both S_1 or S_2 had insufficient evidence for p_1 and p_2 but each failed to recognize it.

Clifford's form of and approach to justification does not solve the problem of multiple evidences or multiple sources of evidence, which is just the problem of religious diversity. What evidence is "sufficient"? The conflict of belief raised by religious diversity is a situation that a Cliffordian model is unequipped to handle except by claiming insufficiency of evidence. While McKim and Feldman follow Clifford's normative, evidential foundationalism, they need another "ingredient" in order to make it work in the situation of conflicting belief. They accomplish this by developing an internalist constraint on belief justification. Flew's argument sheds light on the internalist constraint.

McKim and Feldman ask the question: on what grounds can people hold beliefs while they are aware of the existence of conflicting beliefs? Flew not only develops a system that works in the face of conflicting belief, he in fact requires that every epistemological (belief-forming or utterance-producing) moment include *explicit* reflection on the possible falsifying conditions for belief (these conditions would not only include contradictory beliefs). Flew's concept of meaningfulness depends on whether there are falsifying conditions for belief. Without an explicit internalist constraint on justification, Clifford's evidential foundationalism only goes so far in helping to address the problem of diverse religious beliefs. The addition of an internalist constraint, demonstrated here by Flew, sets the stage for McKim and Feldman to argue that it is necessarily the case that either one belief will prevail over the other or both must fall.

McKim and Feldman's respective strategies are normative: they function to make normative claims about what is requisite for belief justification. They are evidential-foundationalist: first, they assume that all beliefs rest on the foundations of evidence, and second, they are primarily concerned with whether there is better or more persuasive evidence for opposing propositional claims. Finally they are internalists: they assume that it is within the cognitive grasp of the subject to know how and why she holds her belief.

If S_1 knows that p_1 and S_2 knows that p_2, McKim and Feldman adjudicate the conflict between by p_1 and p_2 by asking if S_1 and S_2 are aware of E_1 outweighing E_2; if there is no clear indication that all the evidence (E_∞) is superior for warranting any one belief, then both S_1 and S_2 should let go of their belief, either moderately or entirely. McKim and Feldman make seemingly valid arguments. If a person cannot understand or demonstrate how her belief is more well founded than her friend's belief, then it would seem to follow that perhaps she should give up that belief.

Yet people who are deeply engaged in interreligious dialogue are not as troubled as McKim and Feldman would have them. People who have extensive and thoughtful conversations with others who hold differing religious beliefs, who are recognized to be trustworthy, and whose beliefs cannot be explained away, report the opposite of being epistemically troubled as these epistemological models would suggest they should. Rather than growing more doubtful about their own beliefs (or giving them up entirely), as the following chapter will demonstrate, interreligious dialogue participants often learn to approach others' beliefs with humility *and* grow more fully in their own practices and beliefs.[46]

The contemporary epistemological "solution" to the epistemic situation created by religious diversity hinges on one key move. The move is

---

46. This claim is based on interviews that are a part of my two-year-long research conversation with a women's interreligious dialogue group. This will be discussed in the following chapter.

to argue that religious practice may be maintained even though religious belief may not.[47] In making this distinction between belief and practice, McKim and Feldman attempt to soften the conclusions of their foundationalist, internalist epistemologies; they intend to allow for some aspect of religious commitment to march forward while satisfying justificatory requirements and so present a seemingly practical solution to the epistemic puzzle of religious diversity.[48]

In arriving at this "solution," McKim and Feldman presuppose that an individual's religious belief can be isolated from the communities and practices in which they are formed. They thus only talk about and judge evidential foundations for beliefs apart from the reality in which those putative foundations are situated (when S_1 believes that p_1 on the basis of E_1 but is also aware of p_2 and its basis E_2, McKim and Feldman focus solely on E_1 and E_2 rather than thinking through *what else* beyond E_∞ gives rise to belief). There is no sense that belief and practice are possibly co-constitutive; these epistemologists do not recognize—at least in their epistemological formulations—that a Hindu offering daily *puja* to Saraswati, for example, can nourish, encourage, or give rise to beliefs about Saraswati.

While recognizing the importance of religious practice for day-to-day life (this is precisely why they allow for continued practice), McKim and Feldman overlook the importance of religious practice for shaping belief itself. This oversight is curious for two epistemologists who so greatly emphasize the importance of a believer reflecting on how and why she arrived at and holds her belief. McKim and Feldman so privilege the role that evidential foundations play in belief that they are blind even to the process of internalist reflection that they themselves employ.

The paradigm advanced by McKim and Feldman is flawed in three fundamental ways. First, by their own lights, McKim and Feldman neglect a key locus of epistemological inquiry: the relationship between belief and practice. This produces the curious effect pointed out above, which leads to the second flaw. How can a rigorist internalist not *at least* explore non-foundational factors for belief formation such as continued practice? Third and finally, McKim and Feldman fail to explore real, rather than only hypothetical, examples of interreligious encounter. If they had, they would find experiential accounts of strengthened religious belief rather

---

47. McKim and Feldman (and McKim in particular) themselves seem to be troubled by their own conclusions.

48. This strikes me a concession to their own intuitions about the problems with their rigorist epistemological standards rather than a concession to the religious believers in their readership.

than tentative or suspended belief. Given such accounts, the alternatives are either to claim epistemic privilege (e.g., the believers just have not thought about it enough and so do not realize that they *must* be troubled) or to wonder genuinely and honestly at the question of why the practice does not match the theory. It is the second alternative that I choose. In pursuit of theoretical reflection that *is* accountable to the practical experiences of interreligious dialogue, I now to turn to first hand reports of these experiences.

3

"Evoking the Luminous" in Dialogue

A Case Study of a Women's Interreligious Dialogue Group

ROUGHLY STATED, THE PROBLEM POINTED OUT BY CHAPTER 1 IS THAT theological theories having to do with religious diversity are not epistemologically-minded enough or—if they are—are not systematically so. In chapter 2, the charge brought against philosophies dealing with religious diversity—and particularly with contemporary ones—is that the approach to diversity is misguided by being overly epistemological or theoretical and not appropriately attuned to actual experiences of interreligious encounter. Are these criticisms of theological and philosophical scholarship on religious diversity—"not epistemological enough" and "overly epistemological"—not incongruous? The function of this chapter is to nuance these two criticisms by way of example (a Philadelphia area women's interreligious dialogue group provides a case study) in order to open the door for a new way of thinking about the epistemological significance of religious diversity.

In this chapter, I discuss the comments and ideas of interreligious dialogue participants as articulated in a series of personal interviews as well as in the context of interreligious dialogue meetings. The interreligious dialogue participants of this case study exhibit a kind of "taking-belief-seriously" stance toward diversity and yet, they are not led to place at which McKim and Feldman arrive—that is, diversity does not create an epistemic problem for their beliefs even though they take each others' beliefs seriously as claims to truth. Instead, they find the encounter with diversity through dialogue to provide them with a unique opportunity to form and explore their religious beliefs more deeply.

This chapter is primarily descriptive in nature. It is divided into two major sections. The first section begins with a sketch of the group's history

Virtue in Dialogue

and pattern of functioning. It next moves to a detailed description of the group in terms of (1) its purpose, as understood by the members, both in and beyond the dialogue sessions, (2) the values and standards for dialogue that are mutually cultivated through the group and in the members, and (3) the role the group plays in the women's religious lives particularly in relation to their home religious traditions.[1] Throughout the chapter, I call attention to the ways in which the women's statements are related to the theoretical claims discussed in chapters 1 and 2. I do so to show how the seemingly incongruous demands and evaluations of these first two chapters are actually reconcilable and, moreover, productive toward the end of developing an epistemological theory that is adequate to the experience of interreligious encounter. In this discussion, I also contextualize this women's interreligious group and the significance of their practices by exploring scholarship on women's interreligious dialogue at large.

In the second major section, I analyze the ways in which this group, in general, challenges the assumptions of epistemologists like McKim and Feldman who understand interreligious dialogue as only an occasion of epistemic disagreement. Specifically, I argue that through dialogue, the women of Philadelphia forge a multireligious community that functions as an *epistemic* community. This community has consequences for both the criteria by which they evaluate their own and each other's beliefs and

---

1. This exposition of the Philadelphia women's dialogue group is the outcome of a research project initiated by Jeannine Hill Fletcher in the spring of 2007 and carried out by her and myself since that time. Hill Fletcher began the project out of interest for using ethnographic accounts as a resource for theology. We collaborated to create a plan for this research and, in particular, for using a participant-observer model as our method of inquiry. The project began by contacting the group through formal letters and soliciting their consent. I then initiated the research-conversation by conducting phone interviews with group members about their experiences of interreligious dialogue. After making contact with several group members, I traveled to Philadelphia on several occasions to meet with the women in one-on-one settings (usually in coffee shops or their homes) and recorded our one- to two-hour long discussions. During that period, I attended a dialogue session and observed, but did not record, their dialogue and took notes on their interaction as well as kept in contact with a handful of the women through email. The research culminated in a dialogue meeting in which we the researchers facilitated the formal discussion in the dialogue meeting and then carried the conversation, informally, over a group dinner. Over the course of the interviewing process, I talked with many members on several occasions, recorded these conversations, and draw on my transcriptions of them for this chapter. All interviews were conducted in confidentiality, and the names of interviewees are withheld by mutual agreement. The names supplied throughout the chapter are pseudonyms so as to respect their anonymity.

"Evoking the Luminous" in Dialogue

also for the conditions or circumstances under which they form religious beliefs.

An Interreligious Dialogue Group from Greater Philadelphia

Origins and History

The Philadelphia area women's interreligious dialogue group has been in existence for close to a decade.[2] The group began because a handful of women from Philadelphia, having known one another through the city's longstanding Thanksgiving interfaith service, decided that they wanted more interaction with diverse religious people. The three women who are responsible for organizing the group did so by asking their friends, people from their church, synagogue, and assembly, and others that they knew from the Thanksgiving interfaith event, if they would be interested in meeting regularly throughout the year. As they recruited friends for the newly forming group and held a few small meetings in each other's living rooms, they also decided that it would be beneficial to hold an event for the larger community on the topic religious diversity. Because of the timing of the planned event, which was set to be in the late summer and early fall of 2001, their community program became specifically about responding to the World Trade Center terrorist attacks from a variety of religious perspectives.

One of the group's founding members explains that they had four speakers, "a priest, a rabbi, a Muslim, and a Baha'i" and "invited the public to come and listen."[3] This community program took place in a Philadelphia suburb and is remembered by group members as a success. It was successful both because it brought together members of the community to talk about a sensitive subject at a critical moment and also because it was ultimately the catalyst for drawing in more women to sustain the interreligious conversation. One of the group's earliest members, Joanna, tells

---

2. I am especially grateful to Jeannine Hill Fletcher for extending me the opportunity to work on this research project as well as for her extensive guidance both in writing the narrative of the group and in thinking through the philosophical and theological implications of the women's voices.

3. Interview by Mara Brecht, June 25, 2007, Philadelphia, PA, transcription.

why she thinks the community event planted the seed for the group today: "We all sought to express our feelings in an interreligious setting."[4]

The contrast between the group's community program and the group's present function is noteworthy. In the beginning, as Leila explains, they followed a traditional form for "doing" interreligious dialogue. The priest, rabbi, Muslim, and Baha'i came to the community program to speak as authoritative representatives of and for their tradition. The logic of such a format—where each comes to educate the other about his/her beliefs and practices—ends almost inevitably in the kind of epistemic conflict predicted by the *a priori* formulated religious epistemologies of Feldman and McKim. As the Philadelphia dialogue group grew, however, they changed their model for interreligious engagement. In the group's present form, they no longer place emphasis on which tradition is being represented by whom and neither do they expect that any person can speak for an entire religious tradition.

Group members report sticking with the group in those first years for a variety of reasons: they wanted to express their feelings about the state of the world in general, reflect on their hopes for religious people in American culture following this crisis, and learn about other religious traditions and, in particular, Islam. The dialogue group is not a formal group in the sense that it has a title or a mission statement. It is not registered with any broader interfaith organizations (such as North American Interfaith Network or the Interfaith Alliance) and does not advertise itself or host community events. Without any formal processes, structures, or purpose in place, it is intriguing that the group should be able to maintain itself for over the course of close to a decade.

The group's existence is sustained by the richness of the dialogue that takes place among the women. In the words of one group member, the purpose of the dialogue group is "spiritual conversation and community."[5] In its nascent form, the group met the basic learning needs of its members. That is to say, the women came to learn *about* religious traditions, and the group provided that possibility. As the women continued meeting, however, the group meetings shifted from being a forum to talk about 9/11 or a space for a pedagogically oriented discussion about religions to a group where members came to truly converse with each other about their own religious lives in a rather profound way.

---

4. Interview by Mara Brecht, June 20, 2007, Philadelphia, PA, transcription.

5. Interview by Mara Brecht and Jeannine Hill Fletcher, February 12, 2009, Philadelphia, PA, digital recording.

The group decided to engage in an exercise that would allow this shift—from a pedagogical discussion to a deep conversation—to occur. They refer to this exercise as the sharing of their spiritual autobiographies or faith journeys. For several consecutive months (some members recall the process taking an entire year), they devoted each dialogue session to the spiritual autobiographies of one or two women. In a document describing the process, the Philadelphia group explains the purpose of this exercise as follows:

> We are interested in stories of how our life's experiences, values and beliefs have shaped our religious identification and practice. Sharing our spiritual journeys promises to give life to the distinctiveness and richness of our diverse faith traditions, while deepening relationships and understanding.

Taking the time to listen to each woman recount her journey of faith and answer questions about her story resulted in what one member calls a "qualitative difference" in the group.[6] As another member says, "The group was more superficial before [we shared our spiritual autobiographies] and our conversations were more superficial."[7] Engaging with each other through their own narratives afforded the women stronger bonds of relationships as well as conversations with greater depth.

The spiritual autobiography exercise—and the kinds of practices involved in doing that exercise—functions as a lodestone for the group. It is not only the most important experience in the group's collective memory, it is also the experience back to which they continually refer and the experience that guides their following conversations. The group is characterized and constituted by the spiritual autobiographies. As Elli puts it, "I would say that experience in the women's dialogue . . . has been sharing stories of life's journeys and stories and faith and opinions formed out of that—there's no doubt about it."[8] In their narrative sharing, they became a community and defined for themselves a common "language" and pattern of functioning. The women of Philadelphia understand this community as contributing both to their individual religious lives and to the greater good.

In this evolution—from a group oriented to inform and teach its members *about* religion to a group oriented to creating space for its

---

6. Interview by Mara Brecht, July 20, 2007, Philadelphia, PA, digital recording.
7. Interview by Mara Brecht, July 21, 2007, Philadelphia, PA, digital recording.
8. Interview by Mara Brecht, July 20, 2007, Philadelphia, PA, digital recording.

members to actually engage which each other in their religious practices—the group took on the characteristics of a distinctive community. In the interviews and dialogue discussions, group members acknowledge a range of significant features, characteristics, and associated aims or objectives of their group. The participants' comments are self-reflective. What they say about how they see themselves and what they do in dialogue can be organized into three main categories: first, the women understand themselves as working together toward a greater social good; second, they find that through dialogue they teach one another *both* about their religious traditions and practices *and* how to be more carefully attuned to each other and skilled in entering into each others' religious experiences; and, third, they show that they have built a religious retreat for themselves that complements, rather than stands in competition with, the home they have in their own religious traditions. In the course of discussing each of these aspects, I will call attention to their epistemological implications and suggest in what directions these implications might be developed.

The Features of the Interreligious Dialogue Group

A Shared Endeavor toward a "better way of being"

One member, Rachel, reflects on her understanding of the process undertaken in the group in her own words: "The world demonstrates to us the consequences of living in a world where we are not connected to one another; we see that and ask what is more important to us—being connected? Or, being in the world as it is?"[9] Rachel's comment calls attention to the fact that the group understands itself as transformative for the broader world. There is an ethical impetus for the group: it *makes a difference* that they meet. It offers a community and place wherein its members can discuss how the world is and determine together how the world should be. This description shores up with two closely related theoretical points articulated in the previous chapters. First, their understanding of themselves as creating a space where the discussion of ideas and beliefs generates tangible consequences for the world reinforces Clifford's insight (discussed in chapter 2) that beliefs are dispositions to act. Second, taking Netland's point (discussed in chapter 1) that truth is dynamic and expressions of truth come in forms besides propositional statements, it is possible to see the outcome of interreligious dialogue—that it is transformative in

---

9. Interview by Mara Brecht, July 21, 2007, Philadelphia, PA, digital recording.

people's lives, the community, and so on—as itself an epistemologically significant "statement" or expression of truth.

The space offered by the group is one that crosses the boundaries of particular faith communities of the various religions represented by the group members; it is an interreligious community that has consequences for how its members live and believe in the world. Another member, Ruth, describes something like this when she articulates:

> It's very edifying to be able to understand and to be reinforced in what you think you understand . . . [the dialogue meetings are] really not [focused on] which person is which religion so much as that these are people who are trying to find a better way to be in the world or who are trying to make the world a better place even if it's only for their family, or whoever it's for. And when we share, we are always sharing both richnesses of our own culture or our own religion and frustration.[10]

Ruth expresses the fact that the interreligious dialogue group does more than teach its members about diverse religious traditions. When members come to the group, they do not just say, "I believe x" or "I believe y." They do not make propositional statements alone but dynamically express the truth to which they religiously commit themselves.

Rebecca Chopp uses the phrase "poetics of testimony" to denote "the discourse practices and various voices that seek to describe or name that which rational discourse will not or cannot reveal."[11] The spiritual autobiography exercise initiated a communicative pattern of dynamic, "non-rational" expression that falls into Chopp's category of the "poetics of testimony." "Non-rational" here should not suggest confused, obtuse, illogical, or anti-intellectual expression. Rather, it connotes the kind of expression wherein theoretical claims follow from and grow out of the stories of one's life and experiences, rather than precede one's life and experiences. It is a discourse grounded in *a posteriori* reasoning rather than *a priori* reasoning. The women come together to narrate for each other their understanding of and hopes for the world, through the frame of their own religious experience.

Their narratives are emotive and embodied. Each woman occupies the roles of storyteller and storyhearer at various times in sharing these narratives. Their conversations are not constrained "from above" but rather organically formed "from below." If traditional dialogue is the "rational

10. Interview by Mara Brecht, August 18, 2008, Philadelphia, PA, digital recording.
11. Chopp, "Theology and the Poetics of Testimony," 56.

discourse" that the Philadelphia women break beyond through sharing their journeys of faith, the Philadelphia group's "poetics of testimony" discourse might even be called interreligious *narration* rather than interreligious *dialogue*. In the process of making their relational connections and weaving together their individual stories into a larger fabric through interreligous narration, the women have created a community wherein they gather and are able to be touched and transformed by one another.

The transformative dimension of the women's interreligious narration is a key component to Chopp's notion of the "poetics of testimony." Chopp argues that, by attending to testimony in theological discussions, the method of theology at large will be altered, creating space for theologians to imagine new possibilities for ordering the world.[12] Specifically, Chopp theorizes that the "poetics of testimony" reveal ways for theologians to re-think classic theological problems and to re-order important theological categories such as reason and revelation. Chopp's point that listening to the testimony and voice of someone not previously heard can push one to re-consider both how she construes a theological problem and how she arrives at an answer to that problem is mirrored in the accounts of the Philadelphia women. Since the time the group embraced interreligious narration through sharing their spiritual autobiographies, the very way they experience interreligious encounter radically changed. Through their "testimonial" practice, the group understands itself as not creating just a learning environment, but also a transformative environment.

Two group members, Elli and Hina, offer their descriptions of where they have arrived at through this process. Elli states, "I experience this group as my anchor in time. The group has been a circle of faith—not a support group, but really a faith group. It has been a consistent reminder for me that I need to touch other people of faith."[13] Hina relates her sense of the group as well, "I think it helps us understand each other's religions and thought processes and seeing where each other comes from . . . when we come together we sort of put a salve on each other's wounds. And we try to find out or try to sort through the issues and how they affect us as individuals and us as members of the larger society."[14] The group sees itself as a healing community where members come together to tell each other

---

12. Chopp, "Theology and the Poetics of Testimony," 69n20.

13. Interview by Mara Brecht, June 28, 2007, Philadelphia, PA, transcription.

14. Interview by Mara Brecht, December 16, 2007, Philadelphia, PA, digital recording.

their stories of "a better way of being" in and through a shared experience of faith.

The group's aim is not to get its participants to hold their beliefs tentatively or suspend them entirely but is rather to form a tightly woven, healing community. Neither the sense of connectivity members feel in the group nor their self-understanding as a healing community necessarily means that the participants reach agreement about their differing religious beliefs. As the Philadelphia women demonstrate, the existence of a healing community is not predicated on its participants agreeing on religious beliefs. In this way, their dialogue is intended to foster social flourishing rather than bring about theological uniformity. In dialogue, the group collectively imagines together a vision for social flourishing for themselves as person, for their group and, more broadly, for the world. Their vision for social flourishing—or, as Ruth characterizes it, a "better way of being"—includes freedom from being met with religious prejudice and persecution; the ability to see the "human face" of political issues; the capability to build bridges across social, cultural, and religious rifts; an ever-expanding range of possibilities for religious identity; and, most importantly, authentic engagement with God.[15]

Cultivating the Practice of Dialogue Together

In addition to a conversation that shapes participants in solidarity for transformation of the world and toward social flourishing, members of the Philadelphia area dialogue group demonstrate ways in which they contribute toward the excellence of the practice of dialogue itself and their own ability to participate in that dialogue. The excellent practices and characteristics (such as careful listening, patience in disagreement, and courage to tell one's story) that allow for deep dialogue and full participation can also be called the virtues of dialogue. In chapter 4, I analyze theories of epistemic virtue and lay groundwork for my own theory of epistemic virtue. In chapters 5 and 6, I build the model epistemological model which I argue makes sense of how interreligious dialogue is deeply epistemologically significant for the theology of religious diversity. Before making these theoretical arguments however, I will continue to proceed by way of example. To explain the way in which the dialogue members develop the excellences or virtues of their dialogue practice, it is instructive

---

15. Because this was not an issue the women directly responded to, I have culled this list from all the interview transcriptions and summarized them this way.

to look at the contrast between group members at the beginning of dialogue and later in dialogue.

One participant of the Philadelphia women's interreligious dialogue relates the story of the transformation she has undergone since her membership to the group:

> [A friend] invited me to join [a Muslim-Jewish dialogue] and I said, "No, I won't do that." Interfaith dialogue only works when you have respect for the other people and I had no respect for Muslims, so I wouldn't join that group. And then, when I met [a Muslim member of our group] and she told us about her faith journey and her experiences with 9/11, my attitude changed. My attitude towards [her] and my attitude toward Muslims and everything changed. And that was probably the most significant thing that happened for me.[16]

This group member draws attention to the way her relationships came to shape her understanding of the religious other. It is not the case that this woman's relationships with the group's Muslim members arbitrarily shifted. Rather it shifted *because of* the intentional nature of their dialogue—a nature initiated by the spiritual autobiography exercise. Interreligious dialogue—and the relationships forged in that context—afforded this woman with the opportunity to both challenge her own beliefs and encourage her ability to listen to religious others. The group member notes that she at first "had no respect for Muslims." Through dialogue, she learned to listen to her Muslim dialogue partners and, rather than approaching them with suspicion, approaches them with openness and empathy.

Another group member, Emily, sees a trend with this kind of transformation. She describes other instances of this type and offers a hypothesis about why some people refuse to enter into interreligious dialogue at all:

> In every case I can think of where people actually do engage, their identities—while made more flexible—are strengthened. That is my experience of us here . . . if people go into it thinking, "It's going to be a conflict, so why start it? I already know what I think, so why have the conversation when I am going to lose my identity?" And they get into it and realize, "I actually don't know everything that I think; I am not losing my identity, it is getting stronger; and there are points of convergence and conflict."[17]

16. Interview by Mara Brecht, July 21, 2007, Philadelphia, PA, digital recording.
17. Interview by Mara Brecht and Jeannine Hill Fletcher, February, 12, 2009,

Emily draws a connection between a concern for one's religious identity and seeing dialogue as necessarily conflictual in nature. Emily theorizes that fear of "losing" what she calls "religious identity" halts the interreligious conversation. In fact, to Emily's mind, it is by *not* dialoguing with religious others that one's religious self-understanding becomes reified, brittle, and, finally, capable of crumbling. Entering into interreligious dialogue requires courage against the fear of "losing" one's identity or religious self-understanding.[18] The interreligious dialogue group promotes this kind of courage among its members.

As Emily suggests, the group demands from its members a willingness to admit the partialness and inadequacy with which we understand even our mostly dearly held religious beliefs. Emily states that through dialogue she has come to realize, "I actually don't know everything that I think." The group appreciates the central role that religious beliefs and the practices associated with them play in one's "religious identity." Thus, the group's unspoken expectation for partially-held beliefs is not the same thing as Feldman's requirement for suspended beliefs or even McKim's call for tentatively-held beliefs. Rather than undermining religious belief, Emily here conveys an organically-formed externalist sensibility about religious beliefs and religious self-understanding: dialogue functions to remind individuals that why they believe what they believe may not always be within their grasp, but this does not in principle bar these beliefs from epistemological justification (as it would for Feldman and McKim). People like the woman in the previous example demonstrate back to the interreligious dialogue group the way that one's religious beliefs can be strengthened rather than lost through the interreligious encounter—an encounter which necessarily calls into question the extent to which one can account for (entirely or with adequacy) her beliefs and, by extension, her religious identity.

In another example of how group members draw courage or learn from the group as a whole and, in turn, contribute back to the group through their own acts of creative courage, transformation, and innovation, Leila relates a story about an experience she had in an elevator of an upscale hotel in the suburban Philadelphia.[19] Leila tells of how she and a stranger shared an elevator as they were on their ways to two different parts of the hotel. Both women, Leila and the stranger, were headed to

---

Philadelphia, PA, digital recording.

18. The discussion in chapter 8 will touch on these matters.

19. Interview by Mara Brecht August 19, 2008, Philadelphia, PA, digital recording.

events held by their respective religious communities. They had a polite exchange about going to these events and the stranger asked Leila, "Are you a Christian?" Leila responded that she is not and explained that she is Baha'i. The woman stated flatly, "You are going to go to hell." When Leila recounts the story of this confrontation, her fellow interreligious dialogue participants are astonished. They ask her how she responded, if she felt hurt or angry, or if she took the opportunity to educate the Christian woman about the Baha'i faith. Leila only laughs. She says she could not respond in any of these ways because she was so shocked that someone would condemn her to hell after a brief and otherwise cordial conversation; her only response could be to laugh.

Leila expresses an innovative way to handle interreligious conflict. She could have engaged in argumentation aimed at dismissing her elevator-conversation partner or she could have barked an angry reply back to the Christian woman. Instead, Leila reacted calmly and later laughs about the story. Her laugh disrupts the standard logic of what should happen in an exchange like this one. From her experience in interreligious dialogue, Leila knew that this woman's only interest was in conflict and, moreover, that this woman lacked the "excellences" or "virtues" of dialogue that are key to a productive interreligious encounter. Leila also knew that "what Christians believe" about persons of other faiths was not completely represented by her elevator companion's belief. Instead of engaging in a conflict-destined confrontation in the elevator, Leila brought the exchange back to her interreligious dialogue group, continuing the "conversation" in a different location and for a different purpose.

When Leila brings the story of the elevator meeting back to the group, not one of the many Christians present attempts to explain to her why a Christian might hold the belief that a Baha'i was destined for hell nor does any one attempt to convince her how this woman's logic would make sense from the Christian point of view. Rather, they listen. The group reflects together on Leila's experience of interreligious conflict and discerns together a response. The whole group will learn from Leila's creative response to this moment. The story takes on not only narrative significance for Leila, but also for the whole group, in that they have a model for a creative response on which to pattern their own reactions to situations of conflict generated by religious difference. While Leila occupies the position of "exemplar" (she exemplifies to the group a possible response to her interlocutor's vicious comment), there is a sense in which the group presupposes Leila's response. That is, throughout its existence, the group works to clear a space for imagining alternative ways of dialogically engaging and group members, like Leila, act these ways out.

The women come together not just to share information *about* their beliefs but rather, through sharing stories, they actually *form* a distinctive orientation to the world. This orientation is similar to the "taking belief seriously" stance recommended in the first chapter. It involves an empathetic openness to the experiences of others, a willingness to question how well one has listened before questioning the content of what the other says, and a hope that one's encounter with the religious other will result in amity rather than contention. Finally, the religious beliefs the Philadelphia women eventually form from out of this orientation are concurrently Cliffordian dispositions to act.

In the sharing of religious lives of difference, the distinctiveness of communal practices and religious beliefs inevitably emerges. It is not always an easy or calm process. As one participant put it, "at times members manage to say things that I feel are objectionable."[20] In the words of another member, "Even if you thought you were open-minded there are all sorts of things that challenge that assumption."[21] These women have found that although they desire the reconciled harmony of the many diverse beliefs and practices, and value the spiritual witness offered by their friends of other religious traditions, differences are, at times, insurmountable. The Philadelphia women make it a point to allow for real disagreement because, in their experience, differences and disagreement ultimately provide the group with fresh opportunities for learning to listen to each other better and for putting the virtues of empathy, courage, or patience into practice. This stance toward disagreement (taking it as an occasion for growth) is key as a response to Feldman and McKim's S- and T-principles.[22]

For the group, the most significant example of the challenge of difference concerns the issue of women's roles and statuses in religious communities. On many occasions, group members have questioned others within the group on having a "second class status" within their faith traditions.[23] The participants explain that the women whose home tradition had been critiqued challenged back to the group that there was no such devaluation

20. Interview by Mara Brecht, December 15, 2007, Philadelphia, PA, digital recording.

21. Interview by Mara Brecht, August 18, 2008, Philadelphia, PA, digital recording.

22. This is a prime example of how the women's practice in dialogue informs the epistemological model I develop. This epistemology follows from practice rather than preceding and dictating practice and is therefore *a posteriori* in nature.

23. Interview by Mara Brecht, October 2, 2009, Philadelphia, PA, transcription.

of women. The original questioners remained unconvinced and describe their conversation partners' answer as "unsatisfying."[24] At these times, the group emphasizes the necessity of listening ever more clearly and with humility. Listening clearly and with humility are the excellent practices of dialogue (or virtues) specially cultivated by the Philadelphia group. These practices are not chosen arbitrarily but rather because the group finds that they work; they are the practices that allow the group to draw more closely together and that enrich the content of the conversation. They are the group's "best practices" and are best because they work in this context to promote human flourishing as described above.

In chapter 5, I will argue for an epistemological model that places virtues such as this these—and the practices by which people promote and mutually teach them to one another—at its center. This kind of model, which follows from reflection on best practices and is therefore an *a posteriori* grounded model, stands in sharp contrast to the *a priori* epistemologies of McKim and Feldman. Theirs, I have argued, focus solely on the normative foundation of evidence for explaining how beliefs are formed and justified and result in understanding beliefs and believers as inevitably in competition.

Hina offers her perspective on dealing with conflict and emphasizes the consequences of listening clearly and with humility:

> We try—even as we are bringing out whatever it is that we don't agree with—keeping our views really, really open to listening for another . . . And I think we do try to listen to the other, to a different point of view, which doesn't always answer your question, but at least it recognizes the question and that you have a valid question . . . But then also to open yourself to listen, to what the answer is. And you may not agree with it, but at least it makes you recognize that there is another way of looking at the same problem . . . it untangles the knot a little bit . . .[25]

The women have, as Hina points out, learned to listen to one another openly through their friendships. On a few occasions they have reflected as a group on the issue of how far to push the conversations in sensitive discussions. Emily describes one of these conversations:

> We all kind of said, "Well, yes the highest value is the friendship, but we actually do want to go deeper." So how do we try to

24. Interview by Mara Brecht, August 18, 2008, Philadelphia, PA, digital recording.

25. Interview by Mara Brecht and Jeannine Hill Fletcher, February, 12, 2009, Philadelphia, PA, digital recording.

> maintain the first one? But it was really a great moment to be in the room when that question actually got surfaced. "Are there things we avoid? And why? Are there times when it is actually a higher value to avoid them because the friendship is more?" It was actually a profound moment for me in this group.[26]

Emily's "profound moment" acknowledges the group's ability to balance between addressing real conflict and placing a premium on the friendships that have been fostered through the group. Interreligious friendships do not ignore conflicts or elide differences, but they provide a means by which people can continue communicating with and caring for each other even given these conflicts and differences.

Another member, Barbara, recounts how this has affected her approach at large, "One of the things that I have found is that not only is this a place where we have listened to each other but we also have to listen to ourselves. In my situation, that became kind of a crucible . . . for a multitude of reasons I try to constantly stay within that framework that I had taken refuge in."[27] Barbara's comments give way to the sense that—in interreligious dialogue—there is deep interplay between one's own beliefs and other's beliefs. As Netland, Griffiths, and D'Costa—the theologians of chapter 1 who acknowledge the need for asserting truth rather than just assuming it when developing a theology of religious pluralism—point out, this *ought* to be the case: one should be brought to self-reflection given the encounter with the religious other. Barbara, however, raises an epistemological point that Netland, Griffiths, and D'Costa only gloss over.[28] She states, ". . . but what we also have to listen to is *ourselves*." This suggests that some people, like Barbara, may experience—in the interreligious encounter—a feeling of being overwhelmed by the beliefs of others and an impulse to jettison one's own beliefs.

Barbara implicitly raises an invaluable question about the extent to which we should "trust" our own beliefs in light of religious diversity or what balance ought to be struck between one's own and others' beliefs. There are no simple answers to be given here, but it is important to note—for present purposes—that any epistemological theory dealing with religious diversity must be able to respond to these questions by explaining

---

26. Interview by Mara Brecht and Jeannine Hill Fletcher, February 12, 2009, Philadelphia, PA, digital recording.

27. Interview by Mara Brecht and Jeannine Hill Fletcher, February 12, 2009, Philadelphia, PA, digital recording.

28. They gloss it over because they assume, to a certain extent, that Christianity is true and therefore, if one is Christian, one may trust her own beliefs.

how we can "test" both the beliefs of others and our own beliefs, or, as I argue in chapters 6 and 7, how we can test the processes by which we and others form beliefs in order to figure out what should be the outcome of the interplay between other's beliefs and one's own.

Barbara illustrates her experience of the interreligious dialogue group as a "crucible." The ambiguous meaning of the word is perhaps not insignificant. A crucible can be understood as a place where something is subjected to a severe trial. Epistemologists like Feldman and McKim, who use normative and foundationalist standards and ground their proposals in *a priori* reasoning, see interreligious dialogue as *this* kind of crucible; in dialogue, believers are presented with conflicting religious beliefs and, as such, those beliefs are subjected to trial (e.g., does any person have better or more persuasive evidence?). The outcome, according to Feldman and McKim, is that believers walk away from this trial *without* reason or justification for maintaining their beliefs.

There is another way to understand a crucible, however, and that is as place where something new emerges from the interaction of various elements. Barbara's comment strikes on this usage: interreligious dialogue creates the sort of context and conditions under which it is possible to create something new (the significance of what this "something new" is will be explored in chapter 8 in a discussion on forms of transformation). Indeed, as she points out, there is difficulty and challenge—even trial—in meeting the religious other but this also implies giving birth to something new. For Barbara this has meant learning to be more attentive to her own experiences and religious self-understanding. A view of interreligious dialogue as this kind of crucible calls into question characterizations like those of Feldman and McKim and opens the door to possibilities—possibilities that will be explored at length in the following chapters—for understanding the epistemological significance of religious diversity particularly through interreligious dialogue.

Building an Epistemic Community

Through the sharing of others' religious traditions and the practice of refining their own abilities involved in this sharing process—a process that is sometimes uneasy—group members are opened to a sense of spiritual wonder and the horizon of possibility is widened for thinking about their own spiritual lives and religious practices. One member reflects on her realization that listening to the faith journeys of others especially through

"Evoking the Luminous" in Dialogue

the spiritual autobiography exercise has broadened her own spiritual horizon: "I realized how much more meaningful it was for me to get to know people in the this way [through hearing their responses to] these bigger questions of meaning, God, faith, . . . when you listen and start hearing some patterns [in their stories] . . . for me—it just creates this awareness of a mystery, of the transcendent kind of forces in people's lives."[29]

Through dialogue, the "transcendent forces" in the lives of others are made transparent to this woman. Her statement acknowledges a sense of permeability among the group's individual lives that allows them, in turn, to forge a community among themselves. By telling each other about what they have come to believe religiously through, for example, sitting *shivah*, breaking the fast on the day of *Eid*, or hearing a sermon on Sunday morning, the women of the interreligious dialogue group give others admittance to their home practices. In short, they narratively include others in their own faith communities and are included by others into those home faith communities. In the following examples, group members report that, as a result of the dialogue, they wish to experience and participate in the practices of other religious traditions.

Karen, a committed Christian, talks about how hearing others discuss their practices has sparked in her a desire not only to know more about those religious practices, but even to try them herself. She states, "I just find it fascinating and enriching to learn so much about other faiths and religion . . . sometimes I think that I'd like to, you know, try out a few of those. Not the religion itself but some of those practices: like the spring celebration in the Baha'i [faith]—it was beautiful! And it was different than a Passover, different than an Easter."[30] Elli, who is firmly grounded in her Jewish practice, makes a similar remark about what she feels when she hears other members describe their practices, "If when [another group member] is talking about prayer, or talking about her experience with communion, I can just watch her light up, I want to know what that is about. I want to understand that. If I see it in her, I know it's accessible in me. And I know it's accessible in others. I want to pay attention to that—when she lighted up, talking about her experience on *Hajj*."[31]

Karen and Elli are committed participants in the Christian and Jewish traditions, respectively. Neither of these traditions provide space for ordinary believers as part of their religious practice for "trying out" other

29. Interview by Mara Brecht, July 20, 2007, Philadelphia, PA, digital recording.
30. Interview by Mara Brecht, August 18, 2008, Philadelphia, PA, digital recording.
31. Interview by Mara Brecht, July 20, 2007, Philadelphia, PA, digital recording.

religious practices or make allowances for the validity of other religious rituals in the ways after which Karen and Elli seek.[32] Further, each of these traditions theoretically offers its members the means by which the members can gain fully justified religious beliefs such that there is no room for the justified beliefs of other religious traditions. And yet, Karen and Elli report wanting to delve into other traditions and practices without leaving their own. How can a Christian want to participate in the Baha'i new year when she has her own Easter to celebrate? How can a Jew endeavor to understand the experience of Christian communion or Muslim *Hajj*? These examples suggest that interreligious dialogue grants its participants a sense of permeability about their own and others' traditions—permeability that the authorities of these traditions may explicitly reject—and through that, they become comfortable with and even desire to experience other religious practices.

What is significant here is not that the women want to convert (even temporarily) or desire to "cross over"[33] only for a time to another religious tradition, but rather that they have developed an enduring sense that, through their dialogue, what happens in another's "home" community is opened up to them in their new interreligious community. This sense of being "opened up" has epistemological implications: part of what being "opened up" will entail is subjecting one's beliefs to standards outside of one's "home community." In chapter 1, Griffiths, Netland, and D'Costa collectively suggest something akin to this. Netland, for example, argues that all religious beliefs must be tested according to certain logical principles. These principles are ostensibly remote from the normal tradition-internal

---

32. While religious people who participate in practices outside of their home traditions may not be condemned by those traditions, they are often marginalized by them. Take, for example, Roshi Robert Kennedy, S.J., who is an ordained Catholic priest and a Zen master. Kennedy and others like him are the subject of scrutiny and "concern" for the Catholic Church. The Roman Curia expresses a characteristically wary sentiment for the type of practice exemplified by Kennedy in a Congregation for the Doctrine of the Faith (CDF) letter: "These [proponents of Zen-Christian mediation] and similar proposals to harmonize Christian meditation with Eastern techniques need to have their contents and methods ever subjected to a thoroughgoing examination so as to avoid the danger of falling into syncretism" (*Letter to the Bishops*, §12).

33. James Dunne posits the theory of "passing over and coming back," where a person "passes over" or enters into a time period, set of ideas, or experience other than her own through sympathetic understanding and "comes back" or returns to herself with new insight about her own time, ideas, or experiences. Dunne embarks on a journey of passing over into and coming back from the world religions in his book *The Way of All the Earth*.

standards governing beliefs.³⁴ While Netland (or Griffiths or D'Costa) would not go so far as to say that beliefs should be subjected to the standards of *other* religious traditions (they instead propose generic, external standards such as philosophical or logical ones) there is a pervading sense that the interreligious encounter demands, epistemologically, that believers "open" their beliefs up to alien criticisms and evaluations.

Karen insightfully compares this process of being opened up to something new in dialogue to a pedagogical principle she often used in her professional work in a children's museum. She gives the following account:

> . . . we were working on a project about how and what children learn in a children's museum. And so we were using [the idea of] 'entry points' and how you enter into an exhibit or how you enter into something. And the entry point that has always spoken the most to me is the narrative. Tell me a story. Tell me a story about your belief and how that's affected you.³⁵

Karen calls attention to "storytelling" as a main avenue of communication for the group. In doing so, she homes in on an idea central to scholarship on women's interreligious dialogue and already invoked in the discussion of Chopp's concept of the "poetics of testimony."

Scholars of women's interreligious dialogue raise concerns about the extent to which women's voices are incorporated or granted authority in interreligious dialogue. They offer sharp analyses of why this is the case as well as propose ways to give women's voices greater recognition by revaluing the norms of discourse for interreligious dialogue. The following review of scholarship draws attention to both tasks. Ursula King provides an example of the first critical task. She argues that feminism is missing from interreligious dialogue. King claims, "Women's great invisibility, marginality, and voicelessness in world religions parallels invisibility, marginality, and voicelessness of women in interreligious dialogue."³⁶ She calls for dialogue to become "truly 'en-gendered'"³⁷ and analyzes ways in which traditional dialogue has impeded women from fully entering the interreligious conversation.

---

34. I say ostensibly here because my criticism of Netland is that the so-called disinterested or "objective" standards he chooses are in fact closely allied with the Christian tradition.

35. Interview by Mara Brecht, August 18, 2008, Philadelphia, PA, digital recording.

36. King, "Feminism," 52.

37. Ibid., 43.

Virtue in Dialogue

King and scholars sharing her concerns identify reconstructing the "rationality" of dialogue as one way to counteract the pattern of excluding women and perpetuating patriarchy through dialogue. This coheres with Chopp's idea that attending to the "poetics of testimony" allows the reordering of traditional categories. Interreligious dialogue—like all forms of discourse—carries with it normative modes of communicating (this constitutes its "rationality"). These normative modes of communicating reinforce the positions of those who benefit from the norms. Tinu Ruparell frames it in socioeconomic terms: "When the language of discourse belongs to those in positions of socioeconomic advantage, dialogue must favor that language and that rationality."[38] The upshot is that normative discourse reflects the discourse of those in power; in the case of religious discourse, men historically occupy positions of power, thus excluding women and putative women's ways of discoursing.

In her study of the 2004 Parliament of the World's Religions, Jeannine Hill Fletcher utilizes a taxonomy (male style/feminine style; traditional content/female-focused content/feminist content) developed by Enid M.O. Sefcovic and Diana Theresa Bifiano (scholars in the field of communication) for the purpose of "[distinguishing] different styles of participation in mainstream discourse."[39] While the Parliament of the World's Religions does not represent all women's participation in interreligious dialogue, the Parliament discussions illuminate certain patterns and norms of discourse in mainstream interreligious dialogue. Hill Fletcher's analysis of the style and content of these discussions aims to "underscore how the style of dialogue will impact whether women's voices might make a difference."[40] Specifically, Hill Fletcher notes that instances of the "feminine style" of discourse encouraged women to "[incorporate] personal experience as a source of knowledge" as well as "bring to the table the lived experience of... religions as they are encountered by bodies gendered as female" while the other style ("masculine") did not.[41]

By cultivating their own style of discourse, women's dialogue groups can reject the norms of discourse that reinforce the power of those who have been historically "in charge of" interreligious dialogue and religious traditions and, at the same time, create a role, a voice, and a space for women in the larger interreligious conversation. A Pluralism Project report of

---

38. Ruparell, "The Dialogue Party," 239.
39. Hill Fletcher, "Women's Voices," 13.
40. Ibid., 25.
41. Ibid.

women's interreligious dialogue in the United States describes women's interreligious dialogue groups in the following way: they promote a "culture of listening," "[honor] storytelling," and "relationship building."[42] Uma Narayan proposes an idea that is consistent with both Hill Fletcher's thesis and the Pluralism Project's observations about women's interreligious dialogue and also connects to Chopp's notion of the "poetics of testimony."

Narayan argues that narrative is a distinctive feature of women's interreligious dialogue, which productively conveys what otherwise is inexpressible. She states, "'Non-analytic' and 'non-rational' forms of discourse, like fiction or poetry, may be better able than other forms to convey the complex life experiences of one group to members of another."[43] Narration or storytelling functions in women's interreligious dialogue as a form of "non-analytic" and "non-rational" discourse and it is through storytelling that, as Maura O'Neill writes, ". . . we are really explaining how we acquired our particular way of believing and why we perceive the things the way we do."[44]

Not only does "interreligious narration" allow us to express our own beliefs, it also allows us to understand others' religious beliefs. Along these lines, Helene Egnell notes, "The experience of being listened to in its turn creates a willingness to listen."[45] Narrative thus works on both of "ends" of dialogical interaction—telling and receiving. Women's interreligious dialogue uniquely cultivates this narrative style of discourse so that persons of diverse faith can meet one another. O'Neill sees several specific benefits to placing the "personal" at the center of the group through storytelling; this way of dialoguing "[creates] an atmosphere of trust . . . [clarifies] diverse perspectives . . . [prevents] abstract and irrelevant theorizing . . . [and highlights] points of commonalty and distinction."[46] O'Neill's point is that by disclosing one's experiences one is, at the same time, shedding light on one's theological and philosophical positions.[47] In other words, through storytelling, a close connection is drawn between narrative representation and religious beliefs or theories.

---

42. Lohre, "Women's Interfaith Initiatives," 1.
43. Narayan, "The Project of Feminist Epistemology," 264.
44. O'Neill, *Mending*, 110.
45. Egnell, "Dialogue for Life," 254.
46. O'Neill, *Women Speaking, Women Listening*, 89.
47. Ibid., 49. This is not O'Neill's idea; rather, O'Neill here relates a story of a woman giving a presentation at a conference.

Virtue in Dialogue

Insofar as women's interreligious dialogue encourages this "alternative" type of discourse—a type that has been overlooked and undervalued by epistemological analyses because it does not fit the paradigm of epistemic disagreement—women's interreligious dialogue groups (like the Philadelphia group) offer a unique opportunity for reconsidering the epistemological significance of religious diversity through the frame of interreligious dialogue.

As the women of Philadelphia articulate their religious beliefs through the narrative context of their journeys, struggles, and victories in faith, they create "entry points" through which fellow participants may move. When members step through each other's "entry points," they make porous the boundaries of their home communities; in dialogue, they make a new community, which floats among and overlaps with the home communities. Recall here the "Theology and Falsification" argument discussed in chapter 2. Hare argues that beliefs are both determined by one's *blik*/worldview and justified according to one's *blik* (that is, a belief must be consistent or coherent with one's larger framework if that belief is to be adopted by the believer). Flew makes a powerful criticism of this position. He argues that just because believers *do* justify beliefs according to how the beliefs fit with the believers' worldviews does not mean beliefs *should* be justified in this way. Without taking the epistemologically overly-permissive position that Hare takes, I find that Mitchell makes a sound descriptive point about the conditions for belief, thereby creating an alternative to Flew's stringent position: there are some beliefs that one accepts as "articles of faith," against which evidence cannot count.

The women of Philadelphia articulate their beliefs and demonstrate their practices in the context of this new interreligious community. This community expands or becomes incorporated into each individual's worldview and this broadened worldview. In turn, the women's membership in this community has consequences for what will count against their "articles of faith" thus affecting how new beliefs are formed and justified. The goal of this book is to develop an *a posteriori* epistemology that takes into these factors.

As friendships are fostered and the fabric of relationality sustains conflicts in member's home religious beliefs, there is a larger belief, which grows out of this interreligious community, that is strengthened. Each of these dialogue participants came to the group from a sense of spiritual seeking. Committed to her own tradition, nevertheless, each intuited that there was something more to be gleaned from the encounter with other faiths. As one Jewish member of the group articulates,

> [The group] is my spiritual home in huge, huge ways. So, I find that my spiritual home is where, is with, is in interactions with those who are awed by spirit and awed by divine in whatever form that takes. Which is why this group is so important to me. And the seriousness with which we all hold spirit is what draws me and what nourishes me . . .[48]

Respecting differences of home traditions, the women often communicate through the language of "spirit" or a shared spirituality that they experience as transcending religious differences. It is a presence of spirit "inside" each person that forms the "common bond" they experience when they are together, as one Muslim member comments.[49]

Lucy articulates the sense of security or comfort she feels because of this common bond as follows: "I also want to say that there is a level or a trust that what we bring to the group and that what we share with it will be held in good faith and in good heart and without judgments. And so it's like a huge net into which we can jump."[50] Or, as one Jewish participant echoes, "I think one of the reasons it works when we are together is because we are in deep trusting conversation-relationship, that there is a sense of the sacred presence."[51] Being with the group each month is described, by one of the Christian women, as "important to . . . my personal spiritual core, my spiritual being."[52] This sense of a spirit-sustained relationality reflects the distinctive outcome of the group's dialogue practice; the women describe themselves as being sustained by a shared spirit. One group member characterizes it this way: "[I have the] sense that we can evoke—when we are together, in [this] place—*just something luminous*."[53] The dialogue generates a luminous, shared spirit, and, in turn, this nourishes the dialogue participants.

This cycle of generating and nourishing inevitably leads the group to form beliefs together *about* the spirit that they experience as sustaining them. And thus the content of their interreligious dialogue is often

---

48. Interview by Mara Brecht and Jeannine Hill Fletcher, February 12, 2009, Philadelphia, PA, digital recording.
49. Ibid.
50. Ibid.
51. Ibid.
52. Ibid.
53. Ibid.

implicitly focused on this "something" that transcends and yet sustains them. It is in conversation with each other that these women identify and claim relationships to this sustaining, transcending spirit. Betty sees this as a matter of enriching who and where God is in her life. She states, "If you're in a relationship with someone else and that someone else is in relationship with God it just makes sense that the person's relationship with God would enrich your own relationship with God."[54] Through dialogue, the women come into relation with each other and these relationships, in turn, benefit their personal relationships with God.[55]

For Ruth, the interreligious conversation not only enriches her understanding of or relationship with God, it actually contributes to the very constitution of that relationship. She explains:

> It is so frustrating to try . . . to want to believe in your God—whoever that is, if it's Jesus, if it's the God of the Jews, if it's Mohammed, if it's Bah'u'llah—and look at the world and say, you know, "Where is this God?" and "What is happening here?" and "Why are we doing so much evil in the name of God?" . . . if you don't want to abandon that [belief in God]—if you want to keep your faith—the place to find it, I think, is in people. And not just your *own* people.[56]

Ruth finds God in others and, specifically, in others who are outside of her home faith community. Rachel has a similar intuition: "What comes up for me is that we have to create God in the way that we relate to each other. The more we are connected with each other and respect that, the more we are strengthening the force of what we see as God."[57] Each of these comments brings to the surface the ways in which the women find that boundaries erected by the religious traditions of the world are in fact permeable for persons.

When persons transgress those boundaries, according to the women, they are able to find and enrich relationships with God; they are able to evoke "the luminous" among themselves. The conversation that

---

54. Interview by Mara Brecht, August 18, 2008, Philadelphia, PA, digital recording.

55. The image of Krishna dancing with his milkmaids comes to mind. The poem that describes this dance, called the Rasa Lila, tells how Krishna multiplies himself so that each of the milkmaids (*gopis*) believes herself to be dancing with Krishna at the same time. In images depicting the Rasa Lila, the milkmaids are represented as holding hands and dancing together, connected to each other through their individual dances with Krishna. See Schweig, *The Dance of Divine Love*.

56. Interview by Mara Brecht, August 18, 2008, Philadelphia, PA, digital recording.

57. Interview by Mara Brecht, July 20, 2007, Philadelphia, PA, digital recording.

is sustained by the group gives its members the possibility to compare, contrast, and consider their own beliefs with reference to others' beliefs. Here, members learn from fellow participants not just what others believe but actually *how* to believe. They "act out" for each other how they each relate to God, thus expanding the relational with God imagination of the entire group. Through their experience of deep sharing and cultivating friendship together, the women of the Philadelphia women's interreligious dialogue group come to know each other as members of a religious community—an *inter*religious community—that is not in competition with their home religious communities.

Rejecting the T- and S- Principles

What these accounts suggest is that the spiritual sustenance these women encounter within their own particular traditions can be accessed both in others' traditions *and* when persons of diverse traditions come together. Karen summarizes,

> There was a group—"The Sacred Circle"—at my church which was a group where we spent time looking at our spirituality. What's different about that and this group—and [my church sacred circle group has] been wonderful—is the richness of bringing in the hybridity—of bringing in so many different faiths and then realizing how all those faiths really enrich my own. So the key word to me is enriching.[58]

The accounts indicate a profound interplay *between* bearing witness to the beliefs and practices of a religious other *and* strengthening one's own religious belief and commitment to practice. In this way, the interreligious context gives rise to members' beliefs just as the home communities do. In the following chapters, I will explore in depth epistemological models that help me construct a theory to explain beliefs can gain epistemic justification in the interreligious context.

Elli explains that by learning of her fellow participants' beliefs and hearing their journeys of faith particularly in the spiritual autobiography exercise, she was able to see and experience what her own tradition had been beckoning her to all along: "I got it just by being in relationship with them through all of these years: seeing it manifest, feeling it, *feeling it*. I didn't really know and then, when I read it in my own tradition, and you

---

58. Interview by Mara Brecht, August 18, 2008, Philadelphia, PA, digital recording.

know, I see it's *there*, it's *all there*. And it conjures up that same feeling for me but I never could access it [before this experience of dialogue]."[59] In this example, Elli suggests that the interreligious context not only gives rise to beliefs but also throws into relief the beliefs of one's own tradition so that believers may renew their participation in their home communities. The interreligious context, then, acts as an occasion for the formation of members' religious identities. Emily, for example, remarks on her own religious self-understanding, "I have a strong progressive Christian identity and a strong attachment to [my] church, but I can only understand [my religious identity] in spiritual conversation and community with these women and other people with whom I've been blessed from other traditions. The two are really inseparable for me."[60]

What is characterized as inseparable—one's own religious beliefs and the religious beliefs of others—for the Philadelphia women is understood as in basic opposition for McKim and Feldman. If McKim and Feldman are right that religious belief must be suspended or held tentatively given the interreligious situation, then we are left with the objectionable conclusion that what these dialogue participants claim out of their own experience is theoretically bankrupt or epistemically null. Considering McKim and Feldman's *a priori* reasoned epistemological paradigm in conjunction with the Philadelphia women's accounts presents two possible alternatives: either one must claim theoretical privilege (e.g., say something like "the interreligious dialogue participants just have not thought about it enough or are without the proper epistemological resources and so do not realize that their religious beliefs in fact must be troubled") or pursue an epistemological theory that *can be* accountable to the practical experience of interreligious dialogue. This book chooses the latter option.

Choosing this option means granting credence to the central leitmotif of the women's voices: their membership to the dialogue group is, in fact, membership to a distinctive community. Among the other problems with the epistemological paradigms of Feldman and McKim, which were discussed at length in the last chapter, these epistemologists are hindered by their atomistic and individualistic construction of epistemic agents; for them, S is a single individual, detached from community and context. By failing to do what James and Mitchell demand of epistemologists—which is to analyze believers and beliefs in their appropriate contexts because

---

59. Interview by Mara Brecht, July 20, 2007, Philadelphia, PA, digital recording.

60. Interview by Mara Brecht and Jeannine Hill Fletcher, February 12, 2009, Philadelphia, PA, digital recording.

context determines how beliefs are formed and justified (in this case, for example, the context would be the interreligious dialogue community) and to develop an understanding of the "articles of faith" of believers, against which evidence cannot count—McKim and Feldman can make short work of dismissing as problematic the examples of these women who do *not* suspend or hold tentatively their beliefs.

Feminist epistemologies develop the concept of an "epistemic community" to point out how it is the community, not the individual, that is both the generator and repository of knowledge.[61] Feminist epistemologists, particularly those interested in the philosophy of science and the presumptions involved in scientific inquiry, use the concept of epistemic community to point out the fact that no scientist makes a discovery or advances a theory on his or her own. Rather, scientific developments grow out of a community of inquirers and come by way of dialogic interaction.

Lynn Hankinson Nelson raises the question of whether there are possibilities for extending the idea of an epistemic community beyond the scientific community.[62] The foundational idea here is that individuals have roles in *epistemic* communities and it is only in these contexts that they form beliefs. (Epistemic communities and social communities are distinct, though often related, communities.) Following Hankinson Nelson's lead, it is possible to situate interreligious dialogue communities—groups of diverse religious people gathered together to discuss religious beliefs and practices through the frame of personal experiences and life-stories over the course of time toward the end of fostering respect and mutual understanding for religions other than one's own—as a type of epistemic community.

As I have suggested throughout this discussion, the epistemic community bears on belief formation and justification—both in theory and in practice. Because the Philadelphia women's interreligious dialogue group (following suit with women's interreligious dialogue at large) privileges an alternative type of discourse wherein "truth" is dynamically expressed and beliefs are articulated in the "poetics of testimony," the object of epistemological inquiry—the interreligious encounter in dialogue—is construed differently here than how it is for McKim and Feldman, for example. The notion of an interreligious epistemic community not only has methodological implications, but it also has epistemic implications for believers themselves by reconfiguring the circumstances that are determinative

61. Nelson, "Epistemological Communities," 140.
62. Ibid., 150.

of belief formation and justification. In the following chapters, I explore frontiers in both religious and general epistemology in pursuit of an epistemological model of religious belief that both allows for interreligious epistemic communities and captures the significance of their positive consequences for belief formation and justification.

4

Alternative Contemporary Epistemological Models

IN CHAPTER 1, I ARGUED THAT RELIGIOUS DIVERSITY *SHOULD* BE EXAMined epistemologically. In chapter 2, I looked at contemporary discussions in epistemology and contextualized them by showing their epistemological antecedents in an attempt to get to the bottom of why religious diversity has been construed as an epistemic problem. In chapter 3, I introduced a case study of women in interreligious dialogue to serve as a foil to the conclusions drawn by theorists in the epistemology of religious disagreement. The intent of this chapter is to rethink the epistemological significance of religious diversity given accounts of interreligious dialogue by exploring a range of contemporary epistemological theories. Here, I will begin to build toward an epistemological model that shies away from neither epistemological nor theological challenges and yet is sensitive and attentive to the voices of those who really encounter diversity.

Contemporary A Posteriori Epistemologies

Three voices in contemporary epistemology—Alvin Plantinga, William Alston, and Linda Zagzebski—offer various models for belief formation, maintenance, and justification.[1] Each of these thinkers is more attentive to the processes by which beliefs come into being than either McKim or Feldman were in their *a priori* reasoned epistemologies. Instead of evaluating p on the basis of E (which requires a theory of what the criteria for E are), Plantinga, Alston, and Zagzebski take a more "holistic" look at the way in which S comes to believe *p*, thus creating *a posteriori* or naturalized

---

1. I am aware that there is no paucity of epistemological positions to choose from to guide me in my efforts. Alvin Plantinga and William Alston are particularly relevant to this project because their concerns are explicitly with epistemology in a distinctively religious context. Linda Zagzebski shares this concern, although it is to a less explicit extent.

epistemologies. (Henceforth, "naturalized" will be shorthand for *a posteriori* in contrast to "normative" or *a priori* epistemologies.) For these three, p is only appropriately understood by examining it as the outcome of a broader process, rather than a logical result of E only.

Like James, Plantinga, Alston, and Zagzebski share a commitment to a "best practices approach" or, an approach that descriptively analyzes the conditions in and practices by which we successfully or reliably form beliefs (this makes their epistemologies naturalized). The best practice or reliable method of belief formation that each Plantinga, Alston, and Zagzebski identify become closely connected to their concept of justification. For this reason, these three epistemologists offer a version of reliablist epistemology. They each identify a reliable way by which beliefs are produced and, in turn, assess the justifiability of beliefs with reference to this reliable way. *How* they each explain or understand the reliable way by which beliefs are produced differentiates their epistemologies from each other.

Plantinga, Alston, and Zagzebksi theorize about reliable belief formation; religious belief is one case of reliable belief formation that is under investigation in this book. Because these thinkers consider processes of belief formation (they try to determine which processes are reliable and why they are reliable), their theories necessarily include attention to the contexts in which that process takes place. Because they presuppose context in principle, their theories are amenable to the project of this book, which is to consider belief formed, shaped, and confirmed in a situation of religious diversity such as with the Philadelphia interreligious dialogue participants. If the interreligious dialogue community is an epistemic community, as the last chapter suggested it is, then the reality of diverse religious beliefs can be assumed from the start of the epistemic process instead of being seen as a problem that later appears to overturn already formed belief. Because the notion of epistemic community bears great importance in the projects of both Alston and Zagzebski (although in different ways), their proposals provide this book with the best resources for developing an appropriate epistemological model.

Alvin Plantinga and Properly Formed Basic Beliefs

Alvin Plantinga is concerned with belief in general and religious belief in particular. The goal of his epistemology, labeled "reformed epistemology," is to defend theistic belief. In his reformed epistemological theory,

Plantinga rejects the evidence-based standards for belief justification of McKim and Feldman; he also argues ardently against internalist constraints on justification. Instead, he proposes an epistemology that has an alternative justificatory standard—which is ultimately a type of foundation—and an externalist constraint on justification.

Plantinga's reformed epistemology is a variety of reliablism that remains importantly informed by foundationalism. He structures his discussion through the use of three concepts: warrant, basic belief, and proper function. Simply put, Plantinga's argument runs as follows: beliefs can be justified (warranted) by being based upon certain foundations (basic beliefs); these foundations and the beliefs based on them are formed by reliable processes (proper function).[2] Thus, he develops his religious epistemology to show how basic beliefs are able to be formed reliably by a believer and, in turn, defends theistic belief. The close connection between reliable process and basic belief as a kind of foundation for beliefs is the hallmark of Plantinga's project.

In the previous chapter, I explained that warrant is a term that functions just as justification does. *Justification* is the "special ingredient" that, when added to true belief, makes for knowledge. *Warrant* is a "special ingredient" like justification but with a different connotation. Because Plantinga is in the externalist camp, he uses "warrant" rather than "justification" to differentiate his notion of how a belief obtains this "special ingredient" from internalist notions. In epistemologies with an internalist constraint on justification, a person must be able to give an account of how she has her belief in order for that belief to be justified. It is her epistemic duty to be *internally* aware of how she meets justificatory requirements for her beliefs. An epistemology with an externalist constraint on justification, by contrast, makes no such demands upon a person to have cognitive access to the reasons for why her belief should be justified. A belief can be "justified" or "warranted" for reasons *external* to the believer's own doing.

In Plantinga's defense of theistic belief, a person is warranted in believing that p if p is a properly formed basic belief. P here is a belief such as "God exists." What makes "God exists" a properly basic belief? Plantinga explains that a belief is properly basic, "if and only [if] S [the believer] accepts p in the basic way, and furthermore p has *warrant* for S."[3] "God exists" is a warranted belief (or, a person is warranted in believing that

---

2. Plantinga claims that knowledge is better defined as *warranted* true belief rather than *justified* true belief. In the following paragraph, I discuss why this is so.
3. Plantinga, *Warranted Christian Belief*, 178.

"God exists") if, first, "God exists" is accepted by the believer as basic and, second, if "God exists" has warrant. This definition looks clearly circular at first glance: Plantinga states that one is warranted in having a belief like "God exists" if that belief is basic and warranted.

Plantinga argues, in effect, that a person is warranted in holding a belief if the belief itself has warrant. The "warrant" for belief transfers directly from the belief to the believer with no special or added work. It is easy to see how this theory is externalist in nature: it is not the responsibility of the believer, or perhaps even within her ability, to know how or why she obtained the belief. (In an internalist epistemological model, on the other hand, it would be necessary both for the belief to be justified [it would have to meet a certain standard of evidence, for example] in its own right and for the believer to know why the belief is justified and perhaps even to show why belief is justified in the face of *prima facie* defeaters.) This answers the question of how a belief is warranted. But what makes a belief like "God exists" properly basic in the first place? What makes it any good?

The standard that Plantinga identifies for a "good" belief is two-fold: it must be basic and accepted as such by the believer and must be the yield of a properly functioning belief-forming process.[4] He explains that a basic belief is a belief that is not inferred from other beliefs.[5] Basic beliefs are the foundational beliefs on which other beliefs are built. They are not constructed on the basis of anything else; they are not derived from other beliefs; they do not have evidence to support them. In simpler terms, basic beliefs are "as low as one can go" and are taken as such by the believer.

Plantinga gives the example of "I seem to see a tree" as a properly basic belief. He explains why this belief is basic as follows: "I have that characteristic sort of experience that goes with seeing a tree. I may then form the belief that I see a tree, or that there is a tree there . . . In the typical case, that belief will be basic for me; I will not ordinarily accept the proposition on the evidential basis of other beliefs I hold."[6] The belief that

---

4. It is worth noting that for Plantinga, the process of belief formation can include logical inference. One can infer from the basic belief "I seem to see a tree" that the tree will have properties characteristic of trees, such as sap and roots and so on.

5. Plantinga uses the concept of basic beliefs to argue against what he calls classical foundationalism. Classical foundationalists argue that most of our beliefs are based on inferences made from beliefs we are already have, or, said another way, "on the evidential basis of other beliefs" (Plantinga, *Warrant: The Current Debate*, 68). What beliefs count as foundational—those on which we can legitimately base other beliefs—for the classical foundationalist are extremely limited. Plantinga introduces the idea of basic belief to broaden the scope of what beliefs can serve as bases for other beliefs.

6. Plantinga, *Warrant: The Current Debate*, 71. "I seem to see a tree" is an example

"I see a tree" is not dependent, Plantinga argues, on any other belief (such as, "I am in a forest" or "I able to recognize a tree when I see one").

What ensures basic beliefs as basic and accessible to us as such, he states, is that they have been "produced by properly functioning processes of faculties."[7] Here is where the concept of "proper function"—a characteristically reliablist idea—comes into play. As long as "I seem to see a tree" is the result of clear vision, unobstructed cognitive pathways, and one's own perceptual experience, basic beliefs have been produced properly and so are warranted.[8] The proposition "God is speaking to me now" is like the proposition "I seem to see a tree." If "God is speaking to me now" is not inferred or derived from any other belief and is the result of a properly function belief-forming function, it is a properly basic belief. Theistic belief, which is built on the basic belief "God is speaking to me now," so meets a basic belief justificatory standard and is thus warranted, according to his externalist constraint.

Does Plantinga's theory create a vicious circle?[9] How can a religious person be sure her belief-forming faculty is properly functioning? The main trait of reliablism is that beliefs are justified or warranted because they were formed by reliable belief-forming processes; if a process reliably produces epistemically good beliefs, then the process is reliable. While this line of reasoning is central to all reliablist models, reliablist epistemologists can build checks and tests into their models in such a way so as to protect the reliablist system against the dangers of privatization noted, in

---

of a basic perceptual belief. Plantinga also discusses two other categories of basic beliefs: memory beliefs (see Plantinga, *Warrant and Proper Function*, 61–64) and beliefs about a person's own mental states (ibid., 55–57).

7. Plantinga, *Warranted Christian Belief*, 179 n15.

8. Plantinga does not specifically address the role that language plays in basic belief formation. He does however explain in detail what it would mean for a faculty (here, a person's belief forming faculty) to function properly. This notion of proper function seems to conceptually include language. Like "biological and social scientists [who] continually give accounts of how human beings or other organisms or their parts or organs function" Plantinga too works to outline "how they [here, belief forming facilities] work, what their purposes are, and how they react under various circumstances" (*Warrant and Proper Function*, 6). If the desired end of a faculty—or said another way, if the proper function of a faculty—is to form a warranted belief upon which other beliefs may be soundly built, it is probably fair to assume that this involves articulating that basic belief. It would thus seem that, according to Plantinga, language is inherently a part of our "noetic equipment."

9. It is possible for an argument to be circular, without being viciously so. A vicious circle is one that is drawn very small. A very wide circle of justification may be virtuous, as I argue in chapter 6.

particular, by Griffiths in chapter 1 (Alston also does this effectively as will be demonstrated in the following section). Plantinga employs the reliablist tactic without also offering believers a "way out" or access to a vantage point that would allow them to test the reliability of their processes. In other words, Plantinga's system does not create imaginative space for self-challenge.

In Plantinga's discussion of "God is speaking to me now," he also seems to make a slight leap. Plantinga explains why "God is speaking to me now" is properly basic and warranted, but has he explained why "God exists" is? There is a caveat that Plantinga must address. Even while "God is speaking to me now" is properly basic, Plantinga states that belief in God ("God exists") is only "loosely" a properly basic belief. The distinction of "loose" here is important. Plantinga explains that "specific and concrete" propositions like "I seem to see a tree" and "God is speaking to me now" are properly basic where "general and abstract" ones like "a tree exists" or "there is such a person as God" are not "properly" basic.[10] Even while only the concrete perceptual claims themselves may be deemed properly basic (and so form the foundation of our beliefs), Plantinga points out that the existence of the tree or God are "self-evidently entailed" by the claims "I seem to see a tree" or "God is speaking to me now."[11]

While the belief in God's existence is not strictly properly basic, Plantinga writes, this does not mean "there are no justifying circumstances for it, or that it is in that sense groundless or gratuitous."[12] A person is reasonable in believing *p'* (where *p'* is "God exists") if *p* (where *p* is "God

10. Plantinga, "Reason and Belief in God," in *Faith and Rationality*, eds. Plantinga and Wolterstorff, 81.

11. Plantinga uses the phrase "self-evidently entailed" (ibid., 81) to explain the relationship between "God exists" and "God is speaking to me now." The entailment itself is not defeasible. For it to be defeasible as an entailment, the perception "God is speaking to me now" would have to first be defeated. That is, believing God is speaking to me presumes God as the speaker. One could say, "That's not God; it's the cat." However, this claim defeats the basic belief ("God is speaking to me now" becomes "the cat is speaking to me now"), not the entailment. The only way to defeat my entailed belief ("God exists") is to defeat the basic belief ("God is speaking to me now"), but this cannot be done if the basic belief *is* properly basic. Plantinga does admit that the belief "God exists" can be defeated, but not insofar as it is entailed by "God is speaking to me now." Arguments against "God exists" are not entirely irrelevant. Plantinga states that it is possible for me to accept arguments that would defeat the loosely basic belief "God exists"—even if I accept the belief "God exists" as basic (ibid., 82–84). That however would be a different kind of argument (i.e., free-will defense) and cannot rule out the possibility *prima facie* of the entailed belief "God exists."

12. Ibid., 80.

is speaking to me now") is basic and warranted. This belief in God (p') can be said to be loosely properly basic because the "justifying conditions for this belief" is a properly basic belief.[13] (Again, we might also raise questions about the adequacy of resources Plantinga provides believers with to check the reliability of the foundational belief "God is speaking to me now" in the first place.) The notion of self-evidential entailment is meant to bridge the gap: just as "I see a tree" self-evidently entails that "that tree exists," so "God is speaking to me now" self-evidently entails "God exists." If the entailed belief were false, then the basic belief would be mistaken. Hence the entailed belief can be "loosely" or "functionally the equivalent of" a properly basic belief.

If p is properly basic, a person's belief that "God exists" is not dependent on evidence. Plantinga so distances himself from evidence-based epistemologies like Clifford, McKim, and Feldman. Yet theistic beliefs still rest on foundations—the foundation of properly formed basic beliefs. While Plantinga does not require evidence as foundation for belief, his project has foundationalist attributes because he develops a system wherein believers reliably form foundations (basic beliefs) in order to have warranted beliefs.

What Plantinga does is structure a system whereby believers are warranted in holding beliefs when they have properly arrived at those beliefs even without knowing how or why they have arrived at such beliefs. They are not responsible for explaining how or why "God is speaking to me now" appears to them. (And, because the proposition "God exists" is entailed by the claim "God is speaking to me now," believers are also warranted in holding higher-level propositional theistic beliefs.)

Plantinga's epistemology has been criticized for setting up a system wherein believers have justified belief without understanding the conditions of justification for their justified belief. The idea that believers are not accountable for the origins of or reasons for their beliefs suggests that beliefs are formed involuntarily.[14] In an effort to maintain the principles of Plantinga's theory while avoiding this kind of criticism (that beliefs come about involuntarily), Robert Roberts and Jay Wood make a case for expanding Plantinga's theory of proper function. Rather than arguing that warranted beliefs are the outcome of a person's properly functioning faculties, Roberts and Wood investigate the proper function of the "epistemic agent as a person, so that traits of the person and not merely traits of the

13. Ibid., 82.
14. Zagzebski, *Virtues of the Mind*, 62.

faculties are the basis for warrant."[15] By focusing on the person as a whole (rather than on a particular faculty of a person), Roberts and Wood bring the element of emotion into Plantinga's epistemological model.

They state, "We need to assess not just faculties but their integration into the character of the epistemic agent."[16] In other words, a person does not form belief through a properly functioning faculty or set of faculties alone, but rather she forms a belief through these faculties *as a part* of her very person, which will be determined, to a certain extent, by emotions and desires. For Roberts and Wood, Plantinga's epistemology overlooks a central cog in our epistemic machines. "Emotions," they argue, "determine human epistemic functioning for good and for ill, and so much be taken account of in any construction of proper epistemic functioning."[17] This line of reasoning does not undermine Plantinga's project, but rather only calls for an expansion of it to include the aspect of emotion.

Roberts and Wood explain that emotion enters the model most appropriately through the idea of virtue. Virtues, Roberts and Wood argue, are cultivated "dispositions with respect to emotions" that are used by people to "function excellently."[18] Epistemic virtues, "cultivated excellent dispositions and powers to acquire, maintain, transmit, or apply knowledge," are one type virtue.[19] Virtue here has two interrelated jobs: (1) ordering or controlling emotion and (2) acting as the power by which we form belief. On Roberts and Wood's revised-Plantinga model, "the intellect and will . . . coordinate and interact," thus including emotion in the very process of belief formation.[20] This, in turn, has an effect on belief justification. They write, "not only does bold action come from conviction, but conviction grows out of bold action. And as Plantinga affirms, confidence in belief bears on warrant."[21]

Roberts and Wood's use of Plantinga's theory will become important later when I distinguish Plantinga's theory from other types of reliablist theories (theories that also include the element of emotion and voluntary belief). For the present, it is sufficient to note the general point of this version of Plantinga's epistemology: by introducing the element of emotion

15. Roberts and Wood, "Proper Function," 4.
16. Ibid., 21.
17. Ibid., 19.
18. Ibid., 5, 12.
19. Ibid., 12.
20. Ibid., 8.
21. Ibid., 11.

Alternative Contemporary Epistemological Models

and concept of virtue, they end up not just making the case that some beliefs may be voluntarily formed but rather making the more radical case that belief formation and justification actually can be determined by one's "will" or emotion.[22]

How will Plantinga's epistemological model (or the Roberts and Wood version of it) fare when it interfaces with Griffith's challenge: if an opposing religious claim is deemed to be from a trustworthy source and if there is no good way to explain away the opposing claim, does it not follow that one's own religious belief will be epistemically troubled?

Plantinga states that it is first important to clarify the question raised by religious pluralism. Indeed, he writes, the world presents "a bewildering and kaleidoscopic variety of religious and non-religious ways of thinking." But, he goes on to ask, is the variety itself enough to "defeat" Christian[23] or any particular type of religious belief?[24] According to Plantinga, the mere fact of pluralism is not enough to suggest that Christian belief is problematic. He admits, however, that the fact of pluralism coupled with the fact that one does not "have proof or argument that can be counted on to convince others who disagree" is problematic for Christian belief. Without any leverage for showing that one type of theistic belief (Christian) is superior to any other, maintaining belief would seem to be "self-serving arbitrariness" or "egoism."[25]

There are two strategies to which Plantinga appeals to deal with this problem. The first is to show that there is not really disagreement and, thereby, no problem. Plantinga explains that there is only real epistemic

22. Roberts and Wood's virtue reading of Plantinga's epistemology highlights the connection between a person's beliefs and a person's character. Specifically, Roberts and Wood bring out the affective dimension of this connection. For Roberts and Wood, who a person is trying to become (i.e., a faithful Christian) bears on her belief formation and justification. This epistemological model critically links belief to practice. However, the link (between belief and practice) that Roberts and Wood point out is distinct from the link argued for by Clifford. For Clifford, belief and practice are connected because beliefs are dispositions to act. Thus, there are different warrants for making this connection; Roberts and Wood ground the connection affectively where Clifford grounds it ethically. Moreover, while Roberts and Wood's argument that will bears on belief formation has its merits, their argument that will bears on belief justification is the product of a genetic fallacy. An emotion may be a good warrant and cause for a belief, but it is not necessarily a good justification for continuing to hold a belief.

23. Plantinga addresses this matter from a Christian standpoint and so is concerned about Christian belief. However, for the purposes here, it could just as easily be "Hindu belief" or "Muslim belief" and so on.

24. Plantinga, *Warranted Christian Belief*, 437–38.

25. Ibid., 442.

disagreement when there is epistemic parity between disagreeing beliefs and when the believers are epistemic peers. He argues that a Christian believer, for example, is unlikely to acknowledge other religious believers (who do not accept Christian beliefs and/or who reject Christian beliefs by virtue of believing some other religious belief) as *true* peers.[26] The Christian believer will simply think that the disagreeing believer has some "blind spot" or has not received "special grace" (has not, "found Jesus," so to speak) and so is not a true epistemic peer. The "disagreement" is thus nullified.[27] This is the easy, if not cheap, way out. Furthermore, it does not actually avoid the charge of egoism, which is defined by Plantinga himself to mean "thinking I am in a privileged position with respect to you."[28] It merely broadens the subject and predicate of the claim—"we Christians are in a privileged position with respect to you others"—so as to outwardly diffuse its egoist timbre.

The second strategy Plantinga offers is more substantial because it actually makes use of his theory of "basic belief"-foundationalism. It is the more interesting, though perhaps more insidious, strategy. Plantinga states that it is not the case that a Christian believes her belief simply because it is *her* belief or *her* intuition that it is true. In other words, she does not take her belief as true in a possessive sort of way (e.g., "I hold this belief because it is my own"). Rather, a Christian "non-culpably" believes her belief because she has a "source of knowledge or information" for the belief.[29] "God is speaking to me now" is a properly basic belief that is foundational for her belief about God's existence. This basic belief is not publicly accessible but is instead only cognitively accessible to the believer. This produces precisely the "epistemic haven"-effect that Griffiths warns against in his appraisal of privatization strategies. Basic beliefs are accessible in the way that memories, for example, are accessible to the person who remembers them. It is not arbitrary or merely accidental, according to Plantinga, that the believer holds a particular belief; it is precisely *because of* her basic belief that she does.

Plantinga constructs his epistemology so that beliefs are warranted by virtue of their foundations and, specifically, the foundations of basic beliefs. If a theistic belief rests on a basic belief foundation, Plantinga

26. It is difficult to see how Plantinga seems to think this kind of claim does not display egoism or arrogance.
27. Ibid., 453.
28. Ibid., 444.
29. Ibid., 449.

explains, its warrant is independent of "probabilistic relations to other beliefs."[30] In other words, if a belief is warranted, it is so apart from being considered in relation to other beliefs and even those other beliefs that are also properly warranted. There is a deeply autonomous or even solipsistic tone to Plantinga's epistemology that is thrown into relief when examined in the context of religious diversity.[31]

Plantinga's epistemology is autonomous or solipsistic in two ways. First, because theistic beliefs are warranted by private basic beliefs, there is no public way to evaluate either the derived ("self-evidently entailed") belief or the basic belief. Plantinga's "basic belief"-foundationalism sets up highly privatized system of belief formation. This is compounded by Plantinga's externalism which allows beliefs to be warranted without an account, given by the believer, of why or how she forms the belief she does. The believer is permitted to trust her basic belief foundation without checking it against other possible basic beliefs.

This leads into the second way in which Plantinga's theory promotes a kind of solipsism. There is no sense in which believers are encouraged to engage with other believers regarding their warranted beliefs. Believers are not required to do so. Because the foundation for one's own belief is already warranted by its immediate connection to a reliable process, considering others' beliefs can neither harm nor help that belief. In Plantinga's epistemology, it is as if believers form beliefs out of individual cognitive universes and these universes remain relatively separate. Plantinga's phrase "probabilistic relation to other beliefs" points to this. He explains that we do not form or warrant beliefs by comparing ours to others' and

---

30. Ibid., 442.

31. Also thrown into relief is the "atomistic" structure of Plantinga's epistemology. If a person is warranted in holding a belief independent of probabilistic relation to other beliefs, then self-deception may become warrantable. Take the following example. I am warranted in my belief that "my dog is a good dog." All of my neighbors complain that my dog terrorizes the cats and children of the neighborhood; they tell me that she chases, barks, and nips at the smaller creatures that cross her path. According to Plantinga, if my belief that my dog is good is warranted (she fetches my morning newspaper, never has accidents on the rug and, moreover, I never witness her terrorizing the neighborhood cats and kids), then my neighbors' claims need have no effect on my belief about my dog. While I have presented a relatively prosaic example, self-deception can be highly pernicious (imagine a scenario where a parent refuses to believe his child is a bully in school or an assaulter of women). It is not only problematic but also unsettling that Plantinga's epistemology would allow for it to exist and prosper.

so engaging other beliefs has no real epistemic or epistemological effect.[32] Recall from the previous chapter Barbara's description of the interreligious dialogue group as "a kind of crucible" and the exposition of the two possible meanings of crucible—a crucible is a place of severe testing or a place where something new is forged. On Plantinga's model, neither type of interreligious dialogue "crucible"—negative or positive—would be relevant for religious belief. A person's religious belief—once warranted according to Plantinga's standards—are immune from being affected by interaction with others' religious beliefs.[33]

There is still more that is troubling about Plantinga's theory. It is not only that Plantinga's religious epistemology inherently promotes a kind of solipsism for theistic beliefs, it is also that his system necessarily privileges one type of theistic belief, namely Christian belief. How so? Plantinga's proper function theory viz. theistic belief is modeled on Calvin's idea of "sensus divinitatis."[34] Plantinga summarizes Calvin's model as follows, ". . . the basic idea, I think, is that there is a kind of faculty or a cognitive mechanism, what Calvin calls *sensus divinitatis* or sense of divinity, which in a wide variety of circumstances produces in us beliefs about God."[35] The reliable process (proper function) by which we form basic beliefs about God are, in fact, created by God; that is, the capacity to form the basic belief "God is speaking to me now" is implanted in us by God. According to Plantinga, it can only be explained theologically and, more specifically, according to a theology with a Christian doctrine of God.[36]

Andrew Koehl crystallizes the issue as follows,

---

32. The solipsism for which I criticize Plantinga's theory is only heightened in the Roberts and Wood version. For Roberts and Wood, believers arrive at their beliefs through the conjoined efforts of intellect and will. In their account, the effort to believe reinforces both belief formation (through proper function) and justification. If one can simply *will* her way to justified belief, it is difficult to imagine why she would undermine herself by engaging other possibilities for belief.

33. Not only does Plantinga's theory discourage interaction among diverse religious believers through interreligious dialogue, neither does it do much in the way of encouraging interaction *intra*religiously. For example, Plantinga's model makes it possible for mainstream, "orthodox" Christians—on the authority of *sensus divinitatis*—to dismiss as peers "heterodox" Christians who are on the margins of the Christian community.

34. In fact, the reason that Plantinga's epistemology is labeled "reformed epistemology" is because it is rooted in the theology of Christian reformer Jean Calvin.

35. Plantinga, *Warranted Christian Belief*, 172.

36. This point is significant when talking about the *sensus divinitatis* but should not be overstated with respect to Plantinga's general theory of knowledge.

Alternative Contemporary Epistemological Models

> [For Plantinga] our cognitive faculties are designed so that given certain circumstances we should form particular beliefs in the basic way. Those beliefs which are formed (in that appropriate environment) are properly basic, and Plantinga holds that belief in God and indeed in Christ fulfills these conditions.[37]

Along similar lines, Plantinga writes, "These [theistic] beliefs don't come just by way of the normal operation of our natural faculties; they are a supernatural gift."[38] The proper function argument upon which Plantinga's religious epistemology is requires a Christian ontology: God creates the condition for the human possibility to perceive God.

In fairness to Plantinga, his theory includes an explanation for the teleological status he assigns to proper function (for both mundane faculties and the *sensus divinitas*). Plantinga's epistemology is externalist in character. "Externalism" is typically characteristic of "epistemic naturalism." Naturalized epistemologies provide accounts of the "natural" processes whereby beliefs are formed. An externalist constraint on justification, which does not require believers to know how or why she holds her belief, fits well with a naturalized (descriptive/non-foundational/*a posteriori*) epistemology because, in this type of paradigm, beliefs are the outcomes of processes that are ordinarily presumed to be reliable. In Plantinga's terms, if one's faculties are properly functioning, then the beliefs should be good ones *just because* they are the outcome of properly functioning faculties.

The proper function of our faculties, then, is to attain "true or verisimilitudinous beliefs." From a purely naturalistic-metaphysical perspective, Plantinga explains, there would be no reason to assume that proper function should lead to truth; he states, "natural selection is not interested in truth, but in appropriate behavior."[39] There must be another explanation, then, for why the proper function of epistemic faculties is to attain truth. Plantinga states, "The way to be a naturalist in epistemology is to be a supernaturalist in ontology"[40] A supernaturalist ontology/metaphysic holds that we are designed for truth. John Greco interprets Plantinga's supernatural metaphysic as follows: "From a theistic point of view such design will be by God, but non-theists can also make use of the concept of design. Even non-theists think that, in some sense, a bird's wings are

---

37. Koehl, "Reformed Epistemology" 173.
38. Plantinga, *Warranted Christian Belief*, 245.
39. Plantinga, *Warrant and Proper Function*, 218.
40. Ibid., 215.

designed for flying."[41] Greco is right to point out that Plantinga's general theory of knowledge can be understood from a non-theistic perspective. However, when the design in question is with regard to Plantinga's *sensus divinitatis*, I contend that it is implausible to assert that a designer (God) can be left out of the picture.

Take the following statement from Plantinga: ". . . the fundamental idea is that God provides us human beings with faculties or belief-producing processes that yield these beliefs and are successfully aimed at truth."[42] While a general concept of design may work to explain the faculties of smelling or remembering, God is surely responsible for the *sensus divinitatis* in Plantinga's account. Indeed, Plantinga makes a compelling case for why a supernaturalist ontology best grounds a naturalistic epistemology, particular viz. one's "theistic-epistemic" faculties. What is puzzling, however, is why this designer need be a *Christian* God who creates faculties that then lead to Christian beliefs.[43]

Plantinga's account, perhaps unintentionally, ultimately discredits the epistemic legitimacy of other (non-Christian) religious beliefs. Not only are theistic beliefs only checked by reference to themselves, but also there could be *no* other beliefs against which they might be judged since theistic belief formation is a necessarily Christian process. Plantinga thus does not leave much wiggle room for rethinking the epistemology of religious diversity. He achieves a stalemate: the only warranted religious beliefs that can be formed, on Plantinga's account, are Christian ones.

---

41. Greco, "Catholics vs. Calvinists," 16.

42. Plantinga, *Warranted Christian Belief*, 375.

43. Plantinga's argument, as previous the paragraphs demonstrate, is based on Calvin's theory of *sensus divinitatis*. At first glance, this theory seems generically theistic. Plantinga explains, "The *sensus divinitatis* is a disposition or a set of dispositions to form theistic beliefs in various circumstnaces, in response to the sorts of conditions or stimuli that trigger the working of this sense of divinity" (*Warranted Christian Belief*, 173). As Plantinga carries through with his argument, however, we begin to see that his model implies not only that God implants this capacity in people or designs humans to have it, but also that the Holy Spirit is what allows for the *sensus divinitatis* to work. He writes, "[Beliefs about God] come by the work of the Holy Spirit, who gets us to accept, causes us to believe . . . These beliefs don't come just by way of the normal operation of our natural faculties; they are a supernatural gift" (ibid., 245). The Holy Spirit is thus necessary for perceiving God and this, presumably, leads to or at least strongly favors Christian beliefs.

William Alston and Doxastic Practices

William Alston develops another contemporary alternative to evidentialist epistemologies like those of McKim and Feldman. Alston, like Plantinga, seeks to offer a defense of religious belief. His strategy also works by defining a reliable mechanism or means for belief formation. A belief can be justified if it has been formed by a reliable process. On the surface, this move is similar to Plantinga's. Plantinga argued that a theistic belief such as "God exists" is warranted when it is built on a properly formed basic belief such as "God is speaking to me now."

The difference between Plantinga's and Alston's versions of reliablism is that Plantinga introduces proper function to explain how foundational basic beliefs are formed while Alston uses the notion of a reliable doxastic (belief-forming) practice to show parallels between perceptual belief formation and mystical belief formation. Alston jettisons the need for foundational beliefs whereas Plantinga depends upon them. Alston concentrates on the processes by which S comes to form p in both the realm of general knowledge and the realm of religious knowledge in order to illuminate the way that we organically justify and so "trust" beliefs.

Alston begins by positing that mystical beliefs (M-beliefs) bear a "family resemblance" to perceptual beliefs (P-beliefs).[44] It is imperative to point out that Alston does not claim that M-beliefs are a *type* of perceptual beliefs, but rather that they "look" like each other in terms of function and mode of justification and can be compared analogically.[45] P-beliefs are our most mundane perceptual or sensory beliefs. Alston's argument is that the perceptual practice of seeing, for example, is itself a learned practice. We do not just see with our eyes but rather we learn how to see by way of a doxastic practice. The idea of a doxastic practice has its roots in the philosophical work of Ludwig Wittgenstein and Thomas Reid and

---

44. Alston, *Perceiving God*, 186.

45. Richard Gale raises questions as to whether Alston's analogical argument actually works (though he does so in such a cantankerous way that it makes his reader skeptical of his hermeneutic). Gale points out that Alston denies that his argument is strictly analogical and that he goes to pains to show disanalogies between MP and PP. Gale however thinks that Alston's is indeed an argument by way of analogy. He assesses Alston's epistemology as follows: "This practical justification [offered by Alston] is too thin, because it says nothing about the human purposes that are served by engagement in well established [PPs]" ("The Overall Argument," 139). Gale finds Alston's proposal to do nothing more than offer religious believers practical "pie in the sky" advice (e.g., continue believing because it works) that is ultimately epistemically ineffectual.

is defined as the socially established ways of forming and epistemically evaluating beliefs.[46]

In order to demonstrate that perceptual practices (the practices by which P-beliefs [perceptual beliefs] are formed) are learned, Alston describes a few alternative, imaginary kinds of perceptual practices (PP). (Alston also discusses mystical practices, which are the practices by which M-beliefs [mystical beliefs] are formed, and those are here noted as MP.[47]) He states that there might be a "'Cartesian' practice of seeing what is visually perceived as an indefinitely extended medium that is more or less concentrated at various points" or an "'Aristotelian' [one where seeing is] made up of more or less discrete objects scattered about space" or a "'Whiteheadian' [kind where the] visual field is seen as made up of momentary events growing out a continuous process."[48] These creative examples are intended to show that there are conceivable non-Aristotelian (the mode we generally recognize to constitute PP) ways of seeing. We are "firmly wedded" to the Aristotelian PP, Alston continues, because that is what is socially established. We see in this way because it is the way we have been taught, not because it is necessarily the best way of seeing; we "learn how" through a process in which we may or may not be aware of our participation.[49] Because a PP is the result of social context

---

46. Alston, *Perceiving God*, 6. See also Reid, *Essays*.

47. I use different initials/descriptors than Alston's original work. Perceptual Practice (PP) and Perceptual Belief (P-belief) have been substituted for Alston's terms Sensory Practice (SP) and Sensory Belief (SP). Mystical Practice (MP) is a substitute for Alston's term Christian Mystical Practices (CMP). These substitutes have been made strictly for the sake of clarity and are not intended to stray from his meaning.

48. Ibid., 273.

49. Dr. Charles Fernyhough, professor of developmental psychology at Durham University, explores the early development of newborn babies in his book *1000 Days of Wonder*. In an interview for *Radiolab* with Jad Abumrad, Fernyhough remarks that the book's driving question is, "What's going on for this new person?" Abumrad and Fernyhough discuss the visual and auditory senses in newborn babies as compared to adults. Fernyhough states that newborns see and hear in a way that is distinctive from adult seeing and hearing. For example, he explains that the lens of a baby's eye is "absolutely crystal clear" while an adult lens is yellowed and cracked from time and use. For this reason, babies perceive light in a different (perhaps more intense) way than do adults. There are also neurological differences between adult sense perception and infant sense perception. Fernyhough refers to an experiment done with newborn babies where nets of electrodes were positioned on babies' heads to record the electrical changes that take place in their brain. Measuring the brain's electrical responses through electrodes is a standard (as well as harmless and painless) procedure to "see the way in which particular parts of the brain respond to different stimulus." When an adult is shown a picture, the electrodes record a "spark" in the back portion of the

and practice, Alston states that we do not have "neutral grounds on which to argue effectively for the greater accuracy for our way of doing it [over other (e.g., Cartesian or Whiteheadian) ways]."[50]

Even while it is impossible to argue effectively from a neutral standpoint as to the superiority of one type of PP, Alston holds that this does not mean that its accuracy cannot be checked in any way. Alston explains that what allows us to put stock in our particular practice is its "overrider system." Both PP and MP necessarily include functioning overrider systems. Alston defines an overrider system as "a 'background system' of beliefs against which a particular perceptually supported belief can be checked for possible overriders." Overriders are things that would tend to undermine the belief. Overrider systems provide checks against Griffiths' privatization criticism. Alston gives the following example: if a person sees a flower and thinks that it is purple but has "overwhelmingly strong evidence that there are no purple flowers in [the] garden" or knows that "something about the lighting makes white flowers look purple," her belief

---

brain, where the visual cortex is. If an adult hears a sound, Fernyhough continues, then the auditory cortex, slightly forward of the visual cortex, "would fire and you wouldn't see anything in the visual cortex." When newborn babies are given the same stimuli, however, the results do not match those of the adult subjects. Sometimes, when the babies in the experiment see a picture, there is a spark in the auditory cortex. And, conversely, when they heard sound, the visual cortex sometimes fire. (Fernyhough emphasizes that this *sometimes* happens, while sometimes the babies' brains fire regularly.) Abumrad asks Fernyhough, "Did the picture trigger a sound for the babies?" Fernyhough responds that while researchers cannot know what the pictures triggered for babies *subjectively*, they do know that the part of the brain that normally fires in a developed person did not fire, and the part of the brain that does not normally fire did. Abumrad pushes the point further by asking, "So what you're saying without letting it pass through your lips is that they [the babies] were *hearing* a picture?" Abumrad wants to know if babies can smell sound, taste light, hear smells, and so on. Fernyhough responds, "We don't know what they did [hear or see], but [this research provides] a good basis for saying that when a newborn's brain is developing; these different wirings that lead information into different parts of the brain are still taking shape." Fernyhough does not refer to this experiment to "prove" anything about the development of sensory perception in babies, except to demonstrate just that—that sensory perception *is developing*. Likewise, I refer to Fernyhough's discussion of "seeing sounds" and "hearing pictures" not because I want to make an evidentialist or "scientific" claim about sensory perception, but because I think it puts Alston's point that sensory perception is a learned practice in perspective. There is reason to believe that even the most basic cognitive processes do not arise in humans in finished or fixed form and that it takes practice for humans to get cognitive practices in working order. Fernyhough, interview by Abumrad.

50. Alston, *Perceiving God*, 274.

that the flower is purple will be overridden. As systems, overriders allow beliefs to be methodically checked as reliable.[51]

Both P-beliefs and M-beliefs, Alston argues, are formed through doxastic practices (PP and MP, respectively), which each include distinctive overrider systems. The MP of prayer is like the PP of seeing in that is a learned practice and it involves an intrinsic screening process to discount beliefs if there are overriders. By learning and engaging in MP, people are able to produce M-beliefs. Alston compares the MP for forming M-beliefs to the PP for forming P-beliefs in order to demonstrate how epistemic circularity is involved in "proving" the reliability of either MP or PP.

Alston points out that we accept or trust the reliability of PP even while being incapable of demonstrating its reliability non-circularly (i.e., without reference to the practice itself). He states,

> We must either use sense perception as the source of our premises [for demonstrating why our PP are good], thereby already assuming that it is reliable, or else get our premises from some other source that we would have reason to trust only if we already had reason to trust sense perception. Any such argument is infected by a kind of circularity.[52]

His argument for the justifiability of M-beliefs hangs on the issue of analogous circularity. P-beliefs are "foundationalness" in the same way that M-beliefs are; both are produced through doxastic practices and neither can be justified expect circularly. Why is it the case, Alston asks, that we have more stringent requirements for M-beliefs than P-beliefs if both are produced by doxastic practices?

Alston's answer to this question is that the practices by which M-beliefs are formed are disputed where the practices by which P-beliefs are formed are accepted. However, MPs are not bad or irrational practices unless they are demonstrated to be unreliable for the purposes for which they are used, which is, in this case, to form M-beliefs. The justifiability for engaging in MP is both practical and epistemic. We can engage in MP because it is a socially established doxastic practice that cannot be known to be any more or any less reliable than any type of PP. If the MP turns out to be reliable in a way analogous to the way that PPs are, it follows that properly formed M-beliefs are justified beliefs just as P-beliefs are. Alston works to make a strong case for the weak justifiability of MPs by pointing out that our PPs are just as weakly justifiable.

51. Ibid., 79.
52. Ibid., 107.

Alternative Contemporary Epistemological Models

Alston's justificatory standard is non-foundationalist and is comparable to the non-foundationalism of James, in its attention to the context or circumstance in which beliefs are formed. He points out the broader context (in this case, the doxastic practice itself) in which beliefs are formed just as James does with the genuine option situation in order to set a justifying standard. The implications of Alston's contextually-based non-foundationalism are stronger than they are for James, however, because Alston makes a point about *all* types of belief (that even perceptual beliefs have no real foundations and can only be justified circularly) and not just about belief in one, unique situation.

Like Plantinga, Alston does not hold that believers must be able to explain how or why they privilege their belief-forming processes rather than other types of belief-forming processes, according to his argument, believers *cannot* do so without circularity. Because we tend to refer to the outcomes of our practices to justify those practices, internalist demands are not useful. All types of beliefs, both religious and non-religious, must be understood as the outcome of doxastic practices and can only be justified as such. It is not possible to weigh beliefs neutrally.

Unlike McKim and Feldman, Alston does not presume that all beliefs can be justified on the basis of comparing evidence. Unlike Plantinga, he does not think that reliable practices create *foundations* for beliefs. Alston makes a rather modest, though highly sophisticated, argument. Tilley has characterized the argument as "defensive." Tilley writes, "[Defensive] accounts leave us with indissoluble dilemmas. They may show that religious beliefs are, *pace* the cultured despisers, not irrational."[53] Note Tilley's phrase "not irrational." The goal of Alston's project is to demonstrate only why M-beliefs are *as justifiable as* P-beliefs as long as certain conditions apply (i.e., the result of socially established doxastic practices; pass the test of overriders). It is not to make a positive argument for their independent justification or, here, rationality.

Alston does not dispute Tilley's point, although he states that he prefers to characterize his argument as "internal" rather than defensive. "My argument," Alston states, "for the rationality of (certain) perceptual beliefs about God is 'internal' rather than 'external,' in that it does not aspire to establish that rationality on grounds that are wholly outside the doxastic practice in question."[54] The upshot here is that Alston does not—and indeed thinks he cannot—make a case for the justifiability of any single MP

53. Tilley, "Religious Pluralism," 168.
54. Alston, "Response to Critics," 177.

as compared to another MP. Where, then, are we left when we consider the facts of diverse religious beliefs? Does Alston's epistemology force him to recommend, like McKim and Feldman, that religious beliefs be held tentatively or altogether suspended?

Alston is in agreement with Plantinga about the charge of epistemic egoism; he too sees why it may be problematic to maintain one's belief in the face of conflicting beliefs. Because Alston develops a non-foundationalist justificatory requirement for MP, he is able handle the charge of epistemic egoism more adeptly than Plantinga. The process of belief-justification, in Alston's epistemology, entails a belief being tested against a range of other factors, including evidence and background beliefs (these take the form of overriders). Moreover, as Alston explains, "Prima facie justified perceptual beliefs are subject to further assessment by reference to what we know or justifiably believe about the world, perceivers, and interrelations."[55] Because doxastic practices are social in nature, other people (or perceivers, in Alston's words) and their beliefs are relevant for one's own beliefs. Thus, Alston's epistemology is not subject to the charges of solipsism that Plantinga incurs.

Take for example Alston's discussion of a purple flower. In his example, the belief that the flower was purple could not be justified because it was defeated by the overriders that suggested there was good reason to think the flower was not purple. While Alston is adamant that there are no neutral grounds for judging various MPs, his epistemology explicitly includes the action of testing one's belief against other possibilities. This might be seen as the kind of strategy Flew would advise and the kind of strategy that the women of Philadelphia exemplify in their practice. Not only do the women discuss their religious beliefs with each other, they also invite each other to be witnesses to and participate in (to whatever extent others can) their religious practices—practices which are precisely the MP leading to M-beliefs. For example, when the women gathered to celebrate the Baha'i new year festival, the non-Baha'is were not only able to understand the Baha'i beliefs associated with that religious festival more fully, they were also able to use it is as a point of comparison for their own practices and beliefs.

Alston shows a strong commitment to ensuring the seriousness with which believers and their beliefs come in contact with one another: it is a part of the very system of justification. Rather than claiming superiority or autonomy for one type of belief forming process, it is as if Alston

---

55. Alston, *Perceiving God*, 104.

envisions beliefs as part of a web such that beliefs will be justified with respect to other beliefs. While this assessment of the theoretical implications of Alston's epistemology is rather positive, this still does not answer the question of what the real outcome of epistemic engagement with religious others might be. From what I have explained, it looks as if Alston will arrive at the opposite conclusion from Plantinga: if the process of belief-justification entails being checked by other beliefs as overriders, would not any religious beliefs simply override any other religious belief?

To deal with the fact that one religious belief does not immediately[56] cancel out the justification for another religious belief, Alston draws a distinction between "prima facie" justification and justification by "further assessment." M-beliefs are *prima facie* justified if there are no "sufficient overriders" or "sufficient conditions to the contrary" internal to the MP.[57] M-beliefs might be later subject to "further assessment" by something like, for example, interreligious dialogue that places M-beliefs in relation to other M-beliefs. This is to say that Alston sees gradations of justification and because this is so, it can be the case that diverse, justified religious beliefs coexist.

There is a second distinction that Alston makes in order to avoid the conclusion that the justification of one M-belief would necessarily cancel out the justification of another. He explains that there is an important difference between M-beliefs themselves and how M-beliefs are articulated by believers. Alston states that there are "different ways of conceptualizing, specifying, or identifying appearances [the result of MP]."[58] These ways are determined by the believer's background systems of belief. A Christian's background beliefs will shape the way she formulates her M-belief in one way and a Muslim will articulate her M-belief in a very different way

---

56. Immediate is a technical term. Alston explains that there is a distinction between mediate/indirect justification and immediate/direct justification. Mediate justification is justification by reasons. Immediate justification is by something other than reasons. He states that it is a "wastebasket" category. Immediate justifiers are "(a) experience of what a belief is about, (b) the self-evidence of the proposition believed, and (c) the proposition believed [for example] about one's conscious experience" (ibid., 72). The distinction between mediate and immediate justification is a more exact way of saying what I explain here as *"prima facie* justification" and "justification 'by further assessment,'" whereby *prima facie* justification constitutes immediate justification and justification by further assessment constitutes mediate justification. I have chosen to use more colloquial language to explain this above in an attempt to avoid (more) jargon.

57. Ibid., 72.

58. Ibid., 45.

because of different background beliefs. The fact that there are different background systems, for Alston, is not problematic; background systems are in fact necessary because they are what create overriders.[59]

The conflict of M-beliefs is thus resolved in a two-step process. To summarize, Alston first argues that there are different levels of justification, which allow for the coexistence of diverse justified beliefs. He next explains that background systems will necessarily affect how M-beliefs are articulated. Thus, what we understand to be in conflict is actually beliefs as they are stated and not necessarily beliefs as they really are. And, because we have no neutral grounds for assessing these M-beliefs, Alston remarks, ". . . the sting is taken out of the inability of each of us to show that he is in an epistemically superior position."[60]

The question of whether there is serious conflict between diverse MPs, however, deserves another response. Alston writes, ". . . each of our rival practices [MP] is confronted with a plurality of uneliminated alternatives" and, he goes on to wonder if it is possible, "for supposing any one method to be more reliable that others?"[61] He prescribes the following:

> The knowledgeable and reflective [religious person] should be concerned about the situation, both theologically and epistemically. Actuated by the latter concern, she should do whatever seems feasible to search for common ground on which to adjudicate the crucial differences between the world's religions, seeking a way to show in a non-circular way which of the contenders is correct.

In other words, this is a life long quest,[62] and in the meantime, we can engage in our own practice because it is a socially established, reliable practice.[63]

The take home point for Alston is that if our MP is reliable, the M-beliefs that are the yield of that MP can be justified *regardless of* but not *without regard to* the existence other MPs and M-beliefs. Alston does not circumvent the issue of conflicting religious beliefs as blatantly as Plantinga (whose theory entails the superiority of Christian belief). Alston's

---

59. Ibid., 261.
60. Alston, "Religious Diversity," 443.
61. Alston, *Perceiving God*, 270.
62. In fact, since these practices are social, it is not only a lifetime over which they are worked out, but rather multiple lifetimes of multiple people.
63. Alston also states that there may be "significant independent reasons" for preferring one MP to another but that he will not concern himself with those arguments.

Alternative Contemporary Epistemological Models

epistemology, I have argued, necessitates comparing M-beliefs and MPs to each other. The women of Philadelphia compare their M-beliefs as well as their MPs by both discussing theological topics and demonstrating to each other their religious rituals. For example, in conversation, each woman shares with the others her "image of God." By also inviting others to participate in their religious celebrations (such as the Baha'i new year festival) and demonstrating their religious practices to each other (such as describing in detail circumnavigating the *Kaaba*), the women reveal the ritual methods (their MPs) that lead them each to an "image of God." While Alston himself finally balks at making a case for any positive epistemic consequences of interreligious engagement, his epistemology may allow for this possibility.

Linda Zagzebski and Pure Virtue Epistemology

Linda Zagzebski develops a "pure virtue" reliablist epistemology, or virtue epistemology. For Plantinga, beliefs are warranted by being reliably produced, or, said another way, by being properly formed basic beliefs or beliefs properly derived from properly formed basic beliefs. For Alston, M-beliefs and P-beliefs are equivalently, though, weakly justified by being the product of their reliable doxastic MP and PP, respectively. Zagzebski's argument can be sketched as such: beliefs are justified to the extent that they are the product of an exercise of epistemic virtue. The check for reliability lies with the motivation for and execution of a particular act of epistemic virtue.

To understand where the idea of intellectual virtue in epistemology comes from, it is helpful to look at epistemologist Ernest Sosa briefly. Sosa is the forefather of virtue epistemology. Take the following statement as characteristic of Sosa's theory: "My claim is that to understand knowledge we must enrich our traditional repertoire of epistemic concepts with the idea of *being in a position to know*."[64] Asking if a believer is "in a position to know" is like asking if the believer has the propensity, penchant, or ability to know.[65] In other words, Sosa suggests that focus should be placed on

---

64. Sosa, "How Do You Know?," 118.

65. Lorraine Code is a foremother in the argument about "being a position to know." Where Sosa focuses on the more technical or mechanical aspects of being in a position to know, Code importantly draws out the deeply social and constructed aspects of what it means to be in a position to know and the implications thereof. Specifically, she develops this line of thinking by inquiring into the relationship between gender and knowing. Code first posits this question in her essay "Is the Sex of the

the properties of persons rather than beliefs themselves when considering belief justification.⁶⁶

In her epistemology, Zagzebski follows Sosa's cue that emphasis should be placed on a person's properties and then goes on to deepen it. She has two, interrelated methodological commitments that are instructive for understanding how her project is both related to and distinct from the epistemologies of other reliablists (Plantinga and Alston) and even other virtue reliabilists (Sosa). Her commitments are, one, to bridge the gap between philosophical ethics and epistemology by bringing ethical methods of evaluation to bear on epistemological issues such as justification and knowledge and, two, in doing this, to reposition the lens of epistemology's microscope onto the highly particular subject—a subject who is situated in a community or communities and who forms beliefs—rather than on either the beliefs themselves (as with McKim and Feldman) or on the abstract reliable processes in which the believer participates as a kind of secondary agent (as with Plantinga, especially, and Alston to some extent). In this way, Zagzebski's epistemology has strongly contextualist features and is grounded in *a posteriori* reasoning.

The aim of Zagzebski's epistemology, she explains, is to "assimilate beliefs as well as acts into the domain of moral evaluation."⁶⁷ Here Zagzebski's project bears resemblance to Clifford's: both Zagzebski and Clifford see that beliefs have ethical implications and insist that they can be evaluated as such. However, Zagzebski rejects the kind of deontological approach that Clifford takes. She criticizes the tendency in epistemology to focus exclusively on "rules and procedures," rather than on the agent in the process of belief formation. This criticism employs the very same logic that virtue ethicists make of Kantian ethical theory. Zagzebski shapes her epistemological discussion according to the debate between Kantian-based ethics and virtue ethics. In Kantian ethics, a moral act is evaluated according to how it meets preestablished laws or maxims. In virtue ethics, an act is assessed as right or wrong according to its connection with the "inner traits of a person."⁶⁸

According to "pure virtue theory," used in virtue ethics, morally good acts are understood to be exercises of a person's virtues. This shift in focus in philosophical ethics—from rules and procedures to the "internal

---

Knower," 267–76) and develops it more fully in *What Can She Know?*

66. Zagzebski, *Virtues of the Mind*, 8.

67. Ibid., 230.

68. Ibid., 79.

qualities of a person"[69]—provides a model for a shift in focus in epistemology. Zagzebski makes a case for a parallel form in epistemology: good beliefs are exercises of a person's epistemic virtues. In terms of the global implications of this methodological commitment, Zagzebski wants to remove the wedge that she sees driven between ethics and epistemology. She believes that these two conversations can and should benefit from greater scholarly interaction. Virtue theory centers on person rather than act; the theory presupposes an integrated subject—a person who both acts *and* thinks—and so demands an exchange between ethics and epistemology.

As with Sosa, belief justification, according to Zagzebki, is determined by the belief's relationship to the properties of the believer. Sosa explains this property roughly as "being in a position know."[70] Zagzebski thinks that this definition falls short of a real account of virtue.[71] She so develops a thick account of virtue that gives more content to the sense of "being in a position to know." She uses Aristotelian theory to explain and describe what virtues are.

Virtues are not natural or innate capacities. They are rather dispositions that we train ourselves to have. Yet acquiring virtue is not as simple as learning a skill like being able to tie shoelaces or a technique like being able to swing a hammer properly.[72] Skills and techniques like these are learned by sheer repetition or rote. One can lose skills and techniques because they are formed and used at a relatively surface level. Virtues, once acquired, are an integral part of a person and cannot be shed. Zagzebski writes that a virtue is an "excellence" or "deep trait"[73] that is "entrenched in an agent's character."[74] It involves "knowing-how" that is learned through practice and imitation[75] and ultimately is acquired through habit.[76] Virtues are defined in terms of motivation.[77] For example, as Zagzebski explains,

---

69. Ibid., 59.

70. Sosa begins to develop this position in his famous essay "The Raft and the Pyramid," 3–25) and develops it more fully in *A Virtue Epistemology*.

71. Zagzebski, *Virtues of the Mind*, 8–10.

72. Ibid.,105.

73. Ibid., 89.

74. Ibid., 179.

75. Ibid., 21.

76. Ibid., 125.

77. For example, Zagzebski explains that in her theory "the concept of virtue will be constructed out of the concept of good motivation" (ibid., 82).

Virtue in Dialogue

"Justice is the virtue according to which a person is characteristically motivated to respect others as persons."[78]

Intellectual or epistemic virtues are the epistemic dispositions of persons. They are like virtues such as courage in that they are learned, attained through habit, and defined in terms of motivation. What does all of this have to do with belief formation and belief justification? While it is outside the bounds of this project to discuss the relationship between knowledge and justified belief in significant depth, it is helpful, in this instance, to start with the terms knowledge and know—rather than belief and believe—because that is what Zagzebski herself uses to answer these questions. Briefly outlining Zagzebski's theory of knowledge equips this discussion with resources to get at the issue of justified belief and the role that intellectual virtues play therein.

Zagzebski writes that the "motivation to know is the most basic constituent of intellectual virtue."[79] The motivation for knowledge works toward two interrelated ends. First, the motivation to know pushes believers to develop skills that are associated with particular epistemic virtues (such as fairness of judgment, clarity of expression, curiosity, and so on).[80] Second, the motivation to know incites believers to employ processes that are "truth conducive and whose truth conduciveness [the believer] is able to discover/use by possession of intellectual virtue."[81] Take the intellectual virtue of openmindedness in the following example.

My sister Jessica, who is a teacher, is motivated to know about teaching methods for foreign languages. She realizes that it is necessary to be openminded in her pursuit of knowledge about these teaching methods. Openmindedness is supported by the cognitive skill of listening. She practices the skill of listening when talking to her students, fellow teachers, and principal on the topic of teaching methods. The practice of listening supports her ability to be openminded. When she exercises the virtue of openmindedness, she is likely to reliably attain knowledge of teaching methods.[82] Thus the motivation to know about teaching methods both

78. Ibid., 165.
79. Ibid., 259.
80. Ibid., 135.
81. Ibid., 176.
82. While the virtue of openmindedness involves being open toward new ideas and open toward revising established ways of thinking, it does not imply that one is *wide* open. Openness is always checked by judgment, rationality, and unbiased attention to opposing positions such that those who extol the virtue of openmindedness are protected against having to be openminded about genocide, apartheid, or

gives her knowledge of teaching methods and it also broadens her epistemic skill set that supports her intellectual virtues.

Zagzebski assigns value to each of these two ends—fostering virtue and attaining knowledge—that invert established expectations. Conventionally, knowledge has an absolute value and virtues or other reliable processes have a relative value (they are valuable as a means to the end of knowledge or justified belief). For Zagzebski, however, virtues are valued in themselves and knowledge is valued to the extent that it is the outcome of an act of intellectual virtue. In Zagzebski's paradigm, virtues are absolutely valued and knowledge is relatively valued.

To continue the earlier example, if it turns out that my sister learns nothing about teaching methods, but develops her virtue of openmindedness, Zagzebski would say that it was still a successful endeavor. Virtues have intrinsic value, apart from what they produce (in this case, beliefs about teaching methods).[83] The virtue of openmindedness is good as such. If it happens that my sister acquires a great deal of knowledge about teaching methods, but does so without exercising intellectual virtue (perhaps she is actually very closeminded, but consults one very good and well respected book on teaching methods for foreign languages), Zagzebski questions whether we should think my sister actually *knows* anything about teaching methods.[84]

Assuming that belief is the highest belief state (for present purposes, I assume this epistemological point), it is fair to assume that what has been said thus far about epistemic virtues viz. knowledge applies also viz. justified belief. Zagzebski's theory is that a belief is justified if it arises out of an act of intellectual virtue appropriate to the circumstance. She develops an account of epistemic virtue, premised in general on the motivation to know, in order to explain how virtues give rise to beliefs (which may go on to give rise to knowledge). Zagzebski offers a method by which beliefs are formed and can be justified. In her model, belief justification is considered apart from predefined rules and in such a way that accounts for the highly subjective and contextual process of belief formation. It is therefore naturalized. We can test our beliefs by asking whether an intellectually virtuous person would believe similarly in similar circumstances; this processing of

---

human trafficking, for example. Openmindedness might be better described as critical receptivity.

83. Ibid., 108.
84. Ibid., 312.

testing constitutes the normative—that standard by which epistemologists assess the justifiability of belief—component of Zagzebski's theory.

Even though justification is dependent on the virtuous qualities of other people rather than on external rules (as with Clifford's sufficiency of evidence rule, for example), Zagzebski's epistemology still makes normative demands; it is just that these normative demands are refracted through personal qualities rather than propositional rules. Because of this, there are especially important questions to be raised about the possible forms of elitism (classism, racism, sexism, Eurocentrism, and so on) that may inhere in person-based systems. In other words, are the intellectually virtuous persons—the persons who provide the standard by which beliefs are justified—of a certain privileged type? And, moreover, does the privilege of their position systematically exclude *other* types of intellectually virtuous people and ways of knowing from providing the standard for what counts as justified belief?

Although Zagzebski herself does not answer these highly important (and sensitive) questions, I can develop responses to these questions by using feminist epistemological theory and particularly the work of Lorraine Code. Code's feminist "meta"-epistemological thesis is that theories of knowledge endorse certain forms of life. Mainstream epistemology, Code argues, makes assumptions about the subject (S) of epistemology, which, in turn, affect the normative standards for knowing; for Code, this tends to denigrate women's ways of knowing and honor men's ways.[85] In mainstream epistemology, S is purportedly "neutral"—genderless, colorless, raceless, classless, and so on.[86] In fact, Code explains, *all* knowers have genders, colors, races, and classes and, as such, there is no universal subject of knowledge.

Knowledge—insofar as it grows out of personal experience or, said another way, is the product of variant subjects' knowing processes—is "subjective" or personal. To illustrate the "personal" nature of knowledge, take the following (mundane) example. A person holds this belief about seasonal weather: summer is always hot and winter is always cold. It is shaped be her personal experience of the world, which is specifically informed by her position living in the northern hemisphere. This ordinary belief is relative to her context. Code argues that it is a mistake to read the personal nature of knowledge as necessarily pejorative and she proposes that epistemology fundamentally change the terms of its inquiry to

85. Code, *What Can She Know?*, 29.
86. Ibid., 34.

Alternative Contemporary Epistemological Models

recognize this.[87] In other words, rather than simply deeming this belief about weather as "objectively" wrong (because the weather is just the opposite in the southern hemisphere), epistemologists should make accommodations for the personal nature of belief formation when developing justificatory standards (that is, the faulty weather belief should not simply be dismissed as false, but rather understood as a product of a specific, personal social location).[88] Code's specific interest is in "sex as one of a cluster of objective factors" that constitute subjectivity and thereby knowledge. To this end, the primary mission of Code's prolific work is to examine "women's ways of knowing" particularly in relation to "men's ways of knowing."[89]

If epistemology changes the terms of its inquiry to include a place for the various parts of the "cluster of objective factors," two more features of social location come to the fore: people are active agents rather than "passive recorders of knowledge" and people are "social creatures" in knowing.[90] These insights, taken together, generate the sense that first—with regard to the subject of knowing—knowers are constituted as subjects by the social positions they occupy; secondly—with regard to the process of knowing—knowing does not transcend subjective experience, but rather is deeply informed by it; and thirdly—with regard to the outcome of knowing—knowledge is dependent on social location.[91] In summary, epistemological processes are socially determined. Zagzebski's person-centered, context-based virtue epistemology is closely tied to a view that, like Code's, recognizes the profoundly social nature of belief formation and justification.

Code's model of virtue epistemology shows how her principles about the subjectivity of knowledge play out in practice. For Code, "responsibility" is the central virtue from which all other virtues radiate.[92] She uses

---

87. Ibid., 30, 322.

88. The traditional epistemologist would simply argue that this person has extended her proposition, "winter is cold and summer is hot," beyond its context. That is, she has applied this belief beyond its limited context and, if made aware of weather in the southern hemisphere, she would correct her belief. While this objection stands, it misses Code's point, which is that beliefs formed properly in particular, personal contexts may be justified unless "defeated" in such a way as to require a modification.

89. Code, "Experience, Knowledge, and Responsibility," 167. Nowhere does Code make an argument that these gendered ways of knowing are "naturally" determined. Instead, she investigates how male and female ways of knowing have been constructed.

90. Code, *Epistemic Responsibility*, 137, 167.

91. Code, *What Can She Know?*, 178, 103, 209.

92. Code, *Epistemic Responsibility*, 44.

field research of women who receive welfare in Canada to show how these women (who are of a particular socioeconomic class and educational background) have been denied the opportunity to be epistemically responsible—according to the way this virtue is normally construed—because of their social location.[93] Because Code investigates the "material [and] structural networks" that necessarily impinge on the subjects of knowledge,[94] Code's conception of the virtue of responsibility includes a place for subjects who are otherwise marginalized from epistemic responsibility.

Zagzebski does not address the material and constructed conditions affecting epistemology in the same way that Code does. However, she does recognize the social nature of belief formation, develop an *a posteriori* standard for justification, and create a person-based account. Code's theory is a fitting complement to Zagzebski.[95] The normative component to Zagzebski's virtue epistemology grows out of socially-oriented imagination.[96]

A believer must *imagine* what a virtuous person might believe and, more precisely, what a virtuous person might believe in like circumstances and follow accordingly. This sense of imagination hopefully does not suggest a soft or weak standard for justification—but quite the opposite. To form a justified belief, a person must assess whether a virtuous person would form that sort of belief in that sort of context. This involves a good amount of work and depth of thought on the part of the believer and is a critical part of the (loose) method Zagzebski introduces for belief formation and justification. Applying the example of a belief about seasonal weather to this aspect of Zagzebski's theory, the person who holds that summer is hot and winter is cold must consider this belief in light of what learned persons in her community believe. If the person is part of a community and situated in a social context that lacks resources for understanding the reverse seasons in the southern hemisphere (e.g., even the learned elders of the community are unaware that weather patterns are different in different parts of the world)—and this is Code's point—epistemologists

---

93. Code, "Responsibility and the Epistemic Community," 537–55.

94. Code, *What Can She Know?*, 293.

95. In the following chapter, I propose an epistemological model that is heavily reliant upon Zagzebski; I read and utilize Zagzebski with Code (and other feminist epistemologists) in mind and hope that this feminist-informed approach to virtue epistemology filters out tendencies toward elitism.

96. Zagzebski does not call this an imaginative process; this is my language.

Alternative Contemporary Epistemological Models

should account for this when evaluating the justification for the belief that summer is hot and winter is cold.

The believer is responsible for asking herself if her belief is truly the outcome of an act of intellectual virtue. She can ask herself if she has formed her belief through a virtuous process, one that is motivated by the desire for knowledge rather than the desire to be comforted or consoled, for example. She may also assess whether her belief is in fact the outcome of an act of epistemic virtue by reflecting on whether it is a belief that an intellectually virtuous person would have in a like context. She does all this, not because an epistemologist defines it as her epistemic duty to do so (as with Clifford), but rather because the very notion of intellectual virtue entails this kind of consideration. Although Zagzebski refuses categorization as externalist or internalist (she thinks the terms only frustrate the conversation), she does state that while she does not think S needs to know how she knows p in order to know p, her virtue theory "puts S in a good position" to do so.[97] That is, her epistemology makes realistic, contextually-sensitive demands of believers.

In this theory, the motivation to know is not just a blind aim at knowledge (JTB) but is an aim at a certain kind of knowledge, specifically the kind that arises from the toil and sweat of cultivating and exercising intellectual virtue.[98] Beliefs are reliable and hence justified by being the outcome of acts of epistemic virtues; reliable belief-forming processes (the epistemic acts themselves) are constrained by being properly motivated. This feature of Zagzebski's theory is especially relevant for distinguishing this reliablist form of epistemology from other reliablist types. Zagzebski explains that it is possible, by the lights of other reliablist theories, that belief-forming processes can produce reliable results even while displaying a lack of motivation for knowledge.[99]

This is problematic because, according to these accounts, self-consciousness is only "incidentally related to the good under consideration."[100] In Plantinga's epistemology, good or justified beliefs can come about without a person's motivation, desire, effort, or awareness for it to be so. This kind of theory paints a picture of a problematically disjointed knowing subject: a person whose habits, motivations, and beliefs may not be at all correlated even if her faculties are properly functioning or her doxastic

---

97. Zagzebski, *Virtues of the Mind*, 275.
98. Ibid., 184.
99. Ibid., 207.
100. Ibid., 28.

practice is reliable. Zagzebski demands instead "a unitary account" of one's epistemic life.[101] The sense of disjointedness in Plantinga's theory suggests that the believer is only a secondary agent in the process of belief formation.

Implied in Zagzebski's theory is also a rejection of the opposite extreme that I previously noted as problematic. This position is typified by Roberts and Wood's model of virtue. Roberts and Wood add emotion onto Plantinga's model in order to argue that emotion and virtue (as the exemplification of the motivation to know) can help to determine belief formation *and* justification. The believer in their epistemological model is so fully "jointed"—that is, the intellect and will are perfectly aligned—that beliefs can always be justified (for conviction bears on justification). While Zagzebski argues that epistemology must include a place for desire/motivation (captured by the concept of virtue), her very understanding of virtue rules out the possibility that such desire/motivation leads to self-seeking ends (namely, belief justification). She constructs a necessary relationship between virtue and justified belief, but protects her notion of virtue against a Roberts and Wood-type conclusion wherein a person can simply *will* her intellect to justified belief.

Zagzebski's critics find her theory problematic for mitigating the role that desire and motivation play in belief justification. In Greco's estimation, agent-based theories exhibit unity not only between faculty and desire/motivation (or intellect and will, in the language of Roberts and Wood) but also between belief and believer. Greco contests the extent to which Zagzebski's theory actually is agent-based. He argues that that Zagzebski does not end up with an epistemological model that makes beliefs primarily connected to a person's character.[102] Rather, beliefs are formed from the exercise of virtue per se, which, according to Greco's reading of Zagzebski, a person need not *possess* but only have the characteristic motivation for.[103] In other words, beliefs are formed from the exercise of virtue, which may or may not be representative of a person's character.

Greco highlights this fine distinction because he wants to make clear that Zagzebski is more closely related to Plantinga and Sosa than she bills herself to be. (In fact, Greco states that Zagzebski "misuses the language of virtue" and is not a pure virtue theorist at all but rather a reliablist.[104])

101. Ibid., 51.
102. Greco, "Catholics vs. Calvinists," 17–19.
103. Greco, "Two Kinds of Intellectual Virtue," 183.
104. Ibid., 179.

Alternative Contemporary Epistemological Models

What Zagzebski introduces into the conversation, according to Greco, is not an agent-based theory of knowledge, but instead a theory that makes knowledge "epistemically responsible cognition" through the language of virtue.[105] Thus, the debate has not really become about the person forming beliefs but is still about the processes by which beliefs are formed.

Greco states that "the problem of agent-reliability, or lack thereof, persists . . . the person who acts virtuously has knowledge because she is reliable, not because she manifests any of the other components of Zagzebski-type virtues."[106] But precisely what kind of reliability is Greco after? Zagzebski's virtues guarantees reliability in forming justified beliefs. Greco seems to want a form of reliability that does something beyond creating justified beliefs, but he leaves this reliable "something" as an open—or worse, empty—concept.

Because Zagzebski does not require believers to actually possess the virtues, but only express the motivation characteristic of them, Greco thinks that Zagzebski gives us insight into "the mechanics of human cognition" but not "the conditions for knowledge."[107] Greco's appraisal of Zagzebski helpfully shows a critical feature of her epistemology—namely, that it is rather process-based (instead of being entirely person-based, as Greco hopes it would be). Greco criticizes Zagzebski for constructing a model of virtue epistemology wherein the believer need not possess the virtues in question. For him, this means that she fundamentally misses the meaning of virtue.

Greco's criticism (that Zagzebski is not actually agent-based) and reasoning (that she misappropriates the language of virtue to support her non-agent-based theory) are unfounded. His focus on the distinction between process- and person-based epistemologies (and, consequently, his effort to place her work in one or the other camp) ultimately clouds the central contribution of Zagzebski's work—namely, that she uniquely brings together process- and person-based approaches, revealing that a person's epistemic virtues are always in the process of developing. Zagzebski's agents are not required to possess virtues to produce justified belief. This allows for—in fact, it *demands*—a sense of fluidity: agents' virtues can have potency even while being in the process of maturation (this makes it possible for children or non-neurotypical epistemic agents, for example,

---

105. Greco, "Catholics vs. Calvinists," 29.
106. Greco, "Two Kinds of Intellectual Virtue," 184.
107. Ibid., 184.

to have justified beliefs) and agents can be imperfect in different kinds of virtues while still producing justified belief.[108]

As Greco rightly points out, Zagzebski makes it so that believers do not have to possess virtues to produce justified beliefs, but she does not rule out that they *can and do* possess virtues. This is the piece that Greco misses. Greco reads virtue as though it works with an "on/off" switch: either one has the virtue and it is on or one does not and it is off. But this will not do. Virtue is the *telos* of the habit, not its condition. Zagzebski effectively adds depth to the concept of virtue and she shows how virtues will necessarily be works-in-progress, because she does not, like Greco, draw a hard and fast rule that one must possess a virtue entirely for it to "work." This, *contra* Greco, tells us something important about "the conditions for knowledge."

The point of epistemic inquiry is to aim at a particular *quality* of belief and, simultaneously, to develop one's virtues. Zagzebski is not so idealistic as to say that beliefs are only justified when a believer *possesses* a particular virtue. However, because virtues are valued absolutely and justified belief/knowledge relatively, her theory implies that beliefs formed from acts of pure virtue are of better or higher quality than beliefs formed from epistemic acts that only express characteristic motivations of virtue. This is so precisely because the former (and not the latter) allow for the believer to become a paradigmatically epistemically virtuous person, who will later support others in belief justification and virtue development (by standing as the example by which other's learn virtue through imitation and assess their own beliefs through imagination). Greco faults Zagzebski for not being sufficiently person-based and, in so doing, overlooks the nuance of her theory. Virtues are skilled achievements, and some people achieve better or sooner than others.[109] Zagzebski's theory illuminates this.

What Zagzebski contributes is not just another riff on the reliablist theme. Her theory makes a bold statement about the necessarily social conditions for justified belief or knowledge in that the "condition for knowledge" is that it must be formed socially and measured qualitatively, all with an understanding, on the part of the epistemologist, that virtues are ever in the process of being formed. Zagzebski's theory is both socially-oriented and process-based. By drawing out these two features, her virtue

---

108. This second point will become particularly important as I develop a hybrid virtuous doxastic practice epistemology in the following chapters.

109. Take the following: we would not call a novice carpenter no carpenter at all, but rather on the way to becoming a master of carpentry.

Alternative Contemporary Epistemological Models

epistemology uniquely provides for a variety of conditional spaces for knowledge both across social spectra and through time. In other words, Zagzebski's theory allows for persons to be virtuous at some times and not others and destabilizes what would be fixed social roles for Greco. This opens the field for who can be virtuous (and thus provide the normative standards for belief justification) and countervails elitism.

In conclusion, Greco's reading of Zagzebski is problematic because he utilizes an "on/off" concept of virtue. By re-conceptualizing this understanding of virtue, not only are Greco's criticisms sidelined but important features of Zagzebski's theory can be brought into play.

How does Zagzebski's theory fit with religious belief? She does not develop a particularly detailed answer to this question, but she does offer a few thoughts in various places that provide a constellation of ideas. Most of these points reinforce the arguments she has already made about belief in general and are helpful to repeat here in summary. First, Zagzebski rejects the "well-oiled machine model" argued for by Plantinga (and this could also be applied to a certain extent to Alston) for theistic beliefs.[110] She states that one cannot justifiably believe in God without "contributing something to the process."[111] However, what a believer contributes to the process of "knowing God" is not a rational argument or a stack of evidence but instead is voluntary, cognitive activity.[112] This comes in the form of exercising one's epistemic virtues.

One other critical point she makes in her discussion of religious epistemology, unmentioned by Zagzebski in her discussion of general epistemology, is that religious beliefs are dependent on a community and a communal doxastic structure for justification.[113] For Zagzebski, this community is bound up with traditional religious authority. This comes through, in particular, in her interpretation of justification within the Roman Catholic tradition (Zagzebski's religious tradition). She states, "The possessor of warrant is fundamentally the Church, not the individual, so the conditions for justification of belief are conditions that the Church must satisfy, not Francis or Jane or Edward."[114] In other words, the believer *as a member* of her religious tradition is responsible to the standards of that tradition. What Zagzebski give us is a system where religious beliefs

---

110. Zagzebski, "Religious Knowledge," in *Rational Faith*, ed. Zagzebski, 222.
111. Ibid., 218.
112. Ibid., 209.
113. Ibid., 206.
114. Ibid., 208.

are justified by achieving a balance between (1) being what an epistemically virtuous person would believe in like circumstances and (2) being consistent with the authoritative conventions of a communal doxastic structure.[115]

The case of religious diversity is not one that Zagzebski faces. A strategy like Alston's, which appeals to a distinction between *prima facie* and *ultima facie* justification, can be useful for adapting Zagzebski's epistemology to the context of diversity. Recall that Alston appeals to gradations of justification and distinguishes between the comparison of M-beliefs and the comparison of MPs. M-beliefs may be *prima facie* justified but also subject to later *ultima facie* justification. MPs cannot be neutrally assessed; we are justified in continuing with our practice and set on a road of constantly evaluating our beliefs beyond their *prima facie* justification.

I propose the following: religious beliefs gain justification by being able to imagine what an epistemically virtuous person might believe in *like* circumstances. Examples from the Philadelphia women's interreligious dialogue group discussed in chapter 3 illustrate how people use imagination in the practice of dialogue to understand how both their own religious beliefs and the beliefs of religious others are formed and "justified." When describing her experience with interreligious dialogue, Elli distinguishes between religious "support group" and, in her words, "circle of faith"; in her estimation, the Philadelphia interreligious group is a circle of faith. The distinction Elli draws is based on what she understands each of these groups to provide for its members. In a circle of faith, members *enact* faith together rather than simply talk with others whose experiences resonate with their own, as in a support group. The active quality that Elli notes is confirmed in others members' accounts. For example, Ruth uses the word "edifying" to describe her experience of the group; the women come together and, in dialogical encounter, their own beliefs and religious self-understanding are affected by the stories of each other.

The active and affective characteristics of dialogue may be epistemologically cashed out in terms of imagination. Elli explains how she imaginatively "enters" the experiences of her fellow "circle of faith" group members through listening; she states, ". . . when you listen and start hearing some patterns [in their stories] . . . for me—it just creates

---

115. What Zagzebski fails to acknowledge is that these might be competing demands. Moreover, Zagzebski does not raise questions about traditional authoritative conventions (i.e., who actually has or should have authority?).

this awareness of a mystery, of the transcendent kind of forces in people's lives."[116] It is not that Elli *imagines* (as in "makes up") the presence of "transcendent forces" in others' lives. It is rather that through imagination she is able to understand how they experience that mystery and transcendent force and, furthermore, this "understanding through imagination" has consequences for how she is able to understand, in turn, the beliefs of her dialogue partners.

In another instance, she states, "If when [another group member] is talking about prayer, or talking about her experience with communion, I can just watch her light up, I want to know what that is about. I want to understand that. If I see it in her, I know it's accessible in me. And I know it's accessible in others."[117] Again, through listening and imagination, Elli is able to understand why and how Eucharist, in this example, and the *Hajj*, in a later example, are central to the beliefs of those who participate in these practices. This is not to claim that the Philadelphia women think specifically about epistemological justification. They do, however, work to understand and make sense of each other's beliefs in a genuine and deep way. The effort to "make sense of" a belief is not unlike the epistemological task of justifying belief—both involve considering the belief's sources, the reason for the believer holding the belief, and the role the belief plays in the believer's life. They are epistemologically in *this* context.

The idea that beliefs are assessed according to comparable context suggests that justification is "location specific" or "context dependent," meaning that Christian beliefs are assessed according to a Christian context and Jewish beliefs according to a Jewish context and so on. This sense of inward facing, location specific/context dependent justification is reinforced by the fact that beliefs are also subject to evaluation within the community out of which they grow. If they pass these tests they are *prima facie* justified.

This standard of justification is incomplete and would be problematic if left off there. Even though religious beliefs might be *prima facie* justified internally (by imagining how a virtuous person in like circumstances would act and by testing according a communal structure), this is not the whole story. There is still a question about how to assess the virtues themselves, just as Alston asks how to weigh various MPs. Zagzebski does not give any explicit hints as to how this answer would play out. She either assumes that epistemic virtues are constant across cultures and religious

---

116. Interview by Mara Brecht, July 20, 2007, Philadelphia, PA, digital recording.
117. Interview by Mara Brecht, July 20, 2007, Philadelphia, PA, digital recording.

groups or she is uninterested in addressing variations among epistemic virtues.

Zagebski's theory offers resources to develop a more complete theory of justification. At the very least, I can use Zagzebski's work to argue that (1) we learn virtues through observing and imitating the epistemic virtues and intellectual acts of *others* and (2) justification occurs as when believers imagine what *others* might believe. A Zagzebskian approach encourages interaction between various virtuous people and, thus, various forms of epistemic virtues and *especially* virtuous people who happen to have different religious beliefs. Zagzebski stresses the point that the motivation for knowledge includes the dual aims of obtaining knowledge and fostering virtues. Developing various skills and techniques helps to support virtues.

I argue that the women of Philadelphia exemplify this developing work in their listening practice. They cultivate the virtue of "deep listening" by emphasizing openness, focus in listening, and humility. A remark from Hina in chapter 3 indicates what is involved in deep listening: "We try—even as we are bringing out whatever it is that we don't agree with—keeping our views really, really open to listening for another."[118] Another anecdote from the Philadelphia group indicates the possible effects of the virtue of deep listening: one member admits to being transformed from having little respect for and being suspicious of Muslims to empathizing with the Muslim group members because she learned to *listen*. The women of Philadelphia teach how and encourage each other to listen deeply.

The developing work necessary to cultivate virtues may involve learning about other kinds of epistemic virtues (perhaps even ones outside one's home community) and orienting one's own virtues accordingly. Said another way, developing one's epistemic virtues may involve attention to others' epistemic virtues. Moreover, if we take Greco's reading of Zagzebski seriously (yet divorce this reading from his conclusions about it), then the beliefs formed out of "trying out" others' virtues may gain justification even if the person doing the trying does not posses such virtues. While this is not the argument that Zagzebski makes, her epistemology at least opens the possibility to assign a positive epistemic value to the encounter with religious diversity.

---

118. Interview by Mara Brecht and Jeannine Hill Fletcher, February, 12, 2009, Philadelphia, PA, digital recording.

Toward a Virtuous Doxastic Practice Model for Religious Belief

Because they formulate naturalized epistemologies, Plantinga, Alston, and Zagzebski each offer more substantial accounts of the process of belief formation than the contemporary *a priori* epistemologies discussed in chapter 2. Rethinking the epistemology of religious diversity toward the end of claiming positive significance for it demands a firm grasp on the full complexity of what is actually involved in forming beliefs. As it is now clear, Plantinga's epistemology does not offer many resources toward endowing religious diversity with positive epistemic significance. In the end, only Christian beliefs properly formed through the Christian *sensus divinitatis* faculty can be warranted.

Alston and Zagzebski open up greater possibilities for re-conceiving religious epistemology in the context of religious diversity. I want to call attention to two unique strengths or contributions and two weaknesses or problems to each of their approaches. By themselves, Alston and Zagzebski's projects are equally useful and equally problematic for my purposes, although this is the case for different reasons. Since the theories of Alston and Zagzebski are not mutually incompatible, it is possible to pull resources from both without compromising the fundamental strategy of either.

Post-Zagzebski Assessment of Alston

Alston's Strengths and Contributions

(1) Alston's epistemology shows that beliefs are the outcomes of doxastic practices. Doxastic practices involve a degree of cognitive voluntarism but, at the same time, are not entirely "chosen" by believers in that they are often learned by believers from the beginning of their lives and according to their cultural location and religious context. This achieves a balance between requiring believers to take full epistemic responsibility for beliefs and granting legitimacy to the "here I stand I can do no other"-attitude toward belief. This is particularly helpful when considering the issue of religious diversity because it makes sense of the fact that religious believers who are deeply aware of diversity can develop dual vision toward beliefs. That is, they stake a claim in their own beliefs and at the very same time are troubled by them, given the existence of other possibilities for religious belief.

(2) Alston's epistemology allows for gradations of justification (*prima facie* and *ultima facie*). The fact that there is not an absolute threshold for justification makes it difficult to be dismissive of diverse beliefs or their associated doxastic practices without a substantial and thoroughgoing process of critical reflection. This suggests that forums in which believers come into contact with diverse beliefs (such as interreligious dialogue) may not be, in fact, peripheral to the process of epistemic justification.

Alston's Weaknesses and Problems

(1) While Alston's concept of doxastic practice is laudable for the fact that it can be read as striking the balance noted above, it would be problematic if it were read as a strictly mechanical process. If doxastic practices occur at a level similar to that of seeing, for example, it is possible to imagine how we "choose" to participate in this process on some level (just as we "choose" to stick with our Cartesian practice of seeing rather than opt for a Whiteheadian one). However, that kind of choosing does not involve any emotive elements such as desire, feeling, or motivation—all things that are bound up in the experience of religious belief formation. Any thoroughgoing religious epistemology would need to address this aspect of belief.

(2) Alston aims to make a modest argument; I noted that he makes a strong argument for weak justification (although, as it turns out, according to Alston, perceptual beliefs are just as weakly justified). This is not itself problematic, but this type of approach is not sufficient for this project, which has a significantly less modest goal (perhaps naively so), which is to argue for the positive epistemic significance of religious diversity. Where Alston "plays to not lose," so to speak, the hope for the virtuous doxastic practice theory is to show how believers can "play to win."

Reassessing Zagzebski in Light of Alston

Zagzebski's Strengths and Contributions

(1) Zagzebski's project develops a reliabilist epistemology that demonstrates how belief formation and justification are driven by epistemic virtue. Zagzebski constructs an integrated knowing subject who is firmly embedded in a community. A community shapes a person's epistemic virtues because it is in the community that a believer recognizes epistemic virtues and habituates herself accordingly. Virtues only work and beliefs

Alternative Contemporary Epistemological Models

are only able to be formed and justified because of the communal structure that supports them. This element of community, which is at the very heart of Zagzebski's epistemology, is touched upon by no other epistemologist thus far (Alston comes the closest). Because religious beliefs arise in the context of a religious tradition or culture, attention to the role that communal traditions and institutions play in belief formation is essential for any adequate religious epistemology. Moreover, the question of the extent to which the community shapes one's virtue is left open; the fissure that Greco notices in Zagzebski between virtue possession and belief justification reinforces this point. Thus, it may be possible to show how other religious communities contribute to the development of virtues found in one's own community.

(2) Zagzebski emphasizes a degree of cognitive voluntarism to her epistemology, but the sense of voluntarism has an expanded meaning as well. In the epistemological method she proposes, actual practice and discipline are essential components of belief formation. Epistemic virtues are ultimately formed by habits and buoyed by the skills and techniques associated with those virtues. In terms of religious epistemology, this makes sense of the fact that people actively try, for lack of a better phrase, to get better at believing. They may do things such as read the spiritual autobiographies and writings of people like St. Augustine or Thich Nhat Hanh,[119] join prayer and meditation groups, or even imitate the behavior of persons whom they view as having vibrant religious lives. In fact, believers may sustain their virtues from attention to *all* these things, and not just Christian, or Jewish, or Hindu ones and so on.

Zagzebski's Weaknesses and Problems

(1) It is not clear just *what* epistemic virtues are to be employed viz. religious belief formation or how they are to be employed. This is a limitation of Zagzebski's work rather than as a weakness or problem, since her principal interest is not in developing a religious epistemology per se. In order to go forward with her epistemological model, however, this difficulty must be addressed. There is a range of questions to ask. Are theistic epistemic virtues special or distinct from general epistemic virtues? If they are special, can they be explained without reverting to a *sensus divinitatis* strategy, so as to avoid Plantinga's pitfall? If they are not special, but rather common,

---

119. See for example Augustine, *Confessions*; and Thich Nhat Hanh, *Peace Is Every Step*; idem, *The Miracle of Mindfulness*; idem, *True Love*.

how is it possible to explain why they "work" for some people in forming religious beliefs but do not "work" for others?

(2) The second concern is closely related to the issue of cognitive voluntarism (a point I commended Zagzebski for only a paragraph ago). While it is good to highlight the volitional aspects of virtue development, it would be problematic to construe all beliefs as under agents' control.[120] Recall my earlier criticism of Roberts and Wood's interpretation of Plantinga: if a person can simply *will* her way to justified belief, there is little for epistemology to regulate and nearly anything can count as knowledge. There is thus a critical distinction between the role volition plays in virtue development and the role it plays in actual belief formation.

The issue of voluntarism is particularly thorny when considering justified beliefs about God, the origin of religious virtues, and the motivation for belief in God. Do people just *choose* to believe in God? *Contra* Roberts and Wood, there is a problem with making the epistemological case that agents can will their way to belief about God. However, *a la* Zagzebski, volition is an important component in developing the virtues (and doxastic practices) that lead to the possibility of belief formation. But what if an agent lacks the desire to develop these virtues? Must she be stuck in a state of unbelief? Zagzebski's theory tends in the direction of "responsibilism" (that we are fully responsible for all of our beliefs)[121] and misses any sense of "here I stand, I can do no other." It suggests that believers must be motivated to develop belief in God in the same way and with the same potency, that they are motivated to develop beliefs about, say, teaching methods for foreign languages. Because Alston's theory of doxastic practice is, by nature, a process that goes on at a level beyond the agent's awareness, Alston helps to achieve a balance that pure virtue theory lacks.

---

120. Beliefs are not necessarily under agent control, however agents are responsible for expressions of belief (i.e., actions). While a belief may not be under an agent's control, this does not mean that she is not accountable for those actions rooted in her convictions. A person may not choose to be prejudiced against members of minority ethnic groups (for example, this person was raised in a family and community that encouraged racist ideas, these ideas were engrained in her from early days, and she had little exposure to other, non-racist views), although she would still be responsible for perpetrating a hate crime or violent anti-minority action against any of those persons.

121. I modify John Greco's term "responsibilist," used in his article "Catholics vs. Calvinists," to form "responsibilism." Greco discusses a responsibilist constraint on knowledge to mean, broadly, that what one knows is under one's control (ibid., 26).

Venturing a Theory

Below are the distilled versions of Alston and Zagzebski on the topics of belief formation and belief justification as well as a distilled version of a hybrid form on both topics.

> *Alston "doxastic practice" theory of belief formation*: Beliefs are the outcomes of doxastic practices. These practices are learned practices; are socially established; and include overrider checks for reliability.
>
> *Zagzebski "epistemic virtue" theory of belief formation*: Beliefs are the outcomes of the exercise of epistemic virtues. Epistemic virtues are acquired through habituation and supported by practice/discipline; are developed in the context of community; and involve the imagination of the believer to check for reliability.
>
> *Zagzebski-Alston "virtuous doxastic practice" hybrid theory of belief formation*: Beliefs are the outcomes of doxastic virtue practices. These practices are entrenched in the believer by her communal context; are brought to maturation through observation, habit, practice, and discipline on the part of the believer; and put the believer in a position to reliably imagine possible overriders.
>
> *Alston "doxastic practice" theory of belief justification*: Beliefs are *prima facie* justified if they are the outcome of socially established MPs and if they have not been internally "overridden." Beliefs are *ultima facie* justified by being placed in relation to other (different) beliefs that are the result of other (different) socially established MPs.
>
> *Zagzebski "epistemic virtue" theory of belief justification*: Beliefs are justified if they are what a virtuous person might believe in like circumstances.
>
> *Zagzebski-Alston "virtuous doxastic practice" hybrid theory of belief justification*: Beliefs are *prima facie* justified if they are formed in such a way that coheres with what a virtuous person might believe in like circumstances and have been imagined to be so on the part of the believer. Beliefs move toward *ultima facie* justification by being considered in light of what a virtuous person might believe in unlike (different though relevant) circumstances.

The hybrid model makes a constructive argument about how beliefs are formed and justified. Because this model follows from rather than precedes examples of belief formation, it is a naturalized epistemology. The theory of belief formation shows how beliefs are inextricably tied to communal networks, holds that they are to some extent the outcome of a volitional method and to some extent the outcome of a mechanical process, and demands creative cognitive work on the part of the believer. The theory of belief justification allows for gradations of justification and necessarily includes the consideration of alternative beliefs/kinds of believers.

While the hybrid theory is primarily the result of a marriage between Alston and Zagzebski's theories, as the above summary shows, it is also critically influenced by insights from the ethics of belief and "Theology and Falsification" debates of the past. Clifford's contributions—that beliefs are dispositions to act, in a sense, and as such have ethical implications—fit particularly well with Zagzebski's virtue theory. James and Hare's focus on the determinative character of context and social location for belief formation and justification bolster Alston's notion of doxastic practice and Zagzebski's idea that virtues are borne out of communities. Flew's emphasis on falsifying factors are enlarged and corrected by Alston's notion of overriders. And Mitchell, the great mediator, provides a model for balance between the influencing capacity of evidence and the constitutive character of one's "articles of faith" for beliefs that the hybrid model mimics in describing a balance between the volitional (method) and mechanical (process) aspects of belief formation.

The following chapter fleshes out the skeletal sketch offered in this concluding section for a virtuous doxastic practice epistemological model. Where Zagzebski's project primarily explores the theoretical ramifications of virtue for epistemology, my project takes the next step to discuss, concretely, what the virtues are. Scholarship on Aristotelian virtue provides resources for explaining how the cardinal virtues of Western philosophy can be "retrofit" for epistemology. In the following chapter, I propose four epistemic virtues and two meta-level epistemic virtues. Alston's insistence that epistemic practices include overriders and be socially established provides this proposal with, among other benefits, "guiderails" through which to avoid privatization. Finally, examples from the experiences of the Philadelphia women continue to provide a point of contact for thinking about how these virtues are "practiced" in an interreligious setting.

5

Virtues and Virtuous Agents

Resources from the Aristotelian Tradition of Virtue Theory

IN THE LAST CHAPTER, I EXAMINED THE "RELIABILIST" SET OF CONTEMporary epistemologies, represented by Plantinga, Alston, and Zagzebski. Their epistemologies are reliablist because they understand belief formation and develop justificatory criteria by looking beyond evidence to the processes and practices by which people reliably form beliefs. Code notes that the sort of work done by these epistemologists is different from traditional forms of epistemology in that they "appraise cognitive processes more widely than standard procedures have allowed."[1] In my examination of these three epistemologists and the cognitive processes they appraise, I rejected Plantinga's model as a viable foundation for my project and chose instead to mine resources offered by Alston and Zagzebski.

I argued that Plantinga's "proper function" epistemology rests on the premise that people of other faith traditions do not have the *sensus divinitatis* that Christians do. Consequently, religious others cannot be genuine epistemic peers for Christians. Thus, Plantinga's epistemology cannot account for genuine dialogue.[2] In different ways, Alston and Zagzebski appraise epistemological processes by presupposing a deep connection between a person's practices and a person's beliefs. For this reason, their epistemologies can avoid the criticism that I laid at the doorsteps of the contemporary epistemologists of chapter 2—namely, that they (McKim and Feldman) are unable to account for cases of strengthened rather then enervated religious belief in the face of diversity and that their normativity

---

1. Code, *Epistemic Responsibility*, 120.

2. For a definition of the *sensus divintatis* (also discussed in chapter 3) see also Plantinga, *Warranted Christian Belief*, 172.

is *a priori* constructed. In their move to connect a person's practices and beliefs, Alston and Zagzebski develop agent-centered epistemologies.

I take up Alston and Zagzebski's agent-centered approaches and call the epistemology I construct out of those approaches the virtuous doxastic practice (VDP) model. Recall the outlined forms of the VDP model presented in the last chapter:

> *Zagzebski-Alston "virtuous doxastic practice" hybrid theory of belief formation*: Beliefs are the outcomes of virtuous doxastic practices. These practices are entrenched in the believer by her communal context; are brought to maturation through observation, habit, practice, and discipline on the part of the believer; and put the believer in a position to reliably imagine possible overriders.
>
> *Zagzebski-Alston "virtuous doxastic practice" hybrid theory of belief justification*: Beliefs are *prima facie* justified if they are formed in such a way that coheres with what a virtuous person might believe in like circumstances and have been imagined to be so on the part of the believer. Beliefs move toward *ultima facie* justification by being considered in light of what a virtuous person might believe in unlike (different though relevant) circumstances.

Like Alston's and Zagzebski's, the VDP is a form of reliabilist epistemology: virtue epistemology. Greco concisely notes the defining feature of virtue epistemology: ". . . it makes normative properties of persons conceptually prior to normative properties of belief."[3] The VDP model identifies certain characteristics of persons that make belief forming practices reliable or in some other way epistemically good; these characteristics are the "normative properties of persons" noted by Greco. The concern of this chapter is to discuss the normative properties of persons that inhere in the VDP theory. Some basic and important questions about these properties are, simply, how do people get them and how do these properties work once people have them?

Since the VDP is an agent-centered, the theory must make sense of the relationship between the virtues and the people who exercise them. For that reason, this chapter's discussion is focused on the virtues *qua* normative properties of persons. The following is a summary statement of the theoretical understanding of virtue that I construct in this chapter. Epistemic virtues are the excellent characteristics of persons in a complex and

---

3. Greco, "Two Kinds of Intellectual Virtue," 181.

confusing world. They function in persons as modes of responsiveness to the demands of the world and are pervasive at all levels of cognition. An agent need not possess an intellectual virtue perfectly in order to be said to have it, but she becomes "properly affected" or feels satisfaction when she does exercise virtue. Virtues are learned by social means and are socially attuned. Exercising epistemic virtue contributes both to a person's own virtuous capacity as well as to social flourishing.

This chapter begins with an introduction into the theoretical resources available for discussing the relationship between virtue and virtuous agents. Zagzebski's approach, on which the specifically virtue aspects of the VDP theory are modeled, is Aristotelian in nature. For this reason, I begin discussing the way virtues and virtuous agents are connected by looking to Aristotle and his interpreters. In this first section, I call attention to the risks of elitism possible in my epistemological proposal. In the second section, I discuss the theoretical resources for understanding virtues as normative properties of persons in depth. Specifically, I focus on the theory of human nature implied by the concept of virtue; the function of virtues; the way virtues can be known in persons; the way virtues are communally constituted; and finally, the aims and outcomes of virtues.

The Agents of Virtuous Doxastic Practices

The VDP epistemological model holds that virtuous doxastic practices are the reliable practices by which an agent forms beliefs. Virtuous doxastic practices are reliable practices (like Alston's sense perception) because they are socially established and check for possible overriders. A virtuous doxastic practice is just one type of doxastic practice. Guessing is also a doxastic practice. Alston argues that sense perception is another. The question at stake is whether the practice is reliable. Guessing is an unreliable doxastic practice. Choosing *b* for every question on a multiple-choice test will not reliably lead a student to knowledge (or a good grade, for that matter!).

By contrast, when a person exercises intellectual virtue through a virtuous doxastic practice, the beliefs formed from that VDP may be justified. Virtues, which are normative properties of persons, regulate the reliability of the practice; they account for the epistemic goodness of the practice. How and why? According to the VDP theory, virtues are entrenched in agents, matured through observation, habit, practice, and discipline, and put epistemic agents into a position to form beliefs reliably and imagine possible overriders for their beliefs. Because this is agent-centered epistemology, it is necessary to explain how virtue and agent fit together.[4]

Virtues and Virtuous Agents

When we think about doxastic or intellectual virtue, a range of descriptors comes to mind. Words and phrases such as honest, thorough, receptive to multiple ideas, deep, fair, considerate, openminded, balanced, scrupulous, inquisitive, resourceful, and careful top the list. We might even have a particular person in mind who, in our experience, displays these qualities and characteristics to their fullest degree—a teacher from high school, a character in a novel or movie, a professor in a theology department, a mentor or parent. Aristotle calls this exemplar, a person (man, for Aristotle) of practical wisdom, a *phronimos*.

Philippa Foot claims that our list of virtues (both character or intellectual) will depend upon an account of the human person.[5] She thinks that when we ask ourselves what intellectual honesty is, for example, we implicitly ask ourselves the question: what kind of creature is it that is capable of expressing intellectual honesty to the highest degree? Thus when we think about intellectual virtues, we also think about what it means to be an agent capable of forming and justifying beliefs at all. In a similar way, making a list of the virtues indicates something about what we hope to achieve through intellectual exercise and growth.

Jane Braaten writes, ". . . our own conceptions of intellectual virtues operate as definitions of a *telos* for intellectual development."[6] That is to say, our notion of what an intellectual virtue is involves at least a rough idea of the outcome of virtue. At what does virtue aim? What do we hope to accomplish in exercising virtue? The task to define the intellectual virtues, then, involves more than just stating a set of intellectual characteristics; it touches on central philosophical and existential issues about personhood, rationality, and meaning, and the VDP theory hopes to do at least some justice to that fact.

---

4. I contend that religious belief formation is a distinctive type of belief formation, not because of the way beliefs are formed, but rather because of the content of the beliefs. My claim is that those religious beliefs that are the outcome of VDPs are *religious* because they are formed through religious traditions or are in response to the claims of religious traditions, not because there is a special cognitive faculty for religious beliefs. In short, the VDPs I discuss are not *unique* to religious cognitive processes.

5. Foot, *Virtues and Vices*, 10.

6. Braaten, "Towards a Feminist Reassessment," 4.

Exclusivity and the Risk of Elitism

I argue that when adopted and exercised by agents, virtuous doxastic practices normatively regulate an agent's belief formation and justification and, furthermore, contribute to the flourishing of the ambient community. One of the chief concerns associated with agent-based virtue theories like the VDP model is elitism. Any theory that develops a normative standard or normative *telos*—and particularly any theory that creates normative standards or assumptions about the proper "ends" for *human persons*—is prone to be to some degree exclusionary. In their very nature, normative categories evaluate and exclude. But is this theory elitist in its exclusivity?

The question is not *whether* the normative standards for virtue are exclusive but rather *to what extent* the virtues are drawn with sufficient breadth so as to not systematically exclude any one group of persons from having access to these virtues *as well as* to what extent the expectations for the exercise of virtues are detached from a particular *telos*. The elitism that the VDP theory works against is both with regard to the issue of who can have access to the virtues as well as with regard to the issue of what the expected outcome of virtue is. The VDP theory does not presume a vision for human flourishing, as I will argue in the following pages of this chapter, but rather (following Code, in particular) holds that knowers have different *teloi* for their practices depending on a range of factors, most important of which is their community.

There are three ways in which this theory anticipates or alleviates the risk of elitism. First, as stated in the introduction, my research is guided by a commitment to feminist epistemological principles in particular and feminist critical theory more generally. Indeed, stating one takes a feminist approach does not mean that one always avoids elitism. However, I have researched and written this book with feminist concerns in mind—concerns that importantly include redrawing the knowing subject of epistemology so as to not assert *a priori* "universal" truths but instead to develop *a posteriori* guidelines.[7]

---

7. There are two competing impulses in this project that are running into each other here. The consequent conflict is a classic one; it is a conflict between "the universal" and "the particular." On one hand, the project works to develop a "universal" normative standard that applies to all cases of belief formation. On the other hand, the project works to acknowledge the dizzying particularity of subjects who form beliefs. The epistemology that I develop in this project attempts to balance between these competing impulses by generalizing from the particular people and situations to create a broadly—if not universally—applicable theory of belief formation and justification.

Secondly, as mentioned in the commentary on Code's work in the previous chapter, the benefit of an approach like the VDP theory is that it argues beliefs are formed out of variegated *subjective* experience. In this chapter I will argue that the epistemic virtues—which are exercised through virtuous doxastic practices—provide agents with an ability to understand and evaluate their personal experiences. What these two points (that I do epistemology with a feminist hermeneutic that privileges particular subjects over a "universal subject" and that the VDP theory recognizes that it will be many kinds of subjective experiences toward which people are virtuously oriented) add up to is that, in principle, the VDP theory applies to a wide range of subjects and personal or "subjective" experiences.

Finally, this theory is not "mechanistic." Reliabilist epistemologies, like Alston's, risk elitism in that they appeal to the language of cognitive pathways and perceptive processes. This presumes neurologically typical agents. In other words, for a person to form justified beliefs, her cognitive processes must function "normally" or normatively. To a great extent, Alston protects against the charge of neurotypicality by holding that both perceptual and mystical practices are learned practices that are taught through communities; in other words, it is not about one's *inherited* ability but instead about one's *learned* ability. Even if Alston does not privilege neurotypicality per se is there room in a theory like his for agents whose doxastic practices are "irregular"? Moreover, can an agent who is non-neurotypical or who is differently cognitively-abled engage in these doxastic practices to a full extent?

Insofar as my theory embeds normative properties for belief formation and justification in an agent's *intellectual character* (through the concept of virtue) rather than her *cognitive ability*, the Zagzebskian aspects of the VDP theory help to diffuse these concerns. However, Zagzebski's project has its own elitist-type problem. If an agent's virtuous character forms the normative standard for belief, is it possible that some agents have more or better opportunities for cultivating virtue and thereby have greater success at forming justified beliefs? Does a virtue-based theory assume a certain kind of social status like Aristotle's ethics, which envisioned free male citizens, a small minority in Athens? Insofar as Alston theorizes that *all* epistemic communities carry their own apparatuses for teaching members doxastic practices and that *all* epistemic communities necessarily include their own overrider systems for regulating belief justification, the Alstonian components of the VDP theory helps to diffuse this concern.

Simply put, the VDP theory is a theory of *good* practice. As this is an epistemological project, I am concerned with rationality and knowing subjectivity rather than other features of the human person. As I write from a scholarly Western standpoint, the values of Western scholarship necessarily figure into my theory. However, as my approach uses *a posteriori* reasoning—I generalize from good epistemic practices and virtuous epistemic agents, rather than making *a priori* claims—I hope to avoid the worst forms of elitism. My challenge is both to draw the circle widely enough around each concept of epistemic virtue so as to not systematically marginalize any group from access and to create a productive synthesis of Zagzebski's and Alston's theories that neither conflates intellectual ability with intellectual character nor privileges one communal process of intellectual character formation.

Resources in Virtue Theory for Constructing Virtuous Agents

In the second book of the *Nichomachean Ethics* (abbreviated *NE*), Aristotle discusses virtues—whence they come, what they are, and how they are used. A virtue is an excellence that is brought about through habituation. Virtues are not natural in the sense that individuals are born brave, generous, or magnanimous. Rather, bravery, generosity, and magnanimity "reach complete perfection through habit" (*NE* 2.1.1103a25–27). Simply put, virtues are acquired through habit.[8] Aristotle states that one becomes brave—or acquires the virtue of bravery—by performing brave acts. Here, Aristotle reveals a close connection between character and action, between agent and virtue. This raises a puzzle for his argument. If the virtues were excellences created by habit, would it not be the case that we must already have these excellent capacities so that we can habituate ourselves to be excellent in those ways?

Human Nature and the Virtues

By beginning with Aristotle and his interpreters this section investigates what kind of person is implied by the VDP theory. Precisely what it means

---

8. Habit is a thin word in English when compared to the Greek *hexis* or Latin *habitus*; for English speakers, a "habit" can range from smoking to daily exercise to charging one's mobile phone in the car. For Aristotle, the notion of habit is much richer and is about forming character and intellectual virtues and vices.

to be human, for Aristotle, is to be capable of acquiring virtues. The process of acquiring virtues through habituation is in fact a process of perfecting or making excellent the abilities humans naturally have *qua* being human (*NE* 2.1.1103a25–27). Virtues are thus connected to human nature in this general sense. For example, Jessica is able to acquire the virtue of openmindedness by exercising openminded habits (such as listening carefully to a range of sources). She is able to become openminded because she is human but not because she was born with a special penchant for openmindedness. Though Jessica as an individual takes on the virtue of openmindedness in a special way, all humans have the innate capacity, in principle, to acquire the excellence of openmindedness through habit. Thus, one of the central roles that virtue plays is to fulfill or mature the capacities that are natural to human beings (*NE* 2.6.1106a22–24). The virtues, on this reading, are excellent expressions of general human nature.

Philippa Foot offers a somewhat different interpretation of Aristotelian virtue; her interpretation is problematic, I argue, because it depends on an essentialist view of human psychology. While Foot agrees with the Aristotelian position that the virtues are excellences, she argues that virtues work primarily to correct human unchecked nature. Her position is that virtues are "correctives" to human nature rather than excellent expressions of it. She elucidates:

> Going back to the idea of virtues as correctives, one may say that it is only because fear and desire for pleasure operate as temptations that courage and temperance exist as virtues at all ... If human nature had been different there would be no need of a corrective disposition in either place, as fear and pleasure would have been good guides to conduct throughout life.[9]

Foot's understanding of the virtues as "correctives" is premised on a particular psychological account of the human person, as Foot herself admits.[10] This account understands humans, for example, as fundamentally fearful. The virtue of bravery, in this case, corrects the tendency to cower in risky or scary situations.

Julia Driver criticizes Foot for giving an insufficiently general characterization of human nature. While Aristotle's theory of virtue entails a theory of who or what the human person is, an interpretation like Foot's

---

9. Foot, *Virtues and Vices*, 9.

10. Ibid., 10. She states that the list of virtues and vices will depend on an account of the human person.

needlessly particularizes that account.[11] Foot argues that virtuous tendencies "correct for the presence of prudence in human motivation."[12] But, as Driver points out, there are instances where the virtues "correct even for an insufficient amount of prudence or selfishness."[13] In other words, Foot assumes that people are naturally selfish and self-seeking, and the virtues correct this. However, Driver points out, there may be cases where people are not naturally selfish *enough* rather than *too* selfish.[14] Driver suggests that Foot could nuance her claim by arguing that virtues are correctives for *illegitimate* tendencies in humans; however, Driver goes on, the task to differentiate between legitimate and illegitimate tendencies becomes very muddled very quickly. Constructing virtue according to an essential account of the human person may in fact be an intellectually bankrupt endeavor and the notion of virtue as corrective, according to Driver, would be best left behind.

Foot's understanding of the function of virtue is problematic in that it is predicated on an essentialist (and akratic or, weak-willed) notion of the human person.[15] This notion is what allows Foot to make sense of what the virtues are and how they work. In her paradigm of thinking, the problems to which virtues respond are endemic to humans—that is, they are found regularly in all humans. Because the VDP theory, following Driver, identifies problems with positing a fundamentally specific theory of human nature to undergird its account, the next question to ask is if there a way in which the notion of virtue as "problem-correcting" might be recast?

---

11. Driver, *Uneasy Virtue*, 43.

12. Foot uses prudence in the modern, self-preserving sense, rather than either Aristotelian *phronesis* or Thomistic *prudentia*.

13. Driver, *Uneasy Virtue*, 43.

14. The issue of selfishness/selflessness is of particular importance to feminist thinkers. Feminists point out the troubling effects that promoting selflessness can have on women, who historically occupy the roles of caretakers, nurturing mothers, and so on. Because these social relationships are already defined by the quality of selflessness, theories that emphasize selflessness as a virtue ultimately risk denying women full possibilities for selfhood.

15. Akratic is a technical term, employed by Aristotle, to designate people who do not follow pure reason. This may be the result of being influenced by emotions or a problem with the intellect. Aristotle discusses *akrasia* in book seven of *Nichomachean Ethics*.

Virtue in Dialogue

Occupying a Broken World

MacIntyre parses the function of virtues differently than Foot does, but in such a way that, like Foot, explains its function in terms of human nature. He contends that Aristotelianism depends upon a certain view of "untutored-human-nature-as-it-is" and "man-as-he-could-be-if-realized-his-telos."[16] Any Aristotelian theory of virtue, MacIntyre writes, will "involve at least one central functional concept, the concept of *man* understood as having an essential nature and an essential purpose or function."[17] While MacIntyre may be right that the Aristotelian theory of virtue implies a contrasting view between the human person as she is with and without virtue, it is possible to make this claim without appealing to a notion of how people are in their fundamental nature but rather by pointing out how people are as they flourish in various ways together.

I avoid bolstering the claims of the VDP with a theory of "human nature" because such sketches inevitably universalize cultural or socially specific ideas of what it is to be human.[18] Driver makes a case for understanding virtue as a concept that is functional (though not necessarily functional as corrective) viz. the world rather than viz. the human person. MacIntyre and Christine Swanton also contribute resources toward showing how virtue can function to correct other kinds of problems—namely, the problems of the way humans function in the world.

To paraphrase one virtue ethicist, the only way the concept of virtue really makes sense is against the backdrop of a broken world. That is to say, we have virtues because we need to respond to what is broken. If nothing in the world were broken, we would not need the virtues to help us fix it. In my view, the notion of function can work in regards to the world, and our role in the world, *even without* understanding the world as fundamentally broken. Rather, the world is *functionally* broken and we occupy it without any instructions for that occupancy.[19] Epistemic virtues help us to navigate the demands of the world and to imagine a new future for ourselves in it.

That we imagine a new future for ourselves through exercising virtues is significant because it connotes the collective as well as future-oriented

16. MacIntyre, *After Virtue*, 52.
17. Ibid., 56–57.
18. Avoiding an essentialized view of human nature (for bad or for good) helps to avoid the elitism that valorizes one way of being human.
19. Humans can (and do) "break" the world through bad understanding and bad judgment (both of which yield bad acts), but it does not necessarily follow that the world is in itself fundamentally broken.

dimensions of virtue. Feminist appropriations of Aristotelian virtue theory place special emphasis on these aspects. For example, Ruth Groenhout reviews the role of care in Aristotle's theory virtue. She notes that, on Aristotle's theory, extending care to others has the effect of "[encouraging] others to care in return and so develop their own potential for human excellence."[20] Diana Fritz Cates makes a similar point in her discussion of the Aristotelian notion of friendship. In friendship, and particularly the kinds of friendships that are premised upon the appreciation of each other's character (Cates calls these "character-friends"), people express "[deep], deliberate desires for continued community" and create the possibility for the "co-construction of vision and value."[21] In short, through friendship, people not only unite their desires and hopes, they also extend them toward a new future.[22] The women of Philadelphia epitomize these Aristotelian-derived feminist ethical principles in practice. In their collective imagination toward "a better way of being," the Philadelphia women importantly show how the virtues they cultivate in dialogue together are cultivated specifically to respond to a complex and confusing world.

As with a theory of moral virtue, which posits that we live in a world that demands an ethical response, this theory of epistemic virtue maintains that the world demands an epistemic response from us. Swanton writes, "Virtue [is a] disposition of good responsiveness to an item in its field."[23] Given the epistemic demands of our convoluted world, the way virtues function is to help us formulate our responses. Virtues are therefore not *correctives* to problems in human nature nor are they *correctives* to a desperate world. Rather, the virtues are the abilities that people acquire that enable them to navigate difficult terrain. Driver puts it this way: "Virtues function in social contexts to contribute to human (or social) flourishing and happiness."[24] By following Swanton and Driver's lead to rethink the function of virtue, it is possible to maintain Aristotle's original point that virtues are excellences of the human person without thereby embracing a notion of a corrupt or depraved essential human nature or a fundamentally broken world.

If the basic function of virtue is to provide people with the ability to move through a complex world and communally create a new future for it,

20. Groenhout, "The Virtues of Care," 193.
21. Cates, "Toward an Ethic," 251.
22. Ibid., 245.
23. Swanton, *Virtue Ethics*, 40.
24. Driver, *Uneasy Virtue*, 74.

what does this look like in terms of epistemic or intellectual virtues? The VDP theory makes no claims about the "natural" capacities or "natural" tendencies of epistemic agents except in a general way. The function of intellectual virtues is thus not to correct problematic tendencies or epistemic defects of the human person. Rather, the function of intellectual virtues is to regulate belief formation in our complex world[25] and, as I will show later in this chapter, to do so in such a way that contributes to human epistemic flourishing.

Following Clifford, I have argued that beliefs are dispositions to act. As the women of Philadelphia demonstrated in chapter two, both how one functions in the world and how one relates to others in it—in short, one's actions—bear on belief. The intellectual virtues are at once world-functional and agent-centered. They are the navigational tools that allow people to move through their epistemic surroundings and flourish in doing so. When people exercise epistemic virtue (when they use these navigational tools), they put themselves in a position to form justified beliefs. In this way, their virtuous actions bear on their beliefs.

Satisfaction and Virtue

A key piece of the puzzle—about how virtues function as normative properties of agents—is Aristotle's reasoning for how we can tell if a virtue is really a virtue. (It turns out that the emotional response of pleasure is Aristotle's "litmus test.") Part of the reason that arguments like Foot's land where they do—with a highly particular psychological account of the human person—is because they try to make sense of the role that pleasure and pain play in Aristotle's virtue theory. Aristotle sees a critical relationship between pleasure and pain and virtue. Any theorist who follows Aristotle strictly will be tripped up by the place of pleasure and pain in his account of virtue. The goal of this section is to clarify how agents truly acquire virtue without appealing to pleasure per se. To accomplish this I use the idea of being "properly affected" and feeling satisfaction.

Because virtues are acquired through habit, Aristotle works to ensure that they are distinct from skills or craft, which are also things that people acquire through habit. Having a skill allows a person to accomplish a task successfully. A person is skilled or has skill if she is able to attain her aim.

---

25. Montmarquet, "Epistemic Virtue," 490. Montmarquet states that we desire epistemic virtues because they function to regulate belief. If they (epistemic virtues) did not do this, why we would we want them, Montmarquet queries.

But, according to Aristotle, what this person does not have—if it is a skill but not a virtue—is a certain experience of pleasure that accompanies exercising the skill. For Aristotle, the way to determine whether a person has a virtue or a skill is to investigate her emotional state upon doing an act requiring that virtue or skill. If she feels pleasure, she has a virtue. If she does not feel pleasure, she has a skill.

Driver holds that, for Aristotle, part of being virtuous is being "properly affected." That is, "for an agent to be virtuous, she must have *internalized* good ends."[26] Aristotle writes about the way ends are internalized and how an agent comes to be properly affected; he states that an agent must be appropriately motivated by pleasure and pain (*NE* 2.3.1104b10–11). In other words, if an agent truly exercises a virtue, she takes pleasure in doing so for the sake of the virtue itself and not for the sake of the outcome. Driver dismisses Aristotle on this point. In her interpretation, having a virtue need not depend upon our deriving pleasure from it. An excellence or virtue can be valuable *just because* it produces "good and a significant social benefit."

Driver makes a sound and important argument: virtues are good for the social benefits they produce rather than good for the internal pleasure they bring about. Yet it is not clear that Driver's consequentialist approach (that is, virtues are good for their external consequences) actually satisfies Aristotle's problem. Aristotle employs the pleasure and pain explanation primarily for the purpose of distinguishing between virtue and skill or virtuous act and craft. Aristotle, in other words, has a very particular warrant for bringing up the issue of pleasure and pain, and Driver seems to overlook this point.

If this is the case, then discharging pleasure/pain from the account of virtue does not contribute toward drawing the important distinction between virtue and skill that Aristotle desires. The primary problem that I see with Aristotle's pleasure/pain explanation is that the pleasure and pain factors can cause some confusion for the agent regarding her aim. What precisely does Aristotle want of virtuous agents? Should an agent aim at acquiring and exercising virtue? Or should her aim be to feel pleasure? Working to acquire a virtue and working to feel pleasure do not always comfortably overlap.

While the VDP theory is in agreement with Driver that Aristotle's pleasure/pain explanation is problematic, it (pleasure/pain) must be ushered out of the theoretical account by different means and for different

---

26. Driver, *Uneasy Virtue*, 13.

reasons from those Driver adduces. To avoid the ambiguity inherent in Aristotle's account, the task becomes to incorporate something *like* the pleasure/pain explanation, which can serve as a Rosetta stone for explaining the difference between virtue and skill. To do so without *either* depending too highly on the interior life of virtuous agents (Foot's pitfall) *or* not adequately differentiating between a virtue and a skill (Driver's pitfall), I build on Driver's notion of being "properly affected" to create a standard for determining the presence of epistemic virtue.

James Montmarquet states that Aristotelian virtues are ingrained habits that are entrenched motivationally.[27] A virtuous agent displays a certain kind of motivation and feels a certain way upon exercising virtue, while a skilled agent does not. Bernard Williams writes that on an Aristotelian view, virtues are distinct from skills in that virtues, unlike skills, involve "characteristic patterns of desire and motivation."[28] When a person exercises a virtue, she has certain feelings that are the concomitants of that virtue. These characteristic, concomitant feelings are not "natural" in the agent but are specific to the virtue.

Bringing together Aristotle's interpreters who are troubled by pleasure/pain explanation with Aristotle's interpreters who see that distinction more generically, the problem to distinguish between a virtue and skill can be solved like this: when an agent expresses an virtue, she feels satisfaction at doing so. Take, for example, a marathon runner. Running twenty-six and two tenths miles is not a natural thing for a person to do (recall that the first person who ran this distance fell over dead from doing so). However, because the runner trains and prepares intensively for the race, she "learns" to experience a feeling of satisfaction from running such a distance. The feeling of satisfaction accompanies the "virtue" of long-distance running.

Aristotle uses pleasure to make clear a distinctive feature of virtue; namely, that it involves an agent internalizing the right motivation for its own sake. If an agent is properly affected—that is, if she has taken virtue on in the right way—then she will feel satisfied. Satisfaction is not something *at* which agents aim—that is, it is not the *telos* of virtuous acts. If a person aims at satisfaction, she will not achieve it, for satisfaction always comes from something else. However, a person can aim at a significant goal and feel satisfied upon achieving it. Satisfaction is thus a happy by-product of achievement or expressing virtue. This sense of being properly

27. Montmarquet, "Epistemic Virtue," 486.
28. Williams, *Ethics*, 9.

affected in feeling satisfaction does not paint the VDP theory into Driver's consequentialist corner because the VDP theory looks beyond *just* the outcomes of the exercise of virtue to the ways virtue is constituted in an agent's life.

Satisfaction is a constituent of virtue. A person feels it when she exercises virtue, but this does not necessarily mean that the person *is* virtuous. It is important to here recall the threshold feature of Zagzebski's theory of virtue. According a threshold notion, in Swanton's word, "less than ideal states may count as virtues." That is to say, virtues do not work on an "on/off" switch but rather can be held in varying degrees.[29] Jessica, who strives to be openminded as a teacher of foreign language, may not be openminded, for example, when it comes to teaching art. While she works to investigate a range of pedagogical practices for teaching Spanish, she does not do the same kind of "research" for giving art lessons. Just because she is not perfectly openminded in all aspects of her career as a teacher, she is still able to exercise the virtue of openmindedness as a language teacher and feel satisfaction when she does so. (It is possible and even likely that Jessica's feeling of satisfaction will encourage her to develop the virtue of openmindedness across all her teaching duties.)

The Social Motivation and Orientation of Virtue

Just as agents cannot aim at satisfaction if they are to achieve it, agents also cannot aim at the goal of virtue itself. If Ben wants to be a brave sort of fellow, he will not become brave by aiming at bravery itself. Rather, Ben will become brave by responding to perilous situations in a brave manner. As such, the "aim" of virtue is to be properly aimed rather than to be aimed at a particular target. An example from archery helps illustrate this. If an archer positions her bow such that her arrow is pointing squarely at the bull's eye, but her form for holding the bow and her body are poor, then, on this view, she cannot be said to be properly aimed.

Code captures this idea in terms of "orientation." She writes: "Intellectual virtue is, above all, a matter of orientation toward the world, toward one's knowledge-seeking self, and toward other such selves as a part of the world."[30] Code's notion of orientation complements and fills out the idea of navigational orientation introduced by Swanton earlier. Having virtue is not just about being oriented to navigate the world, but about being

29. Swanton, *Virtue Ethics*, 25.
30. Code, *Epistemic Responsibility*, 20.

oriented to the world in a particular kind of way. Epistemically speaking, when a person is oriented to the world in the "right" way, she puts in herself in a position to form justified beliefs.

What kinds of factors constitute the "right" orientation for intellectual virtue? First, it is critical to note the virtuous "orientation" applies to all levels of cognition, including the most mechanical. In a discussion that accuses virtue epistemology of laxity on the issue of epistemic virtues as *reliable* for belief formation, Baehr writes, "The traits [virtues] in question are reliable only if combined with properly functioning faculties (for example, good eyesight, a good memory, etc.)."[31] Baehr is quite right that an adequate virtue epistemology must construct a theory wherein the intellectual virtues apply and function as reliable across the cognitive board, at both the mechanical and social cognitive levels. For precisely this reason, the VDP theory draws on *both* the insights of Alston *and* Zagzebski.

Alston's basic argument is that perceptual practices are learned practices. Montmarquet reinforces this point; he states that our perceptual beliefs are formed only by means of our abilities to perceive, which is a learned ability. In other words, our training to perceive allows us to see; every epistemic act in which we engage—from the simple perceptual practice of smelling warm bread to the complex practice of relying on the testimony of our elders to form a philosophical belief—comes about because we have learned how to do it.[32] We learn how to acquire virtues—how to engage in virtuous practices—socially. Braaten makes a similar point, "Social abilities may contribute to development of non-social intellectual abilities."[33] While we tend to think of intellectual virtues as being cultivated and employed at higher levels of cognition such as with self-reflective knowledge, they affect basic cognitive processes as well.

Agents learn to rightly orient virtues by social means. At some point, the archer was taught how to hold a bow and shoot an arrow. If the archer is to get better and to aim more accurately, she will practice, take advice from an expert in archery, and compete in archery events against others to make herself better. Aristotle accounts for the social features of virtuous development. His philosophy addresses *zoon politikon* or "political man." He states, ". . . the human being is by nature a political animal" (*Politics* 1.2.1253a-2–3). To be political is to be a member of the community or city. Thus, to be human, for Aristotle, is to be social. Aristotle's account of

31. Baehr, "Four Varieties," 489.
32. Montmarquet, "Epistemic Virtue," 493.
33. Braaten, "Towards a Feminist Reassessment," 10.

how a person learns and exercises virtue (and properly orients virtue) is necessarily an account she does so *in and through* community. In this way, virtues are socially motivated and socially significant.

Martha Nussbaum looks to the emotion of compassion as an essential ingredient in moral development. One's being properly affected, then, is not about "satisfaction" alone. Compassion, Nussbaum states, is a basic human emotion that is based on the notion of the inherent dignity of human persons.[34] For her, it is the fulcrum for ethical action and ethically-based rational deliberation.[35] By feeling compassion we recognize ourselves in the situations of others. The consequence of this is that we deliberate or navigate the world in an ethical or just way. Specifically, Nussbaum argues that although compassion "is not the entirety of justice ... it both contains a powerful, if partial, vision of just distribution and provides citizens with an essential bridge from self-interest to just conduct."[36] In other words, compassion leads to just action.

The epistemic version of ethical compassion can be called sympathetic understanding. Sympathetic understanding orients epistemic agents to factors besides their own epistemic goals and endeavors. Through the feeling state of sympathetic understanding, people become attuned to the beliefs and viewpoints of others. Just as the feeling of compassion has ethical consequences, the feeling of sympathetic understanding has epistemic consequences. Because sympathetic understanding bears on one's virtuous development, it brings about beliefs that are formed in epistemically good ways.

Braaten proposes a set of specifically feminist intellectual virtues that complements this idea of sympathetic understanding. Imagination is an essential part of Braaten's list of virtues; like sympathetic understanding, imagination plays a formative role in how agents acquire virtue and thereby influences the way agents form beliefs. Braaten states that imagination accounts for an agent's ability to "represent alternative subjective points of view." Representing different points of view, she continues, "involves imagining how another person would respond to a variety of ideas, situations and other people." By imagining viewpoints besides one's own, the epistemic agent is shaped by the views of others.

For Braaten, virtues are capacities that are exercised in the context of community and that require an agent's excursion away from her own

---

34. Nussbaum, *Upheavals*, 359.
35. Ibid., 299.
36. Nussbaum, "Compassion," 57.

concerns and to the concerns of another person through imagination. Community is written into Braaten's very definition of virtue. Imagining others' viewpoints involves practicing a certain kind of responsiveness, disciplining oneself to be attentive to others' experiences, and so on. In habituating herself in this way, a person's virtues are socially oriented. This social orientation informs the beliefs that are formed out of these intellectual virtuous practices. Thus, in Braaten's words, an agent comes to "have a better picture of her or his own limitations in making judgments [for example] about persons from different backgrounds."[37]

The virtuous agent's perspective is at once relativized and broadened: her personal viewpoint is relativized in light of her awareness of others' perspectives and it is broadened because she incorporates consideration for others into her own viewpoint. Significantly, the beliefs yielded through her new perspective are different than they would otherwise be.[38] She changes her perspective (and thereby the beliefs that arise from that perspective) not for an expedient reason (like pleasure) or desire for a particular outcome but rather because her virtuous orientation involves attention to others.

Examples of sympathetic understanding and imagination are present in the Philadelphia women's interreligious dialogue group as well. For example, the group discussions often broach the subject of the status of women in religious traditions (and especially the so-called "second-class status" within some religious traditions); the women acknowledge that these conversations can be potentially contentious and impassioned. During these discussions, group members remind themselves of the necessity of listening ever more clearly and with humility. They try to desire less to have their own, self-interested concerns and questions resolved and more to understand what others' perspectives are. And, finally, they collectively remind themselves of the importance of their bonds of friendships. They create virtuous doxastic practices that are socially motivated and developed: listening carefully and with humility *to each other*, recognizing *multiple* points of view even if they are difficult to hear, and keeping *friendship* in the front of their minds.[39]

---

37. Braaten, "Towards a Feminist Reassessment," 6–7.

38. Perhaps the beliefs will be about the same, but more richly appreciated or strongly held.

39. Catherine Cornille identifies five "essential conditions" for "constructive and enriching interreligious dialogue." They are: epistemic humility, commitment to a particular religious tradition, the belief that "the teachings and practices of the other religion[s] are in some way related to or relevant for one's own religious tradition,"

Virtue and Social Flourishing

Now that I have clarified my understanding of the basic function of epistemic virtue for the VDP theory, shown how epistemic virtues can be distinguished from skills, and explored the social motivation and orientation of virtue, it is necessary to explain the overall outcome of epistemic virtue. Aristotle calls the chief good of virtue—the primary outward end toward which all virtue is aimed and all virtuous actions are undertaken—eudaimonia.[40] The standard translation of eudaimonia is "happiness." This translation promotes the idea that the "good life"—which is another way of saying the "chief good"—is itself the happy life. Philosophers struggle to define the features of this "chief good" and labor to identify exactly what constitutes the "good life," which necessarily involves presuppositions about human nature and what makes humans happy.

I argue that the chief good of virtue is to fully exercise the virtues toward social flourishing. In the last section, I drew a connection between epistemic sympathetic understanding and Nussbaum's ethical concept of compassion. For Nussbaum, compassion is the emotion that allows people to act ethically. A person who feels sympathetic understanding is motivated to exercise epistemic virtue. There is a parallel relationship between sympathetic understanding and epistemic virtue, on the one hand, and compassion and ethical virtue, on the other. In order to articulate the outcome of epistemic virtue, I turn to Nussbaum's discussion of the outcome of compassion.

Nussbaum writes that when we feel compassion, we "acknowledge some sort of community" between others and ourselves.[41] Compassion allows us to draw an imaginative connection with those around us. By creating this connection, we conceptually attach the good of others to our own good. To feel compassion for the life circumstances of a suffering, impoverished person, for example, involves a conception of what constitutes a life free from bodily suffering, what circumstances lead to a healthy

---

empathy, and hospitality (*Im-Possibility*, 4–6). The conditions extolled by Cornille parallel the virtues of dialogue exhibited by the women of Philadelphia. There is a difference between Cornille's discussion and my own. Cornille identifies these five criteria as *conditions* for dialogue: they must be in place for fruitful dialogue to occur. In my discussion, I have emphasized how the women of Philadelphia developed their virtues over time and through conversation with one another. That is, the women did not necessarily come to interreligious dialogue with these socially-oriented virtues, but they (the virtues) were brought about through conversation and collective engagement.

40. McDowell, "The Role of *Eudamonia*," 359.
41. Nussbaum, *Upheavals of Thought*, 317.

home situation, what counts as a living wage, and so on. In other words, our latent notions of "the good life" factor into our feelings of compassion. For this reason, Nussbaum writes that there is a "eudamonistic structure" to our compassionate imagination.[42] "Implicit in the emotion [of compassion] itself," Nussbaum states, "is a conception of human flourishing."[43] As this is the case with compassion, so too is it the case with sympathetic understanding: sympathetic understanding is necessarily conceptually linked to a notion of social flourishing.

There are two key components to my understanding of social flourishing. First, the outcome of the exercise of virtue has implications beyond the virtuous agent herself; though an agent exercises a virtue, the outcome of this exercise is not just individualistic. It is communal—hence, *social* flourishing. Secondly, the social implications of virtue cannot be quantified, but rather can only be evaluated qualitatively. More specifically, these implications are evaluated according to the quality by which agents are able to exercise virtue in their communities. It is dynamic—hence, social *flourishing*.

McDowell supports Driver on this point; he defines the concept of eudaimonia as follows: "the life of exercises of excellence is the life that most fully actualizes the potentialities that constitute human nature."[44] On this view, the flourishing of social creatures is not, as Driver puts it, cashed out in terms of pleasure or what makes people happy.[45] Eudaimonia is constituted just by living out and fully engaging one's potentials, regardless of pleasure. The chief good of intellectual virtue, like the chief good of ethical virtue, is not defined by any distinctive features or according to a set of presuppositions about human nature or human happiness. Thus, there is no particular set of principles or specific body of knowledge at which the agent arrives in exercising intellectual virtue. There is no predetermined, objective *telos* of intellectual virtue.[46]

42. Ibid., 388.
43. Ibid., 310.
44. McDowell, "The Role of *Eudamonia*," 370.
45. Driver, *Uneasy Virtue*, 92.
46. Both Riggs and Swanton discuss J. Annas' argument about the "target problem" of virtue ethics. Annas contends that the success component in virtue ethics is misguided because that aim will always be equivocal or ambiguous. How can one be expected to aim at *both* at overall flourishing/contributing to the social good *and* success in that particular scenario? In fact these aims may conflict with each other (Riggs, "Understanding Virtue," 209; Swanton, *Virtue Ethics*). This is a thorny issue for virtue epistemology as well. However, because the VDP model holds that there is

Nussbaum's "capabilities approach" is illuminative for the concept of eudaimonia utilized here. Specifically, Nussbaum develops the capabilities approach to offer a theory of human rights and to argue for what constitutes a properly politically liberal society. However, her theory is more broadly significant for ethical theory and for this epistemological theory of virtue. Nussbaum defines capabilities as the opportunities for functioning or the basic entitlements humans need to function in a politically liberal society.[47] She argues that the capabilities are locally determined yet of universal significance; that is, the capabilities are fundamental to all human beings but they are derived from observations about actual persons in real contexts. Her list of capabilities includes, for example, life—"Being able to live to the end of a human life of normal length; not dying prematurely, or before one's life is so reduced as to not be worth living"—and practical reason—"Being able to form a conception of the good and to engage in critical reflection about the planning of one's own life."[48]

Nussbaum states that her understanding of the capabilities is based on two principles: first, that each person is an end and, second, that there is a social basis for "the good."[49] Her theory of human flourishing privileges the integrity of each person and holds that the only way people can flourish (i.e., function according to their basic entitlements or capabilities) is in the context of community. *What* a person achieves is not an end; *that* a person is capable of achieving is the "end" Nussbaum has in mind.[50] Nussbaum's capabilities approach is helpful for the VDP theory because it articulates a vision for social flourishing that is premised on the good *functioning* of agents in community rather than on the concrete achievements of agents (such as wealth or happiness) as individuals.

The outcome of virtuous doxastic practices is not, then, *just* justified belief. There is also an "economy" of virtue instantiated in the epistemic communities of virtuous agents. People who are motivated to become virtuous epistemic agents create epistemic communities wherein other people can become virtuous epistemic agents as well. The community flourishes

---

no *particular* body of knowledge after which the exercise of intellectual virtue seeks (that is, this theory does not make a claim about objective "truth" that virtue helps us to access; here I would appeal to Kant's noumenal/phenomenal distinction), the best the VDP model can do is say that the aim is to reliably form beliefs through exercising virtue, imagining overriders, testing one's beliefs, and so on.

47. Nussbaum, *Upheavals of Thought*, 416.
48. Ibid., 416–17.
49. Nussbaum, *Women and Human Development*, 56, 81.
50. Nussbaum, "Aristotle," 105.

epistemically not only because the beliefs formed out of virtuous doxastic practices may be (at least *prima facie*) justified but also because the people in the community can grow and flourish as virtuous agents.

In the following chapter, I shift away from this theoretical analysis of virtues and virtuous agents. I fill out the final piece of the skeletal form of virtuous doxastic practices by offering a theory of practice. I then give a descriptive account of the four cardinal epistemic virtues and two overarching virtues, and, finally, make an argument for how believers are *prima facie* justified in their beliefs when the beliefs are the outcome of VDPs.

6

The Virtues in Practice and *Prima Facie* Justification

WHEN RELIGIOUS BELIEFS ARE THE OUTCOMES OF EXERCISES OF INTELlectual virtue, they are *prima facie* justified or immediately justified. A Muslim's claim that the Qur'an is the word of God transmitted through the Prophet Mohammed is *prima facie* justified by being the outcome of a virtuous doxastic practice that is socially established and involves checking the belief for possible overriders and considering it in light of what other virtuous Muslims believe. This chapter offers a thorough treatment of belief formation and *prima facie* justification by continuing the exploration initiated in the last chapter of the two principal parts of virtuous doxastic practice—communal doxastic practices and the virtues. This chapter achieves a comprehensive explanation of how beliefs are formed and *prima facie* justified. In the following chapter, I will shift to the issue of *ultima facie* justification and beliefs in the context of religious diversity. Practically, the question for chapter 7 will be about the justification of a Muslim's belief in the Qur'an as the word of God in a setting wider than Islam.

This chapter begins with the work of MacIntyre. I use his work to develop a theory of practice, so as to demonstrate how people exercise virtues in practice according to the VDP theory. Here, I explore the dual aims of virtuous practice (toward the end of social flourishing, on the one hand,[1] and, on the other, toward the end of an agent's developing virtues)

---

1. Flourishing is one of the terms used to translate Aristotelian *eudaimonia*. Happiness is another standard translation, as I discussed in the previous chapter. Both flourishing and happiness are typically assumed to mean the flourishing or happiness of individual persons, not of social groups. The VDP theory holds that flourishing can only be understood as a social phenomenon and, thus, that a person's flourishing implies the group's flourishing. Take, as exemplary of this notion, Martin Luther King, Jr.'s statement that no person is truly free until all people are. This is captured in Dr.

and the dual roles that virtuous agents (as epistemic agents and as members of epistemic communities) play in those practices.

In the next section, I identify and provide close descriptions of the "cardinal" intellectual virtues of the VDP model; these are steadfastness, judiciousness, prudence, and creativity, which importantly involves one's imagination. I use the literature of American Jewish author Chaim Potok to illustrate the virtues, as well as discuss the role that the overarching virtues (wisdom and integrity) play in the VDP theory. Finally, in the third section, I conclude with a statement on how this account of practices and virtues (or better, virtuous practices) satisfies the requirements for *prima facie* justification and opens the door for new (and more challenging) questions about *ultima facie* justification.

The Practices of the Virtuous Doxastic Practice Model

The skeletal outline of the VDP model of belief formation states that epistemic virtues are embodied by agents in communal contexts. The Alstonian "doxastic practice" element is a critical component of the VDP model. Alston defines doxastic practices as the socially established ways of forming and epistemically evaluating beliefs. Because the VDP model privileges a tight connection between belief and action, it is important to give an even "thicker" account of practice than given by Alston. To do so, I draw on MacIntyre's notion of ethical practices. In the last chapter, I noted the social element of virtues, framed through the concept of sympathetic understanding. This section explores the specific way in which intellectual virtues are learned and exercised through social practice.

A Theory of Practice

MacIntyre defines practice as follows:

> [A practice is] any coherent and complex form of socially established cooperative human activity through which goods internal to that form of activity are realized in the course of trying to achieve those standards of excellence appropriate to, and partially definitive of, that form of activity, with the result that

---

King's 1963 "Letter from Birmingham Jail." He states, "Injustice anywhere is a threat to justice everywhere. We are caught in an inescapable network of mutuality, tied in a single garment of destiny. Whatever affects one directly, affects all indirectly."

The Virtues in Practice and Prima Facie *Justification*

human powers to achieve excellence and human conceptions of the ends and good involved are systematically extended.[2]

In summary, practices are the patterns of behavior in which a social group engages in order to, one, achieve the end at which the practice is aimed and, two, achieve excellence in that practice. MacIntyre's notion of "practice" is akin to a scrimmage or exhibition match. Take for, for example, the sport of soccer. The scrimmage or exhibition match comparison appropriately captures two important features of MacIntyre's practice: (1) the two-fold aim of practice and (2) the relationship between the individual and community in practice. Alex and his soccer team will serve to explain this comparison.

The Two-Fold Aim of Practice

Alex's soccer team meets for daily practice or training sessions. During these sessions, Alex and his teammates run laps, perform dribbling drills, walk through corner kick and direct kick set plays, and compete among themselves in shooting competitions. Daily practice is primarily aimed at achieving excellence as soccer players and at handling a soccer ball. Once a week, Alex's team also has a game or match. In a game, Alex never stops to re-do a "move" with the ball if he does not perform it properly the first time, as he would in practice, nor does he try out a new tactic for playing defense. Why not? During the game, Alex is engaged in serious competition against the rival team; the only thing Alex and his teammates want to achieve is a victory. Game time is not time to get better; it is time to win. The end is distinct—winning—and it is the only end for which soccer matches are played.

Scrimmage or exhibition matches are somewhat different, however. They incorporate aspects of both daily training and official matches. Because the outcome of the scrimmage does not count toward the team's final record, Alex and his teammates are more likely to take chances, experiment with their usual line-up, and test new plays or moves with the ball. The team plays to win and indeed seeks victory, but this is not their only goal; they also want to focus on getting better, similar to how they do in training sessions. A scrimmage differs from a regular game in that the aim for victory (the end of game of the soccer) shares precedence with the aim of developing soccer skills (the standards of excellence appropriate to

---

2. MacIntyre, *After Virtue*, 175.

and definitive of the game of soccer). Only in the scrimmage do Alex and his team exhibit this two-fold aim.

Individual Agency and Membership in Community

A central tenet of MacIntyre's notion of practice is that virtues are cultivated in a community.³ MacIntyre's theory is particularly relevant for the VDP epistemological model because it neatly marries Zagzebskian virtue and Alstonian doxastic practice. The intellectual virtues—that are the epistemic characteristics of the agent that lead to justified religious belief on Zagzebski's theory—are fostered through learned communal practices—that are the reliable processes that lead to justified belief on Alston's theory. MacIntyre's practice not only involves a two-fold aim for every practice, it also illuminates a two-fold role that individual persons play in the communities who engage in these practices: persons are both accountable to themselves and to their fellow community members. Code argues that if epistemologists are to be adequate to real accounts of belief formation (in this case, that beliefs can be strengthened rather than weakened in the context of diversity), they must construct theories such that there is a "vital degree of dependence of knowledge-seekers upon the epistemic community."⁴ Together, MacIntyre and Alston's theories show this relationship of mutual dependence between the individual person and community in the process of belief formation.

Turning again to the scrimmage comparison, Alex is both an individual soccer player and a member of his team. In daily practice, he functions primarily as an individual soccer player. Many of the drills or activities are geared toward Alex developing *his* skills and abilities. In games, Alex functions primarily as a team member. If he plays to set a personal record or is only concerned about whether *he* scores a goal, the entire team is at risk. In a scrimmage, there is a balance between both of these aims—Alex plays both to develop his own skills and abilities and also to contribute to his team's broader success. The relationship individual agents have with their epistemic communities is like the relationship Alex has with his teammates (especially) during a scrimmage. In both cases, the individual works

---

3. MacIntyre actually makes an even stronger claim than this. He states that practices are not only communal but are in fact institutional: "For no practice can survive for any length of time unsustained by institutions" (ibid., 181).

4. Code, *Epistemic Responsibility*, 65. Code argues against epistemologists, like McKim and Feldman, who do not draw this connection.

toward the communal aim but is also afforded space to experiment in his own ways and nuance the communal standards of excellence associated with the practice.

It is the community that teaches and supports individual agents in acquiring and exercising epistemic virtues and the individual who endeavors to "systemically extend" the standards of excellence of that epistemic community. There is, then, interplay between the individual's agency and her role in the community. Code notes that, on MacIntyre's theory, members of epistemic communities are at once "conservers and modifiers of practice."[5] This interplay between conserving and innovating may sometimes be mutually adversarial. There will be times where the individual's aims are not perfectly concordant with the group's aims. For example, Alex may try to beat an opposing defender with a tricky pass that is a permutation of a pass his team often uses, but, in this instance, the attempt fails, and ultimately leads to the opposite team scoring a goal. Alex, as an individual, took a risk that cost his team.[6] Yet his risk was contained by a certain space laid out by team's usual practices. That is, the pass Alex made was but a creative variation of passes he practiced many times before with his teammates.

Any agent in any epistemic community is in a position analogous to Alex. The agent is developing her own intellectual virtues in the context of her community. Take for example, the intellectual virtue of judiciousness (this virtue will be discussed more fully in the following section of this chapter). An agent learns to be judicious about the information she hears from others. She strikes a balance between gullibility and being unreceptive to new thoughts and ideas. Indeed, she acquires the intellectual virtue of judiciousness socially. She learns from her parents, teachers, and friends how judge appropriately information she hears and reads; she learns to exercise judiciousness in the context of and with the help of that community. Part of what being an agent involves is testing judiciousness for oneself. If the agent's role is at once to acquire and achieve intellectual virtue personally and to contribute to the continually developing standards of excellence for the communal practice, the agent must necessarily take risks and experiment just as Alex does during the scrimmage or as a scientist does in venturing novel hypotheses and forging new methods in experimentation; for without risk and experiment on the part of agents, the communal practices cannot continue to achieve excellence.

5. Ibid., 193.

6. This connects to Annas' point about the "ambiguous" aim of virtue. See Annas, "The Structure of Virtue."

Like Alex who tries out new moves with the soccer ball and the scientist who plays with new ideas and methods, the women of Philadelphia experimented with their communal practices by trying to push difficult conversations—such as with the status of women in some religious traditions—to deeper levels. On one occasion, the Philadelphia dialogue group was successful in having productive conversations about contentious issues. They were successful because they drew on their collective skills about how to ask sensitive questions and approach their own biases honestly. Because the agent only knows the virtue of judiciousness by way of her epistemic community (that is, the community is the condition for her possibility as an epistemic agent), the risks she takes and experiments she performs will always be bounded by and to the virtuous doxastic practices of the community.

The Virtues of the Virtuous Doxastic Practice Model

Keeping in mind the theoretical constraints discussed above, the following section lays out detailed descriptions of each of the virtues. It achieves this by following Aristotle's method for illustrating the virtues that includes, first, identifying in which sphere of life the virtue applies and, second, positioning the virtue on a spectrum to show how it tends neither "over does it" nor "under does it."

Aristotle's Golden Mean and Spheres of Application

Aristotle states that the virtues themselves are "preserved by the mean" between excess and deficiency (*NE* 2.2.1104a26–27). Courage, for example, is the intermediate state between too much fear and too little fear. Too much fear is cowardice and too little fear is rashness. Each state of virtue, according to Aristotle, is directed toward a particular aspect or experience of life. For example, the intermediate state (virtue) of generosity is the mean in what Aristotle calls "small" matters between the excess of wastefulness and the deficiency of niggardliness (*NE* 2.7.1107b19–21). Aristotle follows this pattern to define a fairly exhaustive list of virtues: he states an experience, sphere of activity, or aspect of life in which virtues would be exercised and outlines the states of excess and deficiency that would there apply. I utilize this pattern to define the intellectual virtues of the VDP model.

The Virtues in Practice and Prima Facie Justification

Method of Approach

The cardinal virtues of traditional Western philosophy—justice, temperance, fortitude, and prudence—roughly provide the basis for the four primary intellectual virtues of the VDP model. The intellectual virtues are (in order of how they will be discussed) steadfastness, judiciousness, prudence, and creativity.[7] These virtues map onto what I see as four central "moments" of knowing: how an agent's background beliefs figure into her epistemic process, how an agent perceives or receives information, how an agent processes information, and how that agent uses that information.[8] I outline each of the intellectual virtues by, first, offering a summary of its classic virtue parallel; secondly, showing how it works in its epistemological context (that is, what part the virtue plays in the knowing process or where it "maps" on); and, thirdly, utilizing Aristotle's "golden mean" exercise (described in the previous paragraph) to explore the virtue's range.

---

7. The order with which the cardinal ethical or moral virtues are typically discussed does not align with the order in which I explain the epistemic virtues. This is because my discussion is "chronological" according to the knowing process. The cardinal ethical virtues do not require an order, but I list them, first here, according to convention.

8. While the VDP theory relies heavily on Zagzebski, it departs from her work in that it defines a very specific set of intellectual virtues. As the subtitle of her book suggests (*Virtues of the Mind: An Inquiry into the Nature of Virtue and the Ethical Foundations of Knowledge*) her primary task is *theorize* about virtue. The meat of her work is in defining the theoretical constraints on virtue (i.e., acquired by habit, admit of a proper motivation component, etc.), both moral and intellectual (she sees these as separate but closely related categories). The reader is thereby enabled to test "pretheoretical" notions of virtue according to those theoretical constraints. Zagzebski gives a long list of possible virtues; these are discussed from the perspective of variety of philosophers, theologians, and literary authors—from Plato to Locke to Jane Austen. Zagzebski notes the following virtues: courage, generosity, compassion, justice, honesty, carefulness, wisdom, constancy, self-respect, autonomy, benevolence, honor, thrift, wisdom, humility, obedience, gratitude, faith, hope, charity, discretion, perseverance, fair-mindedness, trust, openmindedness, and temperance. She uses examples from this list to illuminate her theoretical account of the virtues. Because my primary interest is to develop a religious epistemology that shows precisely how justified religious beliefs are the outcomes of virtuous doxastic practices, rather than discuss virtue epistemology in general or the theoretical background for using virtue in epistemology, I follow Zagzebski's lead, presume (most of) her theoretical foundations, and then take another step forward by outlining four intellectual virtues that meet the established constraints. While this project is not exactly the fruit and flower of a seed planted by Zagzebski, it is at least the fruit and flower of a genetically modified seed taken from Zagzebski's store. The VDP theory's list of virtues is distinct from Zagzebski's account not because it disagrees with anything on her list, but rather because it is more concrete and systematic than Zagzebski's foundational theory.

Virtue in Dialogue

Following this theoretical explication of the four intellectual virtues, I offer concrete examples from the work of Jewish author Chaim Potok to illustrate each virtue.

Potok's *The Chosen* and *My Name is Asher Lev* tell "coming of age" stories of young Orthodox Jewish men who struggle to assert their intellectual and artistic identities in the context of strict religious communities. *The Chosen*, set in 1940s Brooklyn, focuses on the developing friendship between Reuven Malter and Danny Saunders. Reuven is the son of a yeshiva teacher (who is also a Jewish activist) and dreams of being a rabbi, although he is called "apikoros" (one who is Jewish but denies the tenets of Judaism) by some of his classmates.[9] Danny is a Hasid, destined to be the leader in the Hasidic community in Brooklyn (he will inherit his father's position), and has a photographic memory and an insatiable hunger for knowledge that is considered "goyish" by his community and, especially, his father. *My Name is Asher Lev* features the story of an artistic child prodigy who is also a Hasid. Asher Lev's story takes place in 1950s Brooklyn and centers on his growth as a painter, the emotional duress it places him under, and the tension it creates with his family (and, again, especially his father) and community—a community that is not only unfamiliar with artistic expression but actually shuns iconic representation.

This turn to literature, and specifically the literature of Potok, is motivated by two factors. First, while the Philadelphia women case study provides this project with an invaluable resource for exploring the virtues, it is my conviction that fetching for anecdotal representations of epistemic virtue in literature itself exemplifies an epistemically virtuous task. Using fiction to contemplate acts of virtue and fictional characters as models of virtuous agency contributes toward expanding one's philosophical imagination (recall my position in the previous chapter that Zagzebskian virtue depends upon imagination).[10] The fiction of Potok is particularly relevant

---

9. The term *apikoros* is derived from the Greek word epicurean. It first appears in the Mishnah and is used to indicate a person who has relinquished their Jewish obligations as well as "share in the world to come" (*Encyclopaedia Judaica*, 2nd ed., s.v. "apikoros.").

10. Nussbaum promotes the idea that reading literature expands our ethical imagination in *Cultivating Humanity*. She eloquently states that through narrative engagement (and engagement with art), we are able to see the people of the world who are otherwise invisible to us (*Cultivating Humanity*, 94). Making "invisible" people and cultures "visible" is a necessary component of becoming what she calls "citizens of the world." Nussbaum writes, "We are inclined to be parochial, taking our habits for that which defines humanity" (ibid., 62). When we realize that our habits are particular and that our worldview is limited, and when we see the habits and worldviews of

The Virtues in Practice and Prima Facie Justification

toward the end of expanding one's imagination about virtue in an interreligious context. This leads to the second reason.

Just as his fiction is relevant for its interreligious significance, it is also particularly sensitive for this reason. The examples I pull from Potok's texts to develop conceptions of the epistemic virtues all deal with characters challenging tradition or stepping out of their religious tradition in some way. Though the examples are not precisely interreligious, they are "inter-traditional." The confrontations Potok's characters face are used here as paradigmatic of interreligious issues. Indeed, all of Potok's work is structured around, as he puts it, "core-to-core cultural confrontation" and the response to it.[11] This would seem to imply, in turn, that epistemic virtue comes about only from *rejecting* traditional religious forms. While this conclusion is by no means the position I wish to convey, it is not insignificant that I have chosen as paradigmatic stories (and, moreover, chosen an author whose work is premised on examples such as these) that involve agents forging epistemic virtue in acts of negotiation between themselves and their religious traditions or between themselves and religious others. It is in such negotiations that epistemic virtues are most needed and the presence or absence of these virtues can be portrayed most clearly in such circumstances.

These negotiations-out-of-confrontation, which are manifested at times by shunning tradition, make an impression on the *character* of Potok's characters. Daniel Walden contends that the heroes of Potok's stories are "zwischenmenschen" or "between persons." They occupy both their traditional world and the world that confronts them. By creating viable "zwischenmenschen," Potok offers his readers a new way of conceiving identity in the world; he provides his readers with an example for how to live in the reality of cultural confrontation—that is, as "between persons."[12] While the women of Philadelphia specifically do not now think of their interreligious dialogue as confrontation, there was a time when many of them did. Recall that at the group's inception, their dialogue was formatted

---

others (this happens through narrative engagement), we learn to recognize a "human identity" that "transcends differences" (ibid., 67). Literature "disturbs" us and therefore creates in us a "capacity for openness and responsiveness" (ibid., 98). In short, narrative engagement makes us compassionate; it is, according to Nussbaum, "essential preparation for moral interaction" (ibid., 90).

11. Chavkin, "A MELUS Interview," 147–57. For most of Potok's characters, these conflicting "cores" are manifested in the forms of Orthodox Judaism (especially Hasidism) and Western secularism.

12. Walden, "A 'Zwischenmensch,'" 19–25.

according to the traditional way of comparing and contrasting beliefs and that some members were reticent to talk about their beliefs for fear of conflict. Through dialogue—through "confronting" each others' religious "cultures" (beliefs and practices)—the women of Philadelphia formed themselves into "between persons" who, like Potok's characters, negotiate between their own religious tradition and that of religious others. In short, Potok's stories provide a fictional parallel to the "story" of interreligious engagement told through the women of Philadelphia.[13]

While the specifically religious-traditional confrontations Potok's characters face are outside of my own tradition and religious experience (and likely the tradition and experiences of most readers of this book), Potok expresses the confrontations with the specific intention of addressing what he calls "universal problems." He states that once his readers "get through the costuming and the particularistic cultural elements," they will recognize their own experience of confrontation in his stories.[14] His goal is not only to "convey a broadening moral experience"[15] within the text (through the stories of the characters' confrontations that call into question their religious traditions) but also between the reader and the text. The world of confrontation *within* the stories woven by Potok actually confront the reader as well. Potok invites his readers, as he says, "to continue to encounter new visions of human experiences" through his stories.[16] Although reading outside of one's own tradition must always be done with caution, it is both in the spirit of virtuous imagination and in the spirit of Potok's own hope—and ethic—for his literature that I turn now to explore epistemic virtue and the ways it is exemplified in the fictional stories of Reuven Malter, Danny Saunders, and Asher Lev.[17]

---

13. Even if we do not identify with the experiences "zwischenmenschen" *per se*, the stories told by "between persons" are significant for all people who occupy a religiously diverse world that is complex, confusing, and, at times, bewildering. "Between persons" stand as examples for us when we enter into the life of another person through dialogue or explore another religious tradition through observation.

14. Chavkin, "A MELUS Interview."

15. Marovitz, "Freedom," 129–40.

16. Potok, "Culture Highways," 1–10.

17. I wish also to make two autobiographical or personal notes about this choice to use Potok; these connect rather clearly with the "objective" reasons given in the body of the text. First, reading Chaim Potok's books as a young adult proved pivotal, I think, for my own development as a "virtuous epistemic agent." Potok's work incited me, for lack of a better way to phrase it, to think about thinking and, more specifically, to think about thinking with regard to my religious tradition. While I do not suppose that Potok will affect every person as he did me, I hope that my use of his work here

The Virtues in Practice and Prima Facie *Justification*

The Four Cardinal Epistemic Virtues

Steadfastness and the Role of Background Beliefs in an Epistemic Process

Epistemic steadfastness is modeled on ethical temperance. Although ethical temperance tends to be associated with abstinence from alcohol or puritanical non-indulgence, it more broadly suggests restraint. A temperate person restrains herself from impulsivity and overindulgence. The epistemic version of temperance—steadfastness—has to do with taking a proper attitude toward one's own beliefs in light of other beliefs. Steadfastness is the quality of how an agent holds what she believes. To be not steadfast enough or inconstant about one's belief is to be obstinate, stubborn, or even zealous about what one already knows. This recalcitrant knower refuses to reexamine her background beliefs in light of new information. To be not steadfast enough or to not be constant about one's beliefs is to be tractable about one's beliefs or even acquiescent toward all new ideas. She may be hasty or impulsive about reforming background beliefs. If an agent exhibits steadfastness, she embraces her background beliefs but also shows a willingness to reconsider them in light of new information or new experiences.

Danny, the Hasidic young man in *The Chosen*, displays intellectual steadfastness toward his religiously-infused background in his quest to read literature and master the subjects of philosophy, history, and psychology. Danny is a voracious reader with a brilliant, "photographic" mind; at age thirteen, he becomes interested in psychoanalysis and begins reading Freud. The world Danny enters through reading and study is a world that is disregarded—and even denied—by his religious and social community.

---

will provoke others to think about an author or work of literature that once did or now does engender in them a desire to be reflective about their own intellectual curiosity, integrity, and so on. Secondly, and paralleling the second reason noted in the text above, Potok's fiction forced me to "confront" another religious tradition. The experience of cultural confrontation through text is familiar to Potok's own life story, and motivated him to create such opportunities for confrontation through fiction. Potok suggests this in an interview where he explains his decision to become a writer. He arrived at the decision at the age sixteen after reading Evelyn Waugh's *Brideshead Revisited*. He states, "[*Brideshead Revisited*] brought me into a world I never knew existed and it helped me to experience the loveliness of language, showed me how beautiful language can be to create stories" (Chakin, "A MELUS Interview"). My personal experience of confrontation with Hasidic Judaism through Potok's fiction and, thereby, being opened to a world "I never knew existed" mirrors Potok's experience with fiction and is precisely what Potok intends for his readers.

Danny's father, Rabbi Saunders, expresses deep concern over his son's hunger for knowledge: "I knew already when [Danny] was a young boy that I could not prevent his mind from going to the world of knowledge . . . but I had to prevent it from driving him away completely from the Master of the Universe."[18] Danny's Hasidic community understands the world of "secular" knowledge as an impediment to relating to God. For example, on one occasion Rabbi Saunders tells his congregation, "The world kills us! The world flays our skin from our bodies and throws us up to the flames! The world laughs at Torah! And if it does not kill us, it tempts us! It misleads us! It contaminates us!"[19]

By reading and learning what he does, Danny implicitly contests the fundamental convictions of his community. He is sensitive to this fact and afflicted by it. He tells Reuven, "I want to be able to breathe, to think what I want to think, to say the things I want to say. I'm trapped . . . It's the most hellish, choking, constricting feeling in the world. I scream with every bone in my body to get out of it. My mind cries to get out of it."[20] Though he longs to "think what I want to think," Danny is not reckless in how he goes about learning. He teaches himself German so he can read Freud in the original language; he researches secondary literature and gains a background in the fundamentals of psychology. In reading Freud, Reuven reports, "Danny was as patient, as patient as my father."[21]

Reuven goes on to describe the effect Freud has upon Danny:

> Freud had clearly upset him in a fundamental kind of way—had thrown him off balance, as he once put it. But he couldn't stop reading him, he said, because it became increasingly clear to him that Freud had possessed almost an uncanny insight into the nature of man . . . Freud's picture of man's nature was anything but complimentary, it was anything but religious. It tore man from God, as Danny put it, and married him to Satan.[22]

While, as Reuven reflects, "Danny didn't seem to have rejected what Freud taught"[23] and feels pain at being "trapped," he never simply rebels against his Hasidism as he is tempted to do. He strives to understand Freud as best he can and continues to study Talmud and remain a part of his religious

18. Potok, *The Chosen*, 279.
19. Ibid., 136.
20. Ibid., 202.
21. Ibid., 196.
22. Ibid., 195.
23. Ibid., 196.

community through college. Danny maintains tension between his religious background and his intellectual future. The solution of maintaining tension between oneself and one's tradition is typical of Potok's characters, who, John Timmerman argues, all seek to "find a place in the dynamic flux of [their] heritage."[24] Danny cannot reject his tradition entirely but neither can he remain wholly within it.

Ultimately, Danny leaves Brooklyn to pursue a doctoral degree in psychology and sheds some of the outer symbols of Hasidism (most notably, he cuts his earlocks), though he vows to obey the commandments, he prays three times a day, and he keeps kosher. The beliefs Danny comes to form about Freud are the result of a concerted effort to hold to his religious worldview without clinging to it, and to do so from an informed perspective. His almost magnetic attraction to Freud shows that Danny is willing to question his background and yet his intentional and assiduous approach to Freud reveals an underlying concern to keep Freudian psychology from simply overwhelming his religious worldview. Danny's steadfastness leads him both to pursue his studies more deeply and to a dynamic, reconfigured relationship to Hasidism.

Judiciousness and the Moment of Perception or Reception

The ethical virtue of justice provides the framework for the epistemic virtue of judiciousness. There is a clear parallel between ethical justice and epistemic judiciousness. Ethical actions that are done with justice are done with good judgment, fairness, and good sense. Aristotelian justice is rooted in the idea that persons are given their "due" according to their merits. Thus, notions of ethical justice relate both to the way in which actions are executed and to the way in which agents receive their fair share or what is deserved to them. To be judicious in knowing is to be sensible in how one perceives or receives information. Judiciousness involves making sound judgments about the sources that provoke an agent to perceive and receive; it involves having a balanced perspective, seeing one's sources with clarity, and being openminded about those sources. Judiciousness applies not only to "information" or "data" processing (with tasks such as reading a newspaper article or analyzing a documentary, for example) but also to the dialogical situation of "receiving" information through relationships.

The excess of judiciousness is a tendency toward being circumspect or overly cautious. That is, the epistemic agent takes "good judgment" to

---

24. Timmerman, "A Way of Seeing," 515, 518.

a degree where she actually debilitates herself and is unable to perceive or receive information. On the opposite end of the spectrum, an agent who lacks good sense and judgment could be said to be impetuous, reckless, or perhaps gullible viz. her sources. In matters of testimony, this type of knower would believe whatever she was told and would never bother to "check her sources." In matters of simple perception, an impetuous agent might only give a cursory glance, for example, to a picture before she moved on identifying what is in the picture.

Asher Lev learns and demonstrates the virtue of judiciousness. As a very young boy, Asher begins to draw. He discovers that drawing is his way of expressing himself and understanding the world. He does not like school, has few friends, and has a strained home life. Drawing is a refuge for him. Asher's family is Hasidic and Asher's father, in particular, discourages his art. Repeatedly, he fathers pleads with him, "Asher, will you stop this foolishness?"[25] Asher did stop drawing however desires to learn about art. He convinces his mother to take him to the Brooklyn Museum of Art. As Asher and his mother walk through the galleries, Asher becomes fascinated—almost fixated by—portraits of Jesus on the cross. He stares at them and asks his mother to explain their meaning. His mother is made extremely uncomfortable. She states, "I hope the Ribbono Shel Olom [Master of the Universe] will help me not to hurt your father. Look where it's taken us, Asher. It's taken us to Jesus . . . Painting is for goyim, Asher. Jews don't draw and paint."[26]

Although Asher knows he has hurt his mother by looking at the crucifixion paintings and would most certainly infuriate his father, he returns to the museum the following week to see them again. He rapidly sketches the paintings. He posts them in his room at home and stares at them. His mother, horrified and exasperated, remarks, "Do you know how much Jewish blood has been spilled because of him [Jesus], Asher? How could you spend your precious time doing this?"[27] Asher responds that he needs to capture the expression of Jesus on the cross—to learn to make that expression in his own work.[28] In his artistic pursuits, Asher symbolically

---

25. Potok, *My Name Is Asher Lev*, 105.

26. Ibid., 171.

27. Ibid., 172.

28. In an essay where Potok discusses the Brooklyn crucifix, he explains that while there is no formal prohibition in Judaism against painting Christian symbols, "When a Jew paints a crucifix, he crosses a moral-aesthetic line." Crossing such a line will inevitably be trying. Potok states, "There are no permanently wide-open doors through which you smoothly pass from culture to culture" (Potok, "Culture Highways").

The Virtues in Practice and Prima Facie *Justification*

flees from Hasidism into art (which embodies Western Christian values) and, thereby, implicitly rejects or "shuns" his tradition. While Asher's flight is portrayed as urgent and even necessary, Potok does not describe it as unequivocally good. Joanna Barkess elucidates this point: ". . . to see Hasidism [in the story] as merely repressive and the art world as a utopian place of freedom is to misunderstand Potok's intentions."[29] Rather, Potok lays bare the tension between Asher's world of Hasidism and Asher's world of painting and expresses the agony Asher feels in his struggle negotiate this confrontation.

Asher harnesses the struggle of his cultural confrontation and—through the help of his teacher Jacob—is able to use it toward productive ends. As Asher grows older and becomes a true student of art, his teacher Jacob teaches Asher how to look at and learn from art. Jacob sends Asher to the museum every Sunday for months to study paintings before Asher is allowed to paint them himself. He instructs Asher to make notes on them, to create careful sketches of the paintings, and to read about the artists and their contexts, the historical and religious significance of the crucifixion, and the techniques used to execute the paintings. Asher learns to see the paintings in a way that is very different from how he first saw them. His approach to the crucifixion paintings was greedy and careless, and it involved disregard for the consequences of that approach. Through his teacher, Asher cultivates an ability to see and understand both the form and meaning of the paintings judiciously.

Prudence and the Activity of Forming Beliefs or Hypotheses

A person who displays ethical prudence productively uses practical reason to determine action. Of all the epistemic virtues discussed here, the closest link is between ethical and epistemic prudence. A prudent person chooses carefully and with timeliness and also avoids being swayed by extremes. For example, a prudent person makes a decision without giving into, on one hand, naive hope or, on the other hand, impoverished confidence. In its epistemic context, prudence involves giving due care to the actual experience of knowing. A prudent person forms beliefs with appropriate care and thoughtfulness.[30] She is reflective on her own process of knowledge;

---

29. Barkess, "Painting the *Sitra Achra*," 17–24.

30. Forming beliefs with appropriate care does not suggest that all beliefs are voluntarily formed. In fact, the vast majority of our beliefs are involuntary. Recall that the

she might carefully follow the steps of her logic or candidly think over the rationale involved in forming her belief. She is also sensitive to time; that is, the prudent knower understands the limitations of her own thought processes and is willing to "settle" on a belief. A knower who displays excessive prudence is shrewd to the point of skepticism. Further, she lacks time-sensitivity and is "waiting for the bell," to use James' phrase, that will likely never toll. An imprudent person, on the other hand, is irresponsible about her knowing process. This may mean that she forms beliefs too quickly or she forms beliefs without a thought to her logic, or, often, both. An imprudent knower is a guesser.

Another example from *The Chosen* illustrates intellectual prudence. Reuven is in Talmud class that is taught by a Hasid professor/rabbi and is filled with a number of students who consider him to be an inferior or apikoros Jew. For months, Reuven prepares for each class but is never called on by the professor. He studies the material by drawing on techniques he learned from his father for Talmudic study as well as by recalling the long and intricate Talmudic disputations he witnessed his friend Danny engage in with Rabbi Saunders. Reuven reviews and memorizes the Talmudic passages, reads a wide range of commentaries on them, uses the commentaries to reconstruct various versions of the text, and imagines the possible "tangled questions" the professor could ask about it.[31]

He delves into each passage in depth and, prior to class, recites what he will say if asked to explain the text before the class. Finally, the professor calls on Reuven. For four consecutive classes, Reuven discusses the passage, its difficulties, and the commentaries on it. At the end of his explanation, which Reuven's classmates are awed by, the professor asks Reuven to give his opinion about what he has just spent four days explaining. Reuven answers carefully that he believes it to be *pilpul* or "empty, nonsensical arguments over minute points of the Talmud that have no relation to the world."[32] Potok's description of this "event," characteristically emphasizes the struggle the character (Rueven) undergoes rather than "[allocating] praise or blame" to Rueven's final appraisal or decision.[33]

VDP theory holds that virtues are at work or affect all cognitive levels including mechanical processes. Thus, any belief that is the outcome of a virtuous doxastic practice has been formed with appropriate care (e.g., checked for possible overriders).

31. Potok, *The Chosen*, 242.
32. Ibid., 107.
33. Barkess, "Painting the *Sitra Achra*."

The Virtues in Practice and Prima Facie Justification

Following Reuven's discussion and pilpul pronouncement, the professor asks to speak to him in private. He asks Reuven if there is anything else he would like to say. Reuven says that he thinks that by working from the commentaries to reconstruct the original text, the long and strained arguments—the pilpul—could be avoided. The professor tells Reuven, "It is a joy to listen to you. But you must not use that method in my class. You understand?"[34] The professor wants Reuven to see that his (Reuven's) particular "objective" method is distinctive from the methods employed by traditional Hasidic scholarship. In the traditional Hasidic worldview, study is seen as means by which one can attach oneself to God; appropriately executed, study is a form of prayer.[35]

By reconstructing the text through sophisticated historical and textual criticism, Reuven is able to explicate its various layers. However, Reuven leaves aside theological questions and avoids exploring the text's theological meaning. In his exploration, Rueven does not engage the text with the intention of using his study as a form of prayer. His teacher wants him to be aware of both the different warrants for and the various difficulties of these two distinctive approaches, and particularly, the way that the Hasidic students will perceive the method Rueven has chosen. Reuven is sensitive to his audience and for this reason did not discuss his reconstructed version of the text publicly to his classmates, who are primarily interested in a theological discussion of the text. Rueven prepared for his presentation with great care and attention to detail; he read both widely on the subject and reflected deeply. When it came time for him to form

---

34. Potok, *The Chosen*, 251.

35. To properly contextualize the difference between these two methods of Talmudic scholarships as well as the professor's response to Reuven's method, it will be helpful to outline some features of the Hasidic movement in relation to traditional Judaism. According to the *Encyclopaedia Judaica*, "The rise of the Hasidic movement in the eighteenth century presented a serious challenge to the ideal of Torah study as the supreme religious duty." The Hasid understanding of study subverted the traditional Jewish hierarchy, wherein Talmudic study is held in the highest regard and prayer is an inferior activity. The laws guiding study for traditional Judaism illustrate its importance: "Three benedictions are to be recited before studying the Torah. Since the whole of the Jew's waking life is a time for study these benedictions are recited at the beginning of each day and suffice for the whole day's study" (*Encyclopaedia Judaica*, 2nd ed., s.v. "study."). While Talmudic study plays a significant role in the Hasid movement, it is significant not for its own sake but because it serves in support of prayer. Because Reuven's method of approach does not focus only his relationship with God nor seek answers to strictly theological questions, his discussion of the text is inconsistent with the values of traditional Hasidic scholarship nurtured by the professor in his largely Hasidic student body.

a judgment about the Talmudic passage, he not only processed what he learned with acumen, but he also did so with prudent understanding of the implications his judgment would have for both himself and his classmates.

Creativity and the Actions Taken upon Beliefs

Creativity relates to the ethical virtue of fortitude. To have fortitude is to be courageous and strong, particularly in the face of adversity or difficulty. A person musters fortitude when the stakes are high and when something important is on the line; fortitude involves a willingness to give up present comfort for the sake of a future goal. In short, this virtue is future-oriented; creativity is also future-oriented. In its epistemological context, creativity concerns what one does with a belief and involves imagining how one will hold the belief and the effects it will have. This epistemic virtue is about being innovative. It does not mean that one's knowledge or belief claims are "creative" in the colloquial use of creative—namely, to mean artistic or visionary. Rather, this virtue points to the more basic idea that one's beliefs should be creative toward an end (creative *of* or *for* something) or are nuanced according to how the knower uniquely processes information. Imagination animates the virtue of creativity. The knower imagines the future of her belief—for both herself and her community—and attunes the belief accordingly. The virtue of creativity avoids the excess of being enterprising and the deficiency of being restrained with or insincere about the knowledge one has formed.

The crucifixion portraits, which Asher Lev learned to perceive with judiciousness, play a central role throughout his development as an artist. After years of learning about paintings, training with a master, and reflecting on the experiences he intends to portray in his art, Asher begins to produce his own body of work. By the time Asher is a young man, his relationship with his father is strained to the point of breaking and he is, at best, on the periphery of the Hasidic community. His art makes him an outcast. Asher's story culminates with him painting and publicly showing his two most significant pieces, both of which feature a Christ-like image of his long suffering mother (in the beginning of Asher's story, Asher's mother has a nervous breakdown that she seems perpetually haunted by; the pain caused from watching his mother endure this breakdown is palpable) hanging on a cross.

The process of planning and painting the portraits is not only uncomfortable for Asher, it is tortuous. For a very long time, Asher felt he

The Virtues in Practice and Prima Facie *Justification*

needed to create these paintings, but he resisted the impulse. He states, "And it was then that it [the visions for the images] came, though I think it had been coming a long time and I had been choking it and hoping it would die. But it does not die. It kills you first."[36] Over time and by using his imagination, Asher weighs out various, possible implications of his desire to create these paintings. When Asher finally allows himself to paint the images, he feels an overwhelming sense of relief, "I looked at the drawing. The dread was gone. I had no strength left for fighting. I would have to let it lead me now or there would be deeper and deeper layers of the wearying darkness. And I dreaded the darkness more than I did anything."[37] John Timmerman articulates a basic lesson of Potok's work as follows: "as a pilgrim in the outside world, the seeker may learn better the place that is his last refuge."[38] Asher dreaded the paintings because he knew what it would mean for his family and community (when he showed the paintings, Asher was shut off from his family, banished from his community, and asked by his community's leader to move to a Hasidic community in Europe). What he feared even more was continuing his life *without* expressing himself through his art. In the flight from his community and tradition, Asher takes refuge in his art and that has consequences for what he is able to achieve—artistically, emotionally, and intellectually.

It is not in making the painting themselves that Asher manifests the virtue of creativity, it is rather in how he comes to understand their meaning. When his father reacts with disgust and shame upon seeing the portraits, Asher tells him, "No, I'm not saying these paintings represent the truth; they represent how I feel about things I remembered . . . They're not the truth, Papa; but they're not lies either."[39] Asher, at first, stops himself from making the paintings—which stand as an image of his feelings about the past and his family's relationship with their tradition—because he fears their consequences. He imagines the reactions his parents and religious leaders will have to seeing the painting he envisions. After years of emotional struggle, he realizes that to *not* express himself in this way is an abuse of his memories, feelings, and potential for artistic expression. (He also does not make the paintings out of hubris or to bring him fame—which, in the end, the paintings do.)

---

36. Potok, *My Name Is Asher Lev*, 326.
37. Ibid., 317.
38. Timmerman, "A Way of Seeing," 518.
39. Potok, *My Name Is Asher Lev*, 359–60.

Virtue in Dialogue

By imagining what it will mean to create the paintings, on the one hand, and what it will mean to not, on the other hand, Asher allows his imagination to govern his future choice. When he reckons with his fear through imagination, he is able to paint. He says, "I created this painting— an observant Jew working on a crucifixion because there was no aesthetic mold in his own religious tradition into which he could pour a painting of ultimate anguish and torment."[40] By experimenting with the crucifix as an artistic form, Asher, an observant Hasid, pushes on his community's boundaries and, out of this, not only opens a pathway for his own feelings, but also creatively introduces a new possibility for religious expression.

Conclusion: Combining the Theoretical Components and the Concrete Examples

In the previous chapter, I offered theoretical sketches of epistemic virtue and virtuous agents and, in this chapter, I offered a sketch of practice. The stories of Danny, Reuven, and Asher illuminate these theoretical discussions by providing examples of the epistemic virtues of steadfastness, judiciousness, prudence, and creativity in practice. For example, Reuven learns prudence in the context of community; his father, his professor, and his classmates provide him both with models for prudence and audiences for trying prudence out. Because acquiring prudence involves engaging in various actions associated with prudence, Reuven tests the limits of prudence and, at time, pushes back on what he learns from his community (MacIntyre's theory of practice accounts for this dual aim). We can know Reuven acquires the virtue of prudence based on the motivation and feelings he has that are characteristic of the virtue of prudence (Williams contributes resources for explaining why Reuven exercises the virtue of prudence rather than just a skill of careful learning). The chief aim of Rueven's prudent practices when studying Talmud is not to lead him to a particular interpretation of the text, although his prudent practice may lead him to form a justified belief. Instead, his chief aim is to develop prudence in a more full way, to flourish intellectually as an individual, and to contribute to the intellectual flourishing of his learning community (Driver, Nussbaum, and Zagzebski provide the building blocks for idea of the outcome of virtue).

---

40. Ibid., 330.

The "Meta-Level" Epistemic Virtues

It may seem curious that wisdom and integrity are absent from the epistemic virtue list.[41] They are not present because, first, this list of intellectual virtues models itself on Aristotle's account, which is highly specific about the particular task or application of each virtue. The above account strives to be specific in order to achieve precision or clarity about the virtues. Secondly, and following from this, integrity and wisdom are absent from the list because they stand in unique relation to the individual virtues. Both integrity and wisdom are "higher" or "meta-level" forms of intellectual virtue; it would denigrate their status to suggest they operate in only one realm or aspect of experience. Wisdom and integrity relate to all aspects of life and to the intellectual virtues as a whole. Integrity antecedes steadfastness, judiciousness, prudence, and creativity. Wisdom follows from the unity of steadfastness, judiciousness, prudence, and creativity.

Intellectual Integrity

Intellectual integrity is that which precedes and guides the individual virtues; it is the cause. The virtuous epistemic agent is virtuous because she is able to strike the balance between excess and deficiency. Just as each intellectual virtue (steadfastness, judiciousness, prudence, creativity) applies to a particular realm or aspect of life (background beliefs, evidence, and so on), the virtue of integrity applies to them realm of the virtues themselves.[42] Driver describes it this way, using the language of "ethically

---

41. Honesty might also have been included in this list. I take it that honesty is a component of integrity.

42. Intellectual or epistemic humility is bound up in the virtue of integrity. The claim here is that humility is necessary for locating the place on the spectrum between excess and deficiency where the virtue lies or, said another way, for "ethically sensitive perception." Humility, however, is a problematic concept for an Aristotelian theory of virtue because, for Aristotle, being humble involves at least some level of self-deception if not improper or defective perception. Driver discusses the issue at length in terms of modesty as a "paradigm case": "What the analysis comes down to is this: for a person to be modest, she must be ignorant with regard to her own self-worth" (Driver, *Uneasy Virtue*, 377). If one is humble about one's own ability, she actually underestimates her ability. Underestimating is equivalent to misunderstanding, which Aristotle cannot commend as a virtue. Virtues of ignorance, like modesty and humility, thus do not sit easily with his virtue theory. At least for the purposes of this discussion which, unlike Driver's, is concerned primarily with intellectual rather than character virtues, I take humility to mean a balance between trust in one's own judgment and deference to the judgments of others rather than just ignorance or skewed perception about oneself. If

sensitive perception": "... the virtuous agent must rely on ethically sensitive perception to determine where virtue lies."[43] Ethically sensitive perception with regard to the ethical virtues—the capacity to discern where the virtue is on the spectrum from deficiency to excess—is congruous to what I call integrity with regard to the intellectual virtues. The "meta-level" virtue of integrity in particular highlights the fact that the VDP theory—as it is the case with Aristotle's account—does not depend on rules or norms to govern how a person forms epistemically good beliefs (that is, there is no rule that says what exactly is the mean between excess and deficiency) but rather on a cultivated ability that is applied ad hoc to each situation and according to context.

Wisdom

Wisdom is the result or outcome of the unity of the intellectual virtues; it is the crown. For Aristotle, who divides intellectual and character (or what might be called the ethical or practical) virtues, the virtue of practical wisdom or "phronesis" is that which unites the two. Aristotle states, "wisdom is understanding plus scientific knowledge" (*NE* 6.7.1141a17) and Tilley elucidates, "In short, *phronesis* is the ability to put intellect into action."[44] As with the virtue of integrity, there is no *a priori* defined content to what wisdom is. When an agent exercises all of the virtues—when she is steadfast, judicious, prudent, and creative—it amounts to wisdom.

Limited Unity of the Virtues

Aristotle himself holds what has been called a "unity of virtue" presupposition, which is to say that he argues that one cannot have one virtue without having them all (and, to not display one virtue would make a person not-virtuous). Many contemporary virtue theorists reject the unity of virtue thesis as simply not true to human experience. It is not the case that having one virtue implies that a person could or should have all the others; in fact some virtues seem to be actually incompatible with others. Neera

---

integrity is striking the right balance between excess and deficiency, then the way this can be done is by striking a balance between following one's own intuition and the examples of others (the colloquial phrase "learn from the mistakes of others" might even be applied here). Neither a depraved nor hubristic understanding of oneself is involved in this notion of intellectual humility.

43. Ibid., 5.
44. Tilley, "The Wisdom of Religious Commitment," 3.

The Virtues in Practice and Prima Facie *Justification*

Badhwar helpfully argues that although Aristotle is unrealistic about the unity of *all* virtues, this is not to say that any unity among them should be outright rejected. She argues for a theory of limited unity. The virtues, Badhwar writes, are united in one area, though may be "disconnected across multiple fields."[45] Wisdom here captures the limited unity of virtue theory discussed by Badhwar. While not all steadfast agents are also creative, agents who are wise must also be, by definition, steadfast, judicious, prudent, and creative.

The claim that the precise character of both integrity and wisdom cannot be known in advance highlights the deeply social nature of this theory of intellectual virtue. Neither the individual epistemic virtues nor the meta-level epistemic virtues have definite character. Rather, they are constituted situationally and socially; the virtues gain their character by being exercised and they are only exercised according to the world or social context that demands them.

Sufficiency of the List of Virtues

The objection that the four cardinal intellectual virtues outlined here are insufficient is, however, another kind of objection: it accepts the VDP theory's premises, but impeaches its content. It allows that steadfastness and judiciousness, for example, can lead to justification, it just wonders if there are not more or better intellectual virtues that should be included. The best response to this objection is to state that the goal of the VDP theory is to present concrete descriptions of epistemic virtues and denote their precise tasks. The limitations brought about by this level of concreteness and precision make the VDP theory vulnerable to charges of insufficiency: are there not many intellectual virtues left unmentioned? Is it not possible that we form beliefs by means of other intellectual virtues?

I deflect the charge of insufficiency on the grounds of three points: (1) some epistemic virtues not appearing on the VDP theory list of virtues are simply cognates, components, or analogues of VDP cardinal epistemic virtues (for example, constancy and tenacity are analogue forms of steadfastness where self-respect, honor, and obedience are components of it; involved in judiciousness are discretion, carefulness, and fair-mindedness; prudence's classic virtue cognate is temperance and it takes open-mindedness and demands thrift or a kind of economy in how one acts and thinks; autonomy, courage, and honesty are components of creativity); (2) some

---

45. Badhwar, "The Limited Unity of Virtue," 306.

177

virtues not appearing on the VDP theory list (for example, humility, compassion, gratitude, benevolence, and trust) fall under the umbrella (and specifically not-*a priori* defined) categories of wisdom and integrity (I take it that the virtues parenthetically noted above are constitutive pieces of wisdom and integrity); (3) some epistemic virtues not appearing on the VDP list are culturally or socially specific and, thus, overly particularized (for example, Christian charity, faith, and hope, Enlightenment autonomy, or Victorian chastity). Properly understood, then, this description of the intellectual virtues of the VDP theory is sufficient without overprivileging the virtues of any one social group.

Virtuous Doxastic Practices and *Prima Facie* Justification

In chapter 4, I contended that on Zagzebski's model an epistemic agent tests her beliefs by *imagining* what a virtuous person might believe in like circumstances; this process is what allows for *prima facie* belief justification. Individual agents are responsible for asking if their beliefs are truly the outcome of the virtuous doxastic practices of her community. Practically, this means that, in forming beliefs, an agent relies on members of her epistemic community to provide standards and guidelines for engaging in virtuous doxastic practices. She exercises agency in this way. It is significant that the agent does not look to compare her religious belief with the *beliefs* of her epistemic community, but rather she judges the way she forms beliefs according to the standards for the virtuous doxastic practices of her community.[46] Wayne Riggs states that the "traditional package of knowledge" should include a theory of virtue as well as "some kind of internalism."[47] Zagzebski agrees with this claim. Because reflectivity about one's own intellectual virtue inheres in the concept of virtuous doxastic practice, the VDP model accomplishes the demand Riggs and Zazegbski call for here.

The fundamental claim of the VDP model is that belief formation and justification are derivative of an agent's intellectual virtue and the practices through which that virtue is created and sustained. Thus, when epistemologists examine beliefs, and in the case of this project—religious

---

46. I want to highlight the point that my concern here is with belief and not practice. My theory is meant to create space for innovation, new ideas, and even for tension between new and old beliefs.

47. Riggs, "Reliability," 92.

The Virtues in Practice and Prima Facie Justification

beliefs—the agent's character is, as Code puts it, "of central relevance."[48] The four epistemic virtues presented in the last section—steadfastness, judiciousness, prudence, and creative (guided by integrity and amounting to wisdom)—are the qualities that "contribute to regulating belief."[49] If the agent exercises these epistemic virtues to at least some degree (recall that the VDP model has a threshold standard) in belief formation, the "output" beliefs can be said to be reliable and *prima facie* justified as such. Because exercising virtue involves a doxastic practice like the one MacIntyre describes, these religious beliefs are already subjected to internal tests (for example, imagining overriders) and created in the context of a community—a community that, by its very nature, demands certain standards of excellence and reflective awareness from its agents. The internal tests and standards of excellence used in these tests are significantly different than the kind of tests and standards suggested by Plantinga (and discusses in the previous chapter). Because I theorize that all virtues are socially motivated and socially applied, this theory bars in principle the self-legitimating system Plantinga advances.

The VDP model states that beliefs are *prima facie* justified if they are formed in such a way that coheres with what a virtuous person might believe in like circumstances and have been imagined to be so on the part of the believer. This covers *prima facie* justification. What does all this mean for the concerns of Griffiths and Netland, Flew and Hare, McKim and Feldman? How does this extensive explication of the virtues and the practices of them contribute toward the issue of dealing with epistemic justification in the situation of religious diversity? The question is, in other words, how does a steadfast and creative agent gain epistemic justification that makes senses in the context of deep diversity? In the following chapter, I explore the way by which believers consider their beliefs in light of what a virtuous person might believe in unlike (different though relevant) circumstances so as to move from *prima facie* justification to *ultima facie* justification.

---

48. Code, Epistemic Responsibility, 29.
49. Montmarquet, "Epistemic Virtue," 491.

7

Ultima Facie Justification and Participation through Practice

CHAPTER 6 BEGAN WITH AN EXAMPLE OF A MUSLIM'S BELIEF ABOUT THE Qur'an as the word of God communicated by the Prophet Mohammed. The Muslim is *prima facie* justified in her belief by that belief being the outcome of a virtuous doxastic practice. That a believer gains the status of *prima facie* justification for her belief implies both that the agent exercises epistemic virtue (for example, epistemic prudence) in forming the belief and that the agent learned how to exercise this virtue by participating in a communal VDP. The way that this belief moves beyond *prima facie* justification is by the agent considering it in the interreligious context and in light of what other virtuous people—Baha'is, Hindus, and Buddhists for example—believe. The primary aim of this chapter is to explore how religious believers—precisely through interreligious dialogue—move from being *prima facie* justified in their beliefs toward being *ultima facie* justified.[1]

When a religious believer participates in an interreligious dialogue that creates a community wherein multiple virtuous doxastic practices are exercised together, she has the possibility of being fully justified in the beliefs that are the outcome of this VDP. This argument that a person may be fully justified in holding her religious belief in the context of interreligious dialogue, first, rests on the premise that the VDP epistemological model is itself sound and, second, depends on the supposition that the VDP theory can handle the possible strain and roadblocks that arise out of social situations involving overlapping distinctive cultural traditions. (Interreligious or multicultural situations—where diverse people with

---

1. *Ultima facie* justification is the "all things considered" level of justification (Alston, *Perceiving God*, 225). In other words, it is the kind of justification that takes into consideration *all* relevant factors as opposed to only *immediate* relevant factors, as in the case of *prima facie* justification.

Ultima Facie *Justification and Participation through Practice*

diverse virtuous doxastic practices come into contact and must negotiate these differences—constitute this latter challenge to the VDP theory.) In this chapter I defend the claim that the VDP theory must not only be epistemologically viable but also able to account for situations where multiple virtuous doxastic practices are at work if it is to address the possibility of *ultima facie* justification.

In order to maintain the premise that the VDP model is epistemologically sound, the first major section of this chapter rebuts three possible objections to the VDP theory. These objections are that the VDP theory is epistemologically irrelevant; that the VDP theory has a substantial problem when it comes to the question of epistemic luck; and that the VDP theory promotes relativism. This final (and most powerful) objection on the issue of relativism provides the bridge from this section on the epistemological challenges to the following section on the challenges of diversity. To show how the VDP theory, and particularly the *ultima facie* justificatory component of the theory, does not falter in the face of diversity—but rather fulfills its purpose—the second major section of this chapter deals with interreligious dialogue as a situation of "on the ground" comparative contact that generates, in turn, a creditable standard for *ultima facie* justification.

In order to maintain the premise that the VDP model is able to account for situations of multiple, overlapping virtuous doxastic practices, the second major section of this chapter appeals to the philosophical and theological work of Lee Yearley and Francis X. Clooney to provide the language and theoretical tools to point out how interreligious dialogue mirrors scholarly comparison. Specifically, I argue that in interreligious dialogue, agents talk together in order to compare analogically their beliefs and various religious VDPs to one another and enter into each others' lives through sharing narratives. Through this process, they each play both guide and follower at various times. These shared practices, undertaken by the dialogue participants not despite of, but because of their being formed in differing religious traditions, leads both to the transformation of the religious beliefs, convictions, and attitudes arising from various traditions and to a new context for epistemic justification.

Objections to Virtuous Doxastic Practice Model as a Virtue Epistemology

There are at least three possible objections to the VDP epistemology as an accurate and adequate epistemological account. I raise these objections because, before the VDP model can hold up in the face of religious diversity, it must be able to hold up in terms of questions raised by epistemology—and specifically the epistemology of disagreement—at large.[2] The literature in the area of criticizing virtue epistemology is wide-ranging and highly technical. My hope is not to be consumed by these discussions, but rather to address the most important objections, explain why these objections could be devastating to the VDP account, and use them to be productive toward greater clarity on the VDP theory.

In an essay intended to offer a summary exploration of trends in virtue epistemology, Baehr makes the following provocative judgment: "... any attempt to give the intellectual virtues a central place in epistemology is bound to fail."[3] Baehr is not alone in his hesitancy to embrace the tenets of virtue epistemology. As noted in the introduction of this chapter, there are three primary objections waged by the anti-virtue crowd that are relevant to the VDP theory. These objections are, in order of how problematic they are for the VDP account, as follows: (1) virtue epistemologies ignore the central questions of epistemological inquiry and thus are irrelevant; (2) virtue epistemologies are too permissive about what can count as knowledge because their standards for justification are insufficient and so cannot deal with the problem of epistemic luck; (3) virtue epistemologies are relativistic.

Virtue Epistemology as Irrelevant

Baehr summarizes the first objection concisely. He claims that the central flaw of virtue epistemology is that it works too far outside the realm of traditional epistemology. He writes, "It is difficult to see how a consideration

---

2. The reason I see this is as a necessary move is the very same reason that motivates my criticism of theologians in chapter 1. If theologians are accountable only to themselves, so to speak, and not to those outside of the theological discipline (let alone the community beyond the academy), there is a way in which theology perpetuates only the kinds of debates that are internal to the discipline thereby becoming illegitimate in the perspective of the academic community in general and irrelevant in the eyes of the wider community.

3. Baehr, "Character in Epistemology," 482.

of intellectual virtue could be useful for addressing the questions at the center of the debate between empiricists and rationalists, and principally, the question of whether anything is knowable independently of experience or on the basis of pure thought or reason."[4] This kind of objection misses the point. Because virtue epistemologies do not address the Kantian problematic or worry over Descartes' *cogito* calculation, this does not mean they have nothing to contribute to epistemology. In their commitment to connecting epistemological theory to real epistemic practices, the VDP theory and other virtue epistemologies provide a means of escape from the torrent of speculative, epistemologically-related questions about the world as we know it and the world in itself, the nature of the human mind, and so on.

The real value of virtue epistemologies is that they change the subject of the conversation. Baehr deems this for the worse, but—particularly given the criticisms raised of epistemologists from chapter 2 and Plantinga's speculatively-oriented epistemology outlined in chapter 4—I contend it is far for the better to try new strategies or "change the subject." New developments in virtue epistemology reveal that there is an alternative to the old approach that only leads to conclusions that are simply unsustainable.

The Credit View, Luck, and Explanatory Salience

The second major objection to virtue epistemology is that its justificatory standards are insufficient and, as such, virtue epistemologies like the VDP model are overly permissive about what "counts" as a justified belief. There are various permutations of this type of objection, but this discussion will focus on the "credit view" and the criticisms of it. Greco states that virtue epistemologies describe the concept of knowledge as follows: "knowledge is true belief grounded in intellectual virtue." If knowledge is grounded in a person's intellectual virtue, then attributing justified belief or knowledge to an agent is a way of giving credit to agents.[5] Greco states that the credit view taps into our conventional ways of thinking about the nature of knowledge: that is, our common ways of speaking point to the idea that a person has earned knowledge, in a sense, and so deserves credit for it. The VDP model works similarly. For example, to say that my mother knows that the flowers are crocuses is to say that my mother deserves credit for her belief because that it is the outcome of a virtuous doxastic practice.

4. Ibid., 496.
5. Greco, "A Different Sort of Contextualism," 387.

Jennifer Lackey finds a problem with the "credit view." If we think about knowledge as being creditable to the agent (that is to say, knowledge is the outcome of an agent's exercise of intellectual virtue), we have to also attend to sticky epistemological situations where credit is not, in fact, "appropriately ascribable" to the agent.[6] These situations involve epistemic luck. Lackey tells a story of a tourist who arrives in Chicago for the first time to exemplify the problem she finds with the credit view. A tourist steps out of the subway and asks a person on the street, who happens to be a long time resident of Chicago and very well informed about its landmarks, which direction it is to the Sears Tower.[7] The resident responds and the tourist, Lackey states, has "knowledge" (from perspective of a credit-type view) of the location of the Sears Tower. Lackey wonders whether the tourist—who stumbled on just the right person to ask and happened upon good directions—really deserves credit for knowing the location of the Sears Tower.

On the credit view, Lackey states, the tourist deserves credit because he wisely chose the right person to ask or because he used his listening skills to follow the directions. Either of these things would be a credit to him. Lackey points out a problem with the first reason for ascribing credit to the tourist: it is arbitrary that the tourist chose the right person to ask for directions. The problem with the second ascription of credit is that even if the tourist did use his listening skills (and that is creditable to him), those skills are not the *primary* or *salient* explanation for how he acquired knowledge (rather, the resident who gave him knowledge is the primary or salient explanation). For the credit view to work, Lackey continues, it must be the agent's virtues that hold "explanatory salience" for belief formation and justification. In her tourist example, the virtues do not have explanatory salience.[8]

I argue that Lackey's example is misleading on two counts. First, she conflates "receiving information" with "having knowledge" and, second, she leaves out a crucial epistemic step that would take a person from having information to having knowledge. I will build off Lackey's example to illustrate these points and discuss the implications for Lackey's overarching criticism. By asking for directions to the Sears Tower, the tourist receives "information" about where the Sears tower is. He utilizes that

---

6. Lackey, "Why We Don't Deserve Credit" 347.

7. The name of the Sears Tower was formally changed to the Willis Tower in March 2009. I continue referring to it as the Sears Tower here.

8. Greco, "A Different Sort of Contextualism," 398.

information (i.e., follows the directions) since he has no other options. The tourist takes his informer (the resident) to be reliable—perhaps the informer is assured in her style and so gives the tourist confidence.

The tourist follows the informer's directions, arrives at the Sears Tower, and now knows the location of the landmark. In other words, the tourist has made the transition from having information to having knowledge by engaging in a process for forming justified beliefs—specifically, he walked to the building according to the directions given to him. While the tourist trusted the information he received from the informer prior to acting on the directions, he did not gain knowledge (or justified belief) until he actually tried out the information. At this point, if a second tourist approached the first tourist and asked him for directions, he (the first tourist) would be justified in saying, "I know that it's over there." Had the second tourist approached the first tourist and asked him for directions prior to the first tourist's actually going to the Sears Tower, the first tourist should say, "I've been told it is over there." The tourist may gain true belief ("receiving information") through luck (he luckily asked a trustworthy informer for directions), but he does not have knowledge until he follows the informer's directions.

Lackey's criticism is this: if an agent forms justified belief due to luck rather than virtues, it is not appropriate to say the agent deserves credit for his belief; and if we give credit where credit is *not* due, the account or definition of knowledge is weakened and the value of intellectual virtues are undermined.[9] Epistemic luck (for example, the tourist *luckily* chose the right person to ask for directions) is problematic for the credit view only

---

9. This cursory account of the claim that virtue epistemology has insufficient justificatory standards is barely adequate. Unfortunately, it is outside the scope of this book to explain the problem of luck for virtue epistemology in great detail. It is important to mention here, however, that the specific criticism that Lackey makes is that virtue epistemology puts itself between a rock and a hard place. She writes: ". . . whatever notion of credit the proponent of the Credit View invokes, it has to be robust enough to rule out subjects in Gettier and Gettier-type situations from deserving credit for their true beliefs, yet weak enough to allow subjects in testimonial cases . . . to be deserving of credit for their true beliefs" (Lackey, "Knowledge and Credit," 29). Other important essays, not discussed here but important for informing my hermeneutic on this matter are as follows: Greco, "Agent Reliablism," 273–96; Greco, "A Different Sort of Contextualism"; Greco, "Knowledge as Credit for True Belief," 111–34; Greco, "Knowledge and Success from Ability," 17–26; Greco, "What's Wrong with Contextualism?," 416–36; Greco, "Virtue and Rules in Epistemology," 117–41; Katzoff, "Religious Luck and Religious Virtue," 97–111; Lackey, "Knowledge and Credit"; Lackey, "Why We Don't Deserve Credit"; Pritchard, "Apt Performance and Epistemic Value," 407–16; Pritchard, "Greco on Knowledge," 437–47; Pritchard, "Virtue Epistemology" 106–30.

if the credit view does not require a step by which one transitions from having information to gaining knowledge.

Another way to deal with Lackey's objection regarding the problem of luck for intellectual virtue is to make a distinction among types of chance (Lackey works with one lumped group: luck). Wayne Riggs offers this type of response. He argues that there are least two types of chance that people encounter in forming beliefs and it is necessary to be clear what type of chance, precisely, is problematic for a credit-type view. The first type of chance is luck. Luck is determined by the extent to which an agent plays a causal role in bringing an event about and the likelihood that the event could occur given the agent's "prior given track record."[10] If Martin is dared to kick a field goal from the fifty-yard line, and he has never touched a football in his life yet makes the field goal, this is luck. However, if Martin practices kicking fifty-yard field goals daily, and he makes one on a dare, luck plays only a very minor role. In both cases, Martin's intention plays a role. In the second example in particular it is clear how Martin's track record importantly influences the positive outcome. Accident is the second type of chance. Accident is an event that is not sufficiently caused by the agent's intention.[11] If Martin steps onto a football field and happens to slip on a patch of mud and, in doing so, strikes a teed-up football that then (miraculously) sails through the uprights, this is an accident. Martin's intention had nothing to do with the field goal.[12]

Riggs argues that epistemologists who describe virtues as habits of character need to rule out the possibility that accident, but not luck, is primarily responsible for an agent's belief. For a virtue epistemologist like Riggs, if beliefs can be formed and justified without an agent's intention (or Martin can make a field goal without meaning to do so), then virtue epistemology has a problem.[13] For what would be the point of developing one's virtues (or practicing kicking field goals)? On the other hand, Riggs claims, if an agent forms a belief and luck plays a role (as does an

10. Riggs, "What Are the Chances of Being Justified?," 452–73.
11. Ibid.
12. Austin, "Three Ways of Spilling Ink," 427–40. Austin proposes another way of differentiating luck and the following example illustrates this. If the gun went off while I was hunting and shot my friend in the foot, I shot her accidentally. On the other hand, if I was hunting and aimed at a deer but hit the cow, I shot the cow by mistake. I did not shoot my friend by mistake, but by accident and I did not shoot the cow by accident, but by mistake.
13. This problem, as I construe it here, applies not only to virtue epistemology but also any externalist epistemology, such as Plantinga's.

agent's virtues, intentions, or past action), that belief may be justified and there is no real problem for the habits of character from which the belief is derived. In Riggs' view, then, virtue epistemologists must accept that luck sometimes plays a role in belief formation, and accommodate that fact in their standards of justification.

Lackey's point is that an adequate virtue epistemology must show how justified beliefs are genuinely not the outcome of accepting blithely what she is told, but an outcome of an agent's engagement in a VDP—an agent who exhibits a unity between her virtues, practices, and intention in exercising these practices and who is not being worked on by a force external to her agency. If an agent is able to arrive at knowledge (justified true belief) through luck, in which an agent does not play a causal role, then the reliable mechanism would be discredited as reliable. Lackey's objection is easily dissolved. A person can acquire a belief by luck or information from a source, but these beliefs are not justified until that person properly exercises intellectual virtues.

To a certain extent, Riggs accepts this criticism of virtue epistemology and so draws a distinction between luck and chance to make a partial concession. I, however, do not accept Lackey's objection. On the VDP theory, virtues do not stand alone; they are embedded in doxastic practices. Agents exercise these VDPs to form justified beliefs. These VDPs are the processes by which agents transition from "receiving information" to "having knowledge." By walking the informer's suggested directions, the tourist engages in a process for making this transition possible. This process is the "salient explanation" for the tourist's justified belief about the location of the Sears Tower.

The VDP model contends that believers are justified in their beliefs if those beliefs are the outcomes of virtuous doxastic practices. Belief justification is thus agent-centered. When beliefs are the outcome of the virtuous doxastic practices of those agents, they (the beliefs) can be said to be justified as "shorthand" because they are derived from responsible, virtuous agents' practices. Virtuous doxastic practices imply reliability.[14] When beliefs are *not* the outcome of VDPs, they are *not* justified. This does not mean that unjustified beliefs cannot be true, it simply means that they are not justified. It is possible for a person to arrive at true belief by luck, as the tourist example shows, but not knowledge (*justified* true belief).

---

14. Again, not all doxastic practices accomplish this. Guessing is a prime example of a doxastic practice that is not reliable and thus does not lead to justified beliefs.

Virtue in Dialogue

As an illustration of religious beliefs that are unjustified because they are not formed out of VDPs, take, for example, a person who thinks Muslims are wrong because they take the Qur'an literally. This person also believes the "sword verses" are the most important verses of the Qur'an in Islam and that all Muslims interpret the entire Qur'an in light of *surah* 9:5.[15] When asked, this person says that her belief in the universal love of God is her reason for believing Muslims are wrong. This belief is not only about other people but it is also about others' religious commitments in relation to her own—namely that Muslim convictions stand in opposition to her religious beliefs. This person's belief has been formed with an underdeveloped sense of Islamic theological beliefs and with little awareness of other parts of the Qur'an that hold central for Muslims. There is no evidence that this person exercised, for example, epistemic judiciousness toward her sources on the "sword verses" (i.e., her belief stems primarily from popular media representation of terrorist groups which invoke these verses). For the reasons such as these, her belief is unjustified.

The issue of luck is uniquely important when considering religious belief formation. Charlotte Katzoff states that religious luck—what might also be called in Christian language grace—must be faced when considering "religious virtues," as Katzoff calls them, just as moral luck must be faced when considering character virtues or epistemic luck when discussing intellectual virtues.[16] Although the VDP model makes no distinction between intellectual virtues and "theistic virtues," religious luck is important for considering how VDPs contributes toward religious belief formation. How does religious luck/grace bear on an agent's religious belief formation?

Factors that are outside the agent's control and yet affect the agent's belief forming process—like receiving directions as a tourist—are an inevitable part of the process. Theologically speaking, religious epistemology does not intend to eliminate religious luck or grace from the realm of belief formation. Rather, it makes the basic claim that justified religious beliefs are the outcomes of agent-centered VDPs. There may also be true beliefs that are the outcome of some other means (they may be the outcome of grace or even vicious doxastic practices), but these beliefs do not meet the justificatory standards of the VDP theory. (The tourist forming

---

15. "Kill the polytheists wherever you find them, arrest them, imprison them, besiege them, and lie in wait for them at every site of ambush" (Qur'an 9:5, trans. Tarif Khalidi).

16. Katzoff, "Religious Luck and Religious Virtue," 108.

Ultima Facie *Justification and Participation through Practice*

a true belief about the location of the Sears Tower without following the directions himself is a parallel non-religious example of having a true belief that is not a justified true belief.[17]) Moreover, it may be possible for true beliefs that are the outcome of luck to later gain justification by being reflected upon or redeveloped according to one's intellectual virtue.[18]

Greco writes that not all success is attributable to agents because sometimes the success comes about in the wrong way. We credit an agent when the agent's role in bringing about belief or knowledge is salient.[19] In the case of religious beliefs, those beliefs that are formed in a Paul-on-the-road-to-Damascus type of way are qualified for justification by being further reflected upon and tested by the agent. Like the tourist who receives information (directions to the Sears Tower), believers who are struck as Paul is on the road to Damascus have to take a further step to transition to being justified in their beliefs. Because the VDP epistemology does not eliminate the role of luck (religious grace) entirely in belief formation, it will not account for *all* types of belief formation and neither should it. The VDP theory sufficiently accounts for the formation of justified beliefs through agents exercising VDPs. Virtuous doxastic practices systematically though not flawlessly lead to justified belief. The VDP model gives a picture of belief formation and justification that is generally true, but not rigidly so. Moreover, this fallible quality of the VDP theory may be regarded as something positive rather than negative, in that it is flexible and open to modification.[20]

17. In general, we assume that our beliefs are true. Like the tourist, we rely on others in belief formation and tend to assume the credibility of their testimony. We only work to justify our beliefs when there is reason (such as a conflicting or competing belief) for us to examine them. When a person is challenged in her beliefs, then she may proceed to examine the justification for holding them.

18. It needs to be said that there is an important distinction between epistemological justification and religious or theological justification. My argument is exclusively interested in the epistemological justification of beliefs. I claim *neither* that epistemological justification leads to theological justification (i.e., salvation) *nor* that unjustified (epistemologically speaking) religious beliefs cannot be theologically justified. Rather, mine is a much more modest claim. There may be a good theological arguments—perhaps through the frame of Rahner's insight that the very structure of human knowing has a transcendental quality (see for example Rahner, *Foundations of Christian Faith*, 32) to make about the relationship between epistemological and theological justification, but that is outside the scope of this project.

19. Greco, "What's Wrong With Contextualism?," 419.

20. Driver makes the following statement about her virtue ethical theory, "Virtues systematically though not infallibly lead to good" (Driver, *Uneasy Virtue*, 61). By being fallible, the standards for justification are actually flexible rather than brittle and

Virtue Epistemology and the Problem of Relativism

The final objection is the most theoretically thorny and philosophically troubling. This objection claims that virtue epistemologies generate epistemological relativism. The charge of relativism is not easily dismissed. Here, I will explain the relativism objection, offer one kind of response that is primarily rhetorical in nature, and use this criticism to lead into the following major section of this chapter, which deals with issues related to relativism and specifically issues about making final normative assessments about diverse religious beliefs.

The charge of relativism against the VDP theory looks something like this: the central claim of the VDP theory is that (*prima facie*) justified beliefs are formed through agents exercising VDPs. An agent "moves toward" *ultima facie* justification in these beliefs by considering one's *prima facie* justified beliefs in light of others' *prima facie* justified beliefs. There are at least two problems with this standard of justification. First, and quite simply, the language "move toward" is problematically vague. Is belief always only moving toward *ultima facie* justification? Can *ultima facie* justification ever really be achieved? Second, is the VDP theory of justification just a cloaked way of saying that if agents form beliefs in epistemically good ways (that is, as the exercises of the virtuous doxastic practices), then there is no final way to determine their justification in relation to one another? Does the VDP model remove objectivity?

My first response to this objection is rhetorical. While the VDP model appeals to obscure language and does not take a firm position on how beliefs can be justified in relation to one another, the VDP model is still a *better* option than traditional religious epistemology and especially evidential foundationalism because, as demonstrated in chapter 2, these epistemologies tend to depend upon deliberately ignoring the role religious practices play in religious beliefs. The VDP model ruptures a myopic way of looking at religious beliefs—that justified beliefs are formed on the basis of evidence and are in conflict as such—and carves out a unique place for virtue epistemology to flourish—in religious or theological discourse.

Baehr states, "The problem with [a virtue epistemological] approach is that it fails to specify a set of substantive philosophical issues and questions related to the intellectual virtues that might warrant giving them

---

unyielding, and thus, moribund. Following Riggs, I would also point out that the VDP model need not be read along instrumentalist lines. That is to say, the outcome of knowledge is not the only value to the virtuous doxastic practice (Riggs, "Reliability and the Value of Knowledge," 81).

an important role in epistemology."[21] The VDP model is meritorious, on a macro-scale, precisely for the reason for which Baehr faults other non-religious virtue epistemologies. I have developed the VDP model in response to one specific substantive, philosophical aporia: that "on the ground" accounts of interreligious dialogue attest to strengthened rather than weakened religious belief. Because the VDP model works in relatively unchartered territory (religious virtue epistemology), the charge of relativism cannot or does not apply in the same way that it would in the area of religious epistemology in general. That is to say, the objection itself needs to be reformulated.

As it stands, the relativism charge is as follows: if agents form beliefs in epistemically good ways then they are *prima facie* justified at least in their beliefs, regardless of how those beliefs stand in relation to one another. While I concede relativism for *prima facie* justification, I argue that the approach to *ultima facie* justification (discussed in the following section) is the way to overcome the real force of the charge of relativism. The clause beginning with "regardless" is the critical part. The concern about relativism is that the VDP theory makes it possible for all agents to have equal claim (in terms of justification) on their religious beliefs. The reason traditional epistemological approaches are able to militate against the relativism charge is because they set up epistemological systems wherein agents are actually in competition with one another over epistemic "resources" (evidence) for belief formation and justification. In these systems, belief justification is a zero-sum game. Because the VDP theory grants credibility to a significantly broader swath of epistemic "resources" for belief formation and justification, agents do not compete for these resources and thus it will look as though (from the view of traditional epistemological frameworks) "anything goes."

Keeping the concerns of relativism in view, a more pertinent question to raise would be the following: given the VDP theory of belief formation, how does the theory propose to mitigate *laissez-faire* justification played out on large scale? How do we assess various religious beliefs when we, like the women of Philadelphia, find ourselves continuously engaging with and learning from others who appear to us sincere, thoughtful, and *even justified* in their religious beliefs? The way to respond to these questions is first to acknowledge the disconcerting nature of the objection and then attempt to move forward, provisionally, toward a theory for an assessment of diverse religious belief in relation to each other. This theory

---

21. Baehr, "Character in Epistemology," 497.

is the theory of *ultima facie* justification. In the following (major) section of this chapter, I construct a detailed theoretical account of *ultima facie* justification. This account contributes toward discounting the relativism charge because it permits normative claims to be made (carefully) about beliefs that are the outcomes of virtuous doxastic practices.

Dialogue as "Live" Comparison and the Justificatory Standard of Participative Practice

The motivation for the VDP model is to make sense of the fact that people claim to have their religious beliefs strengthened rather than undermined by the awareness of conflicting religious beliefs. Interviews and discussions with the Philadelphia women's interreligious dialogue group provided the substance for this claim in chapter 3. If the VDP model makes the case that virtues and virtuous doxastic practices are learned in the context of community, how is it possible to claim that an interreligious dialogue community, which involves people from *multiple* religious communities, allows for the exercise of various virtuous doxastic practices?

How do people from diverse religious communities agree upon a set of virtuous doxastic practices in interreligious dialogue? The women of Philadelphia offer examples of strategies for arriving at an agreed-upon virtuous doxastic practice through dialogue. In particular, the guidelines they developed together and drew upon for sharing their spiritual autobiographies testify to this. The following is an excerpt from the instruction sheet of guidelines for the spiritual autobiography exercise:

> Questions [about someone's spiritual autobiography] should be for the purpose of clarification or deepening understanding. This is not the time to challenge assumptions or to offer contradictory or personal experiences . . .] Participants should write their responses to any part of the story heard, to list questions they have or topics about which they would like future clarification. Pause a couple of minutes to do this after each presenter. This will help to constructively channel (and recall) any emotions stirred up by the story and help us to plan the content of future dialogue sessions.

In short, their instruction sheet recommends a listening process, which entails specific "dos" and "don'ts" of deep and respectful listening. They discerned these guidelines through enacting them, thus allowing their experience to structure organically these descriptive "rules." The women's

Ultima Facie *Justification and Participation through Practice*

narrative engagement through sharing spiritual autobiographies depends upon their listening practices, just as believers achieving justification for their beliefs depends upon their virtuous doxastic practices.

Another important question is whether the VDP model effaces difference and makes the relativistic claim that all virtuous doxastic practices are, in the end, the same thing (and this is why beliefs may gain *ultima facie* justification in this particular context)? If not, what are the resources within the VDP theory for negotiating among diverse virtuous doxastic practices and making assessments of them and the beliefs to which they give rise, rather than just resting at the answer of relativism?

Because this is an endeavor to show that members of multiple epistemic/religious communities are able to come together to engage in a VDP and form reliable beliefs out of that practice that may approach *ultima facie* justification—precisely through that practice—it is necessary to introduce a theory of how virtues and VDPs from diverse communities relate to each other. To construct this theory, I weave together the philosophical, theological, and social theoretical insights of Yearley, Clooney, Habermas, and McClendon. None of these thinkers theorize about interreligious dialogue, doxastic practices, or virtue epistemology per se and, yet, their reflections provide important resources for making sense of *ultima facie* justification theoretically.

Because dialogue participants truly engage with each other and witness multiple VDPs, they are presented with real disagreement regarding their religious beliefs and practices. Disagreement demands resolution or, at least, substantial response. In resolving or responding to disagreement, the VDP theory encourages (in Clooney's terms) subtle, provisional, and yet normative assessments of belief justification. Agents form beliefs through the exercise of virtuous doxastic practices; when these beliefs are formed through the exercise of interreligious dialogue *qua* virtuous doxastic practice, they may move toward *ultima facie* justification.

As resources for constructing interreligious dialogue as the distinctive context in which *ultima facie* justification is possible, I incorporate into the VDP theory Jürgen Habermas' discussion of the critical relationship between communication and community and his theory of the ideal speech situation, and James Wm. McClendon's exploration of the theologically transformative power of biography and discussion of participation. Finally, I propose that the VDP theory's standard for *ultima facie* justification is a kind of contextual justification that emulates in several salient ways the "genuine option situation" contextual justificatory standard developed of William James (although the VDP's standard of justification is discontiguous with James' standard in one important way).

Scholarly Comparative Theory and Interreligious Dialogue

Lee Yearley and Constructing Analogues for Comparison

Yearley's central work is a close comparative study of the virtue of courage as theorized by medieval Christian philosopher Thomas Aquinas and fourth century Confucian philosopher Mencius. In the course of actually making this comparison, Yearley also offers a substantial theory of the scholarly method of comparison. In other words, his discussion attends both to the content of the comparison and to the theory supporting that comparison. Yearley contends that comparative virtue theory demands more than a "simple imposition of categories" from one context onto another and instead involves "analogical predication." He defines analogical predication as such: "Through analyzing the ordered relationships among analogical terms, we can preserve both clarity and textured diversity, and thereby fully articulate similarities in differences and differences in similarities."[22] To achieve analogical predication, Yearley argues, the theorist (in the case, Yearley himself) must choose a focal point in his or her "home discourse."[23] His focal point is on a single virtue (courage). He works to give a highly "textured presentation" of courage in his home discourse (in this case, the Western philosophical tradition is his home discourse) as well as in the "other" discourse (Confucian philosophy) before comparing the two.[24]

While Yearley works with great care and precision not to impose categories, he does not imagine that Aquinas and Mencuis are so far apart in their understanding of courage as to be unrecognizable to one another. The very fact that these thinkers are being compared analogically—however carefully—suggests a connection or relation between them. In this work, Yearley advises, "We [comparative theorists] must use our imagination, then, to examine and construct analogues, to set and reset focal

---

22. Lee Yearley, *Mencius and Aquinas*, 188. Yearley continues, "The fact that this approach involves ongoing operations, continuing performances, is extremely important. It does not rest on applying a static structure or a fixed theory to material, and therefore it cannot produce the desired results as would a mechanical implement."

23. Ibid., 191.

24. Ibid., 173.

and secondary meanings and to articulate their relationships."[25] Yearley's imaginative work to bring together Aquinas' and Mencius' respective accounts of courage (setting and resetting focal and secondary meanings) exemplifies his theoretical commitments about the possibility and fruitfulness of comparison.

Although this is not a project in comparative virtue theory, Yearley's observations are indispensable for making sense of how virtues and virtuous doxastic practices across diverse communities may be related to each other. To discern the precise connection between Aquinas and Mencius on the virtue of courage, Yearley invokes the categories of primary and secondary theories. Primary theories, Yearley explains, allow people to "explain, predict, and control most normal situations." They are the implicit background theories that people use to get around in the world. Primary theories will not vary much from culture to culture. They apply to mundane aspects of life such as how to take shelter from the weather or how to collect water. Secondary theories, on the other hand, are those theories that allow people to explain "distinctive, peculiar, or distressing" occurrences. These are culturally situated and express ideas about, for example, gods and supernatural powers; they will vary enormously across cultures.[26] Virtuous doxastic practices function as both primary and secondary theories (or better, have functions on both primary and secondary levels) and these distinctive functions (as "primary" or "secondary") are rooted in both their Alstonian and Zagzebskian heritages.

Virtuous doxastic practices, insofar as they are derived from Alston's theory of doxastic practices as the processes through which we reliably form justified beliefs, work on one level like Yearley's definition of a primary theory. Doxastic practices are the processes that allow people to "explain, predict, and control" normal epistemic situations and they are relatively invariant across cultural contexts. For example, every culture instills in its members a doxastic practice for seeing. Religiously speaking, for example, every religious tradition teaches its followers a doxastic practice for perceiving God or truth about reality. When the Roman Catholic members of the Philadelphia women's dialogue group narrate their experiences of receiving Holy Eucharist as a means through which they commune with God and their community, the other women can understand this because they can identify a practice in their own tradition

---

25. Ibid., 200.
26. Ibid., 176.

that likewise allows them to commune with God and their community.[27] Here, various distinctive VDPs are compared at their primary level.

Virtuous doxastic practices, insofar as they bear resemblance to Zagzebksi's theory of virtue as a character disposition embodied in persons in the context of specific communities, can also be likened to Yearley's definition of secondary theories. The way that virtuous doxastic practices are learned and utilized will be specific to cultural context. Thus, for example, different cultures will teach their members different ways of seeing and will do so by different means. To draw on Alston's example, it might be the case that some cultural groups teach their members Aristotelian "sight" while others teach Whiteheadian visual perception. Thus, different religious traditions will have vastly distinctive virtues embodied by their followers and patterns for embedding these virtues in their followers. While Catholic Eucharist is recognizable to the non-Catholic interreligious dialogue members as a process for communing with God and community on a primary level, it is—on a secondary level—a highly specific and contextual way through which members of the Catholic faith engage religiously that cannot precisely mirror any other type of practice.

Yearley's idea and use of primary and secondary theories is fundamentally a heuristic device that provides a key for understanding the various layers involved in the process of comparison. Just as the comparative theorist follows the comparative method that Yearley advocates, those involved in interreligious dialogue also must use their imagination to examine and construct analogues between their own virtuous doxastic practices and the virtuous doxastic practices of their companions—this collective act of comparative imagination is precisely the "virtuous doxastic practice" of an interreligious dialogue community. "Primary" and "secondary" are simply heuristic tools that are used—either organically or explicitly—to get a handle on how these analogues are effectively constructed and employed.

The process of dialogue, I argue, is itself live "comparative" contact with diverse religious believers. We hear the women of Philadelphia tell about their efforts to listen to each other with more keen ears and with greater sympathy in their own comparative process. Hina's comment in chapter 3 suggests an example of this effort: "We try—even as we are bringing out whatever it is that we don't agree with—keeping our views

---

27. Elli shares the example of listening to Catholic members talk about receiving communion. Interview by Mara Brecht, July 20, 2007, Philadelphia, PA, digital recording.

really, really open to listening for another . . . And I think we do try to listen to the other, to a different point of view, which doesn't always answer your question . . ."[28] She notes that the women of the group continue to listen not only when they do not agree but also even when their questions are not being answered. This kind of listening—the kind that listens to even what is difficult to hear—is a discipline. This collective discipline is in line with Yearley's proposal for careful and ardent comparative theoretical work in constructing analogues and moving out of the comfort of one's home discourses. People presume a certain level of familiarity with others' "primary" virtuous doxastic practices and, in attentive comparative conversation, they hash out and make sense of their unique "secondary" ones together.

Francis X. Clooney and Artful, Comparative Reading

Clooney, a long practitioner of comparative theology, offers his wisdom on the possibility of religious comparison. Clooney's reflections on theoretical method of comparison, like Yearley's, can be translated appropriately for the context of interreligious dialogue. These reflections are invaluable for understanding how VDPs function across contexts and how the beliefs that arise out of those practices can be tested for justification in an interreligious context. Clooney's comparative scholarship has largely been focused on the comparison between the Roman Catholic tradition, texts, and theology and Hindu traditions, texts, and theology.

Comparison, Clooney states, "is ultimately an art."[29] As an art, comparison is neither formulaic nor necessarily constrained by disciplinary boundaries. That is to say, comparison does not follow a strict method or draw only on one canon of resources; it will be *sui generis* in both how it proceeds and what comparative material it engages. This does not mean, however, that there are not more or less proper ways of entering into comparison and more or less fruitful methods for comparison. Clooney notes some of these ways according to his own kind of "best practices" approach: he draws on his years of experience and the insights he has learned from other comparative theologians to delineate "how we might best read religiously" and engage in comparison.[30]

---

28. Interview by Mara Brecht, December 16, 2007, Philadelphia, PA, digital recording.

29. Clooney, *Comparative Theology*, 47.

30. Ibid., 59.

His approach to comparative theology can be summarily articulated as follows: "Comparative practice occurs," Clooney states, "when *acts* of reading have been undertaken, as we read back and forth across religious borders, examining multiple texts, individually but then too in light of one another."[31] Significantly, these acts of reading ought to be guided by authorities of the other tradition. He writes, "Reading *with* readers in the other tradition entails accountability, learning with deference."[32] Comparison is an art that takes place through acts of reading that engage multiple religious texts in multiple settings and that yield to the insights of those within the tradition from which the text is drawn.[33]

Clooney's own mode of comparison is primarily textual and "read" is the appropriate verb for describing his method. "Read," however, may be construed more broadly to encompass a range of activities (e.g., one can "read" a piece of art, an expression on a friend's face, or a social situation) that fit the purposes of this book's discussion (i.e., interreligious dialogue). Using this inclusive understanding of "read" and recalling Yearley's language in his reflections on comparison, it is possible to take the following away from Clooney: comparison most fruitfully takes place when a person examines or "reads" something (a religious text, tradition, object of worship, piece of art) from within her home discourse, then from within the discourse community out of which the object comes, and then back again—all of which is guided by the authorities of one's own and the other's tradition.

Through dialogue, interreligious dialogue participants "read" each other by traversing the boundaries of their home communities and returning again and repeating the process. The dialogue participants act for each other as authoritative guides to "reading" the various practices and beliefs introduced through dialogue. They organically construct analogues and sort out the primary and secondary levels of their virtuous doxastic practices. Karen gives an example of this process in her description of the

31. Ibid., 58.

32. Ibid., 64.

33. Another central feature of Clooney's understanding of comparative theology is that it be done from the perspective of "faith seeking understanding" (ibid., 10). Comparative theology is fundamentally an "alliance of faith and inquiry" (ibid., 36) and, thus, religious faith (of some sort) is a prerequisite for real comparative work. Because I am dealing with interreligious dialogue, I presume, in accordance with Clooney, that this work grows out of faith commitment. While it is not necessarily the case that all people who participate in interreligious dialogue claim membership to a religious tradition, on some level they share a common, faithful desire for understanding or relating to the religiously ultimate.

Ultima Facie *Justification and Participation through Practice*

group's participation in a Baha'i new year celebration. Lelia, a Baha'i member of the interreligious dialogue group, hosted a Baha'i new year's festival for the group and guided them through the event, both ritually and theologically. Karen reflects on how taking part in this religious holiday (with Leila as her guide) provided her with the opportunity to see points of comparison and contrast between Easter and Passover (two religious celebrations in which she and her family regularly take part) and also imagine ways in which aspects of the Baha'i ritual might shape how she takes part in her home religion's celebration.[34] Karen's reflections support Clooney's contention that what we learn about others' religious beliefs and practices will affect what we "know" about and how we live out our own.

Interreligious Disputes and the Role of Normative Assessments

In interreligious dialogue, just as in scholarly comparative theology, persons of "different linguistic and cultural dispositions"[35] interface with each other. In conversation with Yearley and Clooney and through the examples offered by the Philadelphia women, the previous section was directed toward showing how interreligious dialogue participants organically sort through the primary and secondary levels of various VDPs in order to effectively compare various practices and the beliefs that arise out of those practices. In many cases this comparative process will lead to substantial disagreement or conflict among beliefs and practices.

Clooney gives an example from his scholarship on the comparison between Aquinas' understanding of *imago Dei* in the *Summa* and the issue of likeness with God in Vedanta Desika's *Essence of the Three Holy Mysteries* to illustrate the movement from "interreligious comparison" to a sophisticated "interreligious dispute."[36] Similarly, the women of Philadelphia note on multiple occasions that conflict bubbles to the surface regularly throughout the course of their decade-long, extraordinarily rich "comparative" conversation. For my purposes here, the details of the dispute between Aquinas and Desika that Clooney discovers and the conflicts that come about in the course of the Philadelphia women's conversation are ancillary. Of crucial significance is *how* disputes arise from careful comparative work and, more importantly still, what the outcomes of these disputes are.

---

34. Interview by Mara Brecht, August 18, 2008, Philadelphia, PA, digital recording.
35. Clooney, *Comparative Theology*, 164.
36. Ibid., 120.

Virtue in Dialogue

In the second chapter, I examined epistemologists (McKim and Feldman) who advise tentative or suspended belief in the face of diversity. They do so, I argued, because of their normative, evidential foundationalist, and internalist commitments: these epistemological principles led them to see religious diversity as entailing epistemic disagreement. This project has been, in large part, an effort to overturn that epistemological way of understanding religious beliefs and, thereby, the epistemological significance of religious diversity. And yet, I here commend scholarly and "live" comparative work for bringing about dispute and conflict. Is this not a contradiction?

Feldman, McKim, and others like them are problematic not because they suggest that epistemic conflict grows out of religious diversity, but rather because of the way they trace this conflict. What is at issue is how they understand religious belief; namely, that beliefs are *a priori* in conflict on foundational (evidential) grounds (i.e., the very ways that religious beliefs come about and are grounded in conflict). The conflicts these epistemologists identify are conflicts generated from diverse religions—religions that are constructed as isolated monads—bumping into one another. They are never the conflicts generated by interreligious comparison or dialogue. In other words, their epistemological models rule out—in principle—real conversation among members of diverse religious traditions and instead deal only with anticipated conflicts.

The epistemological model I develop is meant to allow for real conflict and dispute that *follows from* interreligious engagement. In chapter 1, I advocated a "taking belief seriously" stance and also adopted Griffiths' "uneasiness" conditions. Taking this stance and recognizing these conditions entails seeing that religious traditions are richly textured, that the members of these traditions make real claims to truth, and that the virtuous doxastic practices exercised by believers bring about distinctive religious beliefs, which—at times—will be in conflict. Both Clooney and the women of Philadelphia draw out examples of what is truly *interreligious* conflict rather than the conflict of religious diversity.

The conflicts and disputes realized by Clooney and the Philadelphia women lead to questions about both the beliefs and VDP practices of one's home communities and those of the communities of religious others. This, in turn, leads to normative questions about both one's own and others' VDPs and the various beliefs that arise out of those practices. Clooney writes, ". . . truly comparative work does not stop with detail, but must grapple also with the normative issues and truth claims always implicit

Ultima Facie *Justification and Participation through Practice*

in comparative study."[37] Insofar as interreligious dialogue participants engage in live comparison and "read" each other's traditions through dialogue, they will, like Clooney, be brought to questions about the truth or justification of their diverse beliefs.

Clooney's comparative scholarship ". . . does not seek a theory by which to account for all religions or to rank them from one's tradition's perspective"[38] nor does he presume an ". . . overarching narrative that explains, already and in advance, how we are to make our own the multiple religious insights and experiences of the human race."[39] Still, Clooney aspires to make some evaluative and normative claims. He states, "Subtler, provisional theological assessments become the norm [in comparative theology]."[40] The VDP theory, likewise, aims at similar kinds of assessments about the epistemological justification of believers.

The VDP theory is not designed to be a method for objectively arbitrating diverse religious beliefs as they are propositionally formulated. That is, this theory cannot be employed to create a ranked list of the religious claims, for example, "Atman is one," "Allah is God and Muhammad is his prophet," and, "On the third day, Jesus rose from the dead." At the same time, however, the VDP theory does not leave us without resources for distinguishing among religious beliefs that believers are unjustified in holding, religious beliefs that believers are *prima facie* justified in holding, and religious beliefs that believers may be *ultima facie* justified in holding. The epistemological assessments that are the outcome of applying the VDP theory are subtle, provisional, and—to add to Clooney's list—nuanced.

Participative Practice as a Justificatory Standard

In the course of dialogue, religious believers participate together in a virtuous doxastic practice unique to their interreligious dialogue community and test their beliefs for possible *ultima facie* justification. The VDP theory of justification runs as follows: Beliefs are *prima facie* justified if they are formed in such a way that coheres with what a virtuous person might believe in like circumstances and have been imagined to be so on the part of the believer. Beliefs move toward *ultima facie* justification by being considered in light of what a virtuous person might believe in unlike (different

---

37. Ibid., 50.
38. Ibid., 111.
39. Ibid., 105.
40. Ibid., 112.

though relevant) circumstances. *Ultima facie* justification functions as a higher state of justification than *prima facie* justification. It is an ideal state for believers to achieve in their beliefs.

Participation in the religious lives of others through live comparative contact is what brings one to test for possible *ultima facie* justification. Thus, the work done in interreligious dialogue is the condition for the possibility of *ultima facie* justification. Importantly, the women of Philadelphia do not claim to reach agreement with each other about their religious beliefs when they have sophisticated interreligious disputes. The epistemological "end state" of interreligious dialogue as a virtuous doxastic practice, then, is not that all diverse believers' beliefs converge into one unified set of beliefs; moving toward *ultima facie* justification is not synonymous with reaching agreement.

Rather than reaching agreement about beliefs, the women of Philadelphia claim to find "a better way of being" and to "evoke the luminous" together through their dialogue—a dialogue which, I have argued, allows for real interreligious disputes and raising serious normative questions. In the following subsections, I place the women's "on the ground" formulation (that dialogue results in finding a better way of being and evoking the luminous) in conversation with the theoretical work of Habermas and McClendon to hypothesize about the precise function and standard of *ultima facie* justification.

Jürgen Habermas and the "Ideal" of Ultima Facie Justification

Habermas' social philosophy and moral ethical theory illuminates two, interrelated features of the function of *ultima facie* justification. First, *ultima facie* justification is an ideal epistemic state. The word "ideal" connotes that it is a state to which we constantly aspire. Second, *ultima facie* justification is closely linked to social community. *Ulitma facie* justification, I have stated, is ultimate justification that takes into consideration all relevant factors. It is an ideal state not because it is utopian or nonexistent but rather because it is constant in its demand. Braaten argues that Habermas' work, generally speaking, is therapeutically—as opposed to diagnostically—focused. In other words, Habermas' social theory attempts to offer a therapy or "method of treatment" for society rather than simply diagnose its problems.[41] (Habermas' particular interests are with

---

41. Braaten, *Habermas' Critical Theory of Society*, 10.

creating a true democracy that allows for the full social participation of all its members.)

To achieve full participation, Habermas develops a theory of human communication and advocates the "ideal speech situation" as one means by which participants can gain their voice and have agency as members in a social group.[42] The principles of this situation are: (1) all people who are able to speak and act are allowed to take part in a discourse; (2) all people have the right to question any statement made in the discourse; (3) all people are allowed to make any statement in the discourse; (4) all people are allowed to express their feelings, desires, and needs; (5) no people are allowed to prevent others from participation.[43]

---

42. The ideal speech situation is a model circumstance where all people have equal opportunity to participate in the conversation. Habermas develops this notion with an eye for how democracy ought to work (that is, the ideal speech situation grows out of a larger political theory) and for how consensus might be achieved in the public square. The way this situation comes about is by each participant in the conversation giving concrete attention to the concerns and voices of the other participants. In this, participants may be guided by agreed-upon rules for discourse. Habermas has been criticized for implicitly reinforcing an Enlightenment narrative that is invested in the notion of objective reason and ignores the reality of power imbalances among people. In chapter 3, I discussed feminist objections to the hegemonic, patriarchal form of discourse underwriting traditional interreligious dialogue. Specifically, feminists argue that interreligious dialogue traditionally involves a normative mode of communicating, which, in turn, reinforces the positions of those who benefit from such norms (male authorities of religious traditions). This feminist critique of dialogue applies also to Habermas and my invocation of him. It is possible to respond to this objection by arguing that while Habermas' theory may not account *a priori* for multiple forms of reason or power imbalances among participants, it also does not *a priori* rule out employing multiple forms of reason in discourse and adjusting power imbalances through discourse. Thus, it is possible to make a feminist appropriation of Habermas that takes into consideration the fact that patterns of communication reinforce particular social position and thereby constructs the ideal speech situation so as to reinforce the positions of those who have been systematically excluded, marginalized, disenfranchised, and so on. Moreover, because Habermas' ideal speech situation is communally constituted—rather than governed by external, abstract rules—it is up to the discourse community to define its own pattern of communicating and functioning. In this way the kind of "feminist appropriation" of Habermas' ideal speech situation comes "from below" rather than "from above."

43. Habermas, "Discourse Ethics," in *Moral Consciousness*, 89. These five principles relate to what Habermas calls the "rhetorical level of processes." Processes here is shorthand for "process of communication" (ibid., 88). The rhetorical level of processes is one of the three "levels of presuppositions of argumentation" that Habermas adopts from Aristotle. The other two levels are the "logical level of products" and the "dialectical level of procedures (ibid., 87). If participants in dialogue follow these five rules, they create and foster optimal conditions for conversation. Habermas states that

Virtue in Dialogue

Habermas uses the ideal speech situation, which is built upon the above five principles, to show a critical connection between the communicative patterns of a group and the social actions of a group.[44] For Habermas, Braaten argues, all human communication is ultimately oriented toward social relationships. To achieve relationships within social groups, communication must first aim at mutual understanding.[45] Habermas develops the notion of the ideal speech situation to propose how mutual understanding (and, following, rich social relationships) can be achieved through communication. The ideal speech situation functions, in his theory, as a device for gauging how well participants communicate and, following from that, what kind of actions they will undertake as a group.

While Habermas' theory has been criticized for being hopelessly unrealistic (and modernistic), it is precisely as an *ideal* that it is an illuminating concept. The ideal speech situation, like *ultima facie* justification provides an ideal standard by which groups may judge the circumstances of their comparative conversation, consider their progress in making assessments within that conversation, and determine what kinds of communal actions can be achieved out of that conversation. The Philadelphia women's interreligious dialogue group operates with principles that have the same aim of inclusivity as Habermas: they have rotating leadership so no single or few persons define the function of the group; they regularly reflect on their own processes and conversations to ask if they are going "too deep" or "not deep enough"; and they approach different theological topics and religious questions from a variety of angles and in a variety of ways, not all of which are dialogical (for example, they discuss the religious significance of fasting in different religious traditions but they also join together to celebrate Islamic *iftar*, the breaking of the fast, and hear about people's different types of fasts in their spiritual autobiographies).[46] These are a few examples of ways in which the women of Philadelphia experiment to achieve an ideal situation of dialogue where all the members can participate and make valuable contributions.

---

his goal is to make it so that participants in dialogue do not just see these as "mere *conventions*" but instead as "inescapable presuppositions" (ibid., 89).

44. Simpson, *Critical Social Theory*, 132–33. Habermas' statement, for example, that communicative reason is always embedded in the contexts of lifeworlds supports Simpson's analysis (Habermas, "Conceptions of Modernity," 152).

45. Braaten, *Habermas' Critical Theory of Society*, 57–58.

46. Group interview by Mara Brecht, February 12, 2009, Philadelphia, PA, digital recording.

Ultima Facie *Justification and Participation through Practice*

The collective Philadelphia women's VDP thus anticipates the very strategies Habermas suggests for achieving an ideal speech situation. In the context of interreligious dialogue, dialogue participants may invoke practices like those of the Philadelphia women as well as ask themselves questions that follow on Habermas' lead to act as "checks" on how they go about their comparative engagement: To what extent are others allowed to tell their stories? Do group members pay careful enough attention to the feelings and desires of others? What are the ways in which some people are implicitly or explicitly excluded from the conversation?

Habermas theorizes a direct and immediate relationship between communication and community. The women of Philadelphia also suggest a close relationship between the way they engage with each others' beliefs and the effect that has on both their dialogue community and the way they situate themselves in relation to the world. When the women of Philadelphia are able to imagine and live out a better way of being in the world through dialogue with diverse others—a dialogue that even provokes disagreement and dispute—and are able to "evoke the luminous" together, they are matching what Habermas would call an ideal speech situation. They are successfully communicating, achieving mutual understanding, and, finally, creating a social situation where all members can be full participants.

JAMES WM. MCCLENDON JR. AND THE BROAD CIRCLE OF PARTICIPATION

The epistemological "end state" of interreligious dialogue—for the purposes of this project—is ideally *ultima facie* justification. The goal of *ultima facie* justification is about participation rather than conformity or unity of belief. In a book titled *Biography as Theology* (2002), McClendon argues for a new direction in theology and, in doing this, he offers a rich insight into the meaning of participation for theological thinking. His basic premise, as he writes, is that theology "must at least be" biography. Said in other terms, theology is best done when it works from the lived examples of others and, in particular, "significant persons" (he examines the lives of Dag Hammarskjold, Martin Luther King, Jr., Clarence Jordan, and Charles Ives). McClendon states, "If by attending to those lives, we find ways of reforming our own theologies, making them more true, more faithful to our ancient vision, more adequate to the age being born, then we will be justified in that arduous inquiry."[47] There is a sense here that the

---

47. McClendon, *Biography as Theology*, 22.

work of using biography to inform one's theology, rather than simply the biographies themselves, is transformative.

McClendon elucidates further what happens when one studies biography:

> The character we investigate in a biographical study is always character-in-community. None of the persons we examine can be understood unless we understand his participation in ("participation" does not exclude controversy with and alienation from) communities of faith, and other human communities as well . . . If the voice is human, we can understand it at least in part. If it is interesting, let us listen.

McClendon contends that the task of entering into the life of another—listening to her stories, understanding her growth, seeing her as a member of her community—transforms one's own theological reflection.

A person is able to be transformed by another's biography because she has brought that person into the "orbit" of her own universe, so to speak. In other words, when others (through biography) become central to a person's life, she can be transformed by them. McClendon calls this the "circle of participation." He writes,

> The images [a person] discovers [in biographies] need not be mere metaphors, the convictions he finds mere propositions. They cannot be. To discover them in these lives is in some measure to incorporate them into one's own. The remedy for bias, then, is participation, and as the circle of participation widens, the center from which one began becomes ever less important. I do not mean that good theological work will lose its personal and individual flavor. Our circles of work overlap without becoming identical. The unity thus produced by the joint work of many workmen may be . . . composed of disparate elements often juxtaposed in unexpected ways, and often displaying no resolution prior to the resolution of the cosmos itself.[48]

McClendon's notion of circle of participation mirrors Habermas' ideal speech situation in that it represents a state of affairs where conversation with others breaks the dominance of one's own priorities, beliefs, and feelings in the horizon of one's awareness. As more people participate in the circle of conversation—and participate in a substantial and meaningful way—each person becomes increasingly attentive to the "human voice" of the others. This exemplifies the notion of sympathetic understanding

48. Ibid., 170.

discussed in chapter 5. A person does not lose sight of her own beliefs and concerns; instead she becomes invested in those of others.

While McClendon's interest is with the discipline of theology broadly, the notion that participation through biography can be theologically transformative is apposite to this discussion of interreligious dialogue. Examining interreligious disputes through the guided narrative "reading" of other's religious experiences, I contend, transforms the beliefs that are formed through virtuous doxastic practices. A circle of participation does not aim at leveling the concerns or beliefs of its members. Rather, it aims at allowing all participations to understand each other, to form mutually enriching relationships, and to have their beliefs (and themselves) transformed as a result. Participation is not only a remedy for bias, but it is also a remedy for relativism.

Participation in interreligious dialogue is thus not only theologically transformative as McClendon describes, but so too is it *epistemically* transformative. Clooney is sensitive to these kinds of transformations. He writes, ". . . as we learn another tradition in some depth, we will then begin also to re-read our own in light of that other."[49] In dialogue, we exercise our VDPs together. The comparative process thus can affect one's beliefs as well as help agents to reaim and develop their virtuous doxastic practices substantial and practical ways. Comparative contact can, Clooney holds, "change the dynamics of how we learn from another tradition and how we understand what we are doing when we name God in theology and prayer."[50]

As an example of the kind of transformation Clooney points to and McClendon calls for, recall from chapter 3 Elli's description of her reaction to hearing a dialogue partner's narrative account of the *Hajj*. Elli states, "I can just watch her light up, I want to know what that is about . . . If I see it in her, I know it's accessible in me. And I know it's accessible in others. I want to pay attention to that—when she lighted up, talking about her experience on *Hajj*."[51] Elli moves beyond simply listening to her dialogue partner's experience to raising a very profound question about that experience (e.g., what *is* it at work that religiously ignites my friend?) and, at the same time, allowing that question to shape her own practice (e.g., how do I enable that igniting power to animate my own practice?). Participation in interreligious dialogue may properly transform one beliefs and perfect ones VDPs in the way the Elli and Clooney describe. At the very least,

---

49. Clooney, *Comparative Theology*, 60.

50. Ibid., 123.

51. Interview by Mara Brecht, July 20, 2007, Philadelphia, PA, digital recording.

participation in interreligious dialogue may transform (by expansion) the context within which one tests her beliefs.

Epistemological theories, like the VDP model, which make sense of belief formation and justification through "context" (i.e., beliefs arise out of and are justified according to an agent's epistemic context and community) are commonly impeached on the grounds of their standards for justification. Specifically, the legitimacy of contextual justification is called into question as follows: if beliefs can only be justified in the context out of which they grow—rather than by external, universal standards like evidence—it promotes a narrow or circular form of justification.

When the context for justifying believers in their beliefs, however, is as wide as it can be given the circumstances, the criticism that a practice or theory is *only* contextual loses most of its force. Because interreligious dialogue involves virtuous agents and engages VDPs from a range of religious traditions, it is an example of a wide context for justification. I contend that the wide context created by interreligious dialogue allows for a standard of justification that is more rigorous and more authentically "human" than any of the standards suggested by traditional religious epistemology.

The women of the Philadelphia interreligious dialogue group enter into each other's lives (biographies) by recognizing the "human" voice of the other (to use McClendon's language) and (to use Yearley's language) imaginatively construct analogues with their own experience. They "read" each other's narratives together and allow themselves to be guided by the storyteller—on questions of clarification, points of interpretation, and issues of meaning—(to use Clooney's language) rather than stumble blindly through another's story. In doing this, they exemplify in practice what Yearley, Clooney, Habermas, and McClendon propose theoretically and, consequentially, widen the circle in which they participate and in which their beliefs become justified. The wider the circle of participation is, the more it is like the "ideal speech situation" and the closer one gets to *ultima facie* justification as a result of being in it.

Interreligious dialogue as a VDP can open the way toward *ultima facie* justification because it can provide the conditions wherein believers may reflect on their justified religious beliefs in light of what other virtuous persons might believe in unlike (different though relevant) circumstances. It is precisely through engaging in "live" comparative contact with religious others and entering into the lives of others through the stories of their experiences in a transformative way that believers become able to meet the other, in her different but relevant circumstances, and see her

Ultima Facie *Justification and Participation through Practice*

as a virtuous agent who expresses virtuous doxastic practices in her own right. Participants in interreligious dialogue can move toward *ultima facie* justification in their beliefs precisely because they forge these beliefs in conversation with the religious other.

The effort to engage comparatively and enter into the others' biographies is an unending task. Clooney writes that this kind of scholarly comparison is an ongoing and extended process that "cannot be undertaken merely to get to results known already"[52] and that "requires institutional as well as rational insight, practical as well as theoretical engagement."[53] The standards for comparison described by Clooney here illustrate well my claim about *ultima facie* justification—namely, that we always *move toward* rather than *possess* it. A process that draws on such a breadth of intellectual and social resources and activities (institutional insight, rational insight, practical engagement, theoretical engagement) and that is only responsibly undertaken as an open-ended task only reaches fulfillment by protracting the process and forestalling its conclusion.

The Justifying Standard for *Ultima Facie* Justification

Where McKim and Feldman follow in the epistemological footsteps of Clifford in developing an evidence-based justificatory standard for belief, the justificatory standard in place in the VDP theory bears some resemblance to James and his notion of the genuine option situation. The genuine option situation, for James, occurs when an option is presented to a person and that option has the characteristics of being living, forced, and momentous. If a person forms a belief in this kind of circumstance—where the option for belief is living, forced, and momentous—then the person may be justified in her belief, according to James.[54]

In a parallel way, the VDP theory of justification holds that if a person forms a belief in the situation of interreligious dialogue and that person had performed (epistemically) everything demanded of her (she engages in comparative contact in the responsible ways theoretically suggested by Yearley and Clooney; she forms her belief through an exercise of virtue; she considers her belief in light of what other virtuous people

---

52. Clooney, *Comparative Theology*, 61.

53. Ibid., 10.

54. This is not to say that religious belief is chosen *without regard to* evidence, but rather that belief, if chosen, is chosen because of the circumstance and not because of the amount or quality of evidence.

believe in both like and unlike circumstances), then the person may be or may be close to becoming *ultima facie* justified in her belief. The justificatory standard for *ultima facie* justification might be called, picking up on McClendon, a "broad circle of participation."

To repeat, McClendon writes, "The remedy for bias, then, is participation, and as the circle of participation widens, the center from which one began becomes ever less important."[55] The justificatory standard of a broad circle of participation is like James' genuine option situation in the sense that it has an unfixed, evolving, and circumstantial quality. More importantly still, the broad circle of participation is Jamesian in that it involves hope. James insists that—in a genuine option situation—it is "better and wiser to yield to our hope that it may be true" rather than wait to find out if what we believe is really true.[56] Belief formation in this circumstance, James writes, is a "certain particular kind of risk."[57] In short, James claims that we ought to be hopeful about the risk we take. Participants in interreligious dialogue make the choice to engage in interreligious dialogue because they, like James, recognize that something bigger is at stake.

Dialogue—and all that it carries with it (i.e., its unsettling and transformative possibilities)—is a risk the women of Philadelphia are willing to take because they are hopeful about its outcomes. Rachel's insightful comment points to precisely this idea: "[We] ask [ourselves] what is more important to us—being connected? Or, being in the world as it is?"[58] The women of Philadelphia draw a distinction between the world as it is and the world as it might be. Translating Rachel's comment into McClendon's language, the women of Philadelphia see their dialogue group as a creating a broader circle of participation (new world) wherein they are connected together through sharing their stories. Participants in the conversation have the opportunity to develop their epistemic virtues, to influence how their conversation partners are virtuously oriented to the world, and to put into practice their vision for their collective epistemic flourishing. As the circle becomes broader, it becomes more like the ideal speech situation. They will inevitably be transformed by the broad circle of participation they create, and, I argue, will move toward *ultima facie* justification in the beliefs they form in this context.

55. McClendon, *Biography as Theology*, 170.
56. James, *The Will to Believe*, 27.
57. Ibid., 26.
58. Interview by Mara Brecht, July 21, 2007, Philadelphia, PA, digital recording.

Ultima Facie *Justification and Participation through Practice*

The new world the women of Philadelphia create stands in contrast to the "world as it is," as Rachel puts it. This sense—that their conversation matters for creating a new way of being—also shores up with Habermas' thesis that there is a critical connection between communication and community. While the comparison to James illuminates how the broad circle of participation works as a contextual justificatory standard that importantly involves risk and hope, it is here that the comparison fails. For James' genuine option situation is unlike the VDP's broad circle of participation in that it is wholly individualistic. James develops a theory of justification that is concerned exclusively with individual persons. McClendon, Habermas, and Rachel all foreground community in their theories and reflections.

The concept of a broad circle of participation is a communal concept. Thus the justificatory standard for the ideal state of justification (*ultima facie* justification) in the VDP theory is communally based. James' justificatory standard, by contrast, is situationally based and individualistically oriented. In chapters 4 and 5, in particular, I argued for the necessity of an agent-centered epistemological model. The broad circle of participation justificatory standards shows that the VDP approach is not only agent-centered but, more radically, is agent*s*-centered.

In dialogue, people do not reject the particularity of their *prima facie* justified religious beliefs, biographies, theological reflections, or traditions. Rather, they learn to open themselves to plurality and the particularity of others' beliefs, biographies, reflections, and traditions. Their goal is not to achieve a *single* set of justified beliefs or a *unified* theological narrative. The outcome is that they widen the circle of participation in which they sit, speak, risk, hope, and form justified beliefs and, in so doing, their beliefs can move toward *ultima facie* justification.

The theory of virtuous doxastic practice developed here is built on a set of normative properties of agents and a systematic account of practice. The task of defining normative properties and giving a systematic account—both of which have a sort of "universal" quality—would seem to be in tension with the concluding assertion of this chapter. This assertion is that particular and situated religious beliefs may be finally justified only in the non-conventional context of a religiously diverse community. This is so not because these beliefs there merge into one coherent communal set of beliefs, but rather because there, in that context, religious beliefs are fashioned, scrutinized, and laid bare before the religious other. It is this tension between, on the one hand, a textured and yet "universal" account of epistemic agents/religious believers and, on the other hand, an understanding of the highly particular way in which religious beliefs are formed and justified (as the outcome of socially established, communal virtuous doxastic practices) that the VDP theory relies on in order to make sense of believers who are strengthened and, moreover, *justifiably strengthened* in their beliefs in the situation of religious diversity.

Believers may never reach *ultima facie* justification so long as intractable religious disagreements remain. In this case, the women of Philadelphia continue to persist in their beliefs, but recognize that it is impossible to discern at this time and place which of them, if any, is *ultima facie* justified in holding their beliefs. In the process of being "true to" each other, they may not be able to justify their beliefs fully. The VDP theory, at the very bottom, grants *the possibility of* an epistemological stalemate *in any situation that "falls short of" Habermas' ideal speech situation*. I have two responses to any objections to this declaration of stalemate. First, any position that does not conclude with a stalemate—at least on some level—presumes that epistemology is, as I previously put it, a zero-sum game. A large portion of this project has contributed toward demonstrating that these kinds of epistemologies are mired in insoluble problems. Epistemology may be *ideally* a zero-sum game, but in the real world with its limited resources and discourse communities, disagreements between beliefs may be intractable.

Secondly, my position is importantly influenced by the view that the imagined practical implications of a theory ought to shape that theory. Francis Schüssler Fiorenza argues that ". . . a theory is more warranted to the degree that it can guide praxis." He uses the term "retroductive warrant" to identify the practical criteria, which "structure praxis and guide forms of life," that function as warranting factors for theories.[59] David Tracy makes a similar point in different terms. He contends that theologians must pay attention to the "history of effects" of various theologies when shaping these theologies.[60] In other words, Fiorenza and Tracy incite theoreticians to imagine the outcome of their theories and allow those imagined outcomes to inform them.

The "retroductive warrant" and anticipated "history of effects" of the VDP theory is best captured in the words of the women of Philadelphia: there is a distinction between the world as it is and a world that nurtures "a better way of being." As I develop the VDP epistemological theory, I

---

59. Schüssler Fiorenza, *Foundational Theology*, 307.
60. Tracy, "Theological Method," 48.

am guided by consideration for what theory of religious belief best allows religious believers to put "salve on each other's wounds," to be members of a tightly connected circle of faith, and to "evoke the luminous" together. If the future I envision (through the VDP epistemology) encourages the kinds of insights into the religious ultimate and the sorts of enriching relationships among diverse people like those that have been forged in the Philadelphia women's dialogue group, it is my position that admitting a possible epistemological stalemate is a risk I am willing to take.

The conclusion of this chapter, then, is not that religious believers should forfeit their commitments to tradition or their commitments to orthodoxy. Interreligious dialogue, understood as the context wherein *ultima facie* justification of religious believers is made possible for believers, does not supplant or replace traditional religious communities; in fact, religious traditions and communities remain indispensable for agents to acquire virtue and become properly affected. Interreligious dialogue does, however, have important theological consequences—consequences that have gone heretofore largely unacknowledged—for those traditions and communities.

In the following chapter, I explore those consequences for the Christian church, broadly construed. I examine a document of instruction (*Dialogue and Proclamation*) issued by the Pontifical Council for Interreligious Dialogue and both formal and informal statements made by the World Council of Churches to show the way in which the church actively encourages dialogue as well as expresses openness to the transformation that may result from it. While both Catholic and Protestant church leaders offer positive appraisals of dialogue in these documents and display a genuine hope that dialogue fosters Christian faith, they also betray an underlying suspicion about the dangers of syncretism, which purportedly may be brought about by dialogue. In an effort to address (and allay) this suspicion, I identify three forms of transformation and pair each with a particular epistemic virtue. This proposal for a model of virtue-based transformation seeks to show the way by which distinctively *Christian* virtuous doxastic practices retain an ongoing epistemic and theological relevance for the transformed dialogue participant, regardless of the type of transformation she undergoes.

8

Christian Views of Interreligious Dialogue and Forms of Transformation

The previous seven chapters have worked toward building an epistemological model that makes sense of strengthened religious belief as an outcome of encountering religious others. Two guiding commitments of the virtuous doxastic practice epistemological model are to maintain a close—even indivisible—relationship between belief and practice and to take an agent-centered approach to understand belief formation and evaluate justification. Through dialogue, we exercise our multiple virtuous doxastic practices together. In this chapter, I explore forms of transformation brought about by interreligious dialogue.

I first examine a group of documents that addresses the issue of religious pluralism for the Christian community. These documents are authored by superintendent Christian bodies from both the Catholic and Protestant Christian communities, including the Roman Catholic Church and the World Council of Churches. *Dialogue and Proclamation*, which is the Roman Catholic Church's systematic statement on interreligious dialogue, encourages Christians to enter dialogue with an open attitude and to be prepared for transformation. While *Dialogue and Proclamation* acknowledges interreligious dialogue as something good and worthwhile, it also portrays dialogue as falling under the umbrella of evangelization and occupying an ancillary status in the faith lives of Christians. Likewise, the World Council of Churches gives an ambiguous estimation of dialogue. Its documents both encourage Christian participation in dialogue and also caution against problematic outcomes, such as syncretism.

Considering the arguments of epistemologists like McKim and Feldman that interreligious dialogue will lead to weakened religious belief, it is rather astonishing that official religious institutions would encourage dialogue at all. The purpose of this chapter is to begin from the positions

Christian Views of Interreligious Dialogue and Forms of Transformation

of the Christian Church (as reflected in *Dialogue and Proclamation* and multiple World Council of Church documents) and, in the second major section of the chapter, to discuss the virtuous doxastic practice model in relationship to these views of dialogue toward the end of explaining *how*, *why*, and *in what ways* dialogue is transformative. As a concept, virtue leads to or inherently allows for comparison (that is, the structure of virtue "naturally" sets up comparison). Therefore, comparison is an elemental component of engaging in virtuous doxastic practices. Interreligious dialogue is the stage on which this virtuous comparison plays out and is the way by which religious people can be transformed in the beliefs, convictions, and attitudes that are the outcome of virtuous doxastic practices.

The focus of my project has been to make epistemological sense of the accounts of the women of Philadelphia. In the final part of this chapter, I make *theological* sense of the accounts of the women of Philadelphia and interface with statements from the Christian tradition at large so as to widen the relevance of my claims about the transformative nature of interreligious dialogue. To accomplish this, I introduce three possible forms of transformation—the transformation of recommitting to one's tradition or "returning home," the transformation of double religious belonging or hybridity, and the transformation of conversion—and discuss them in connection with specific virtues—steadfastness, judiciousness, and prudence. In dialogue we exercise our practices together in a diverse community and thus critically examine and transform, when appropriate, our religious beliefs, attitudes, and convictions.

My interpretation of the transformation of returning home is inscriptive or affirmative while my expositions of the transformation of hybridity and the transformation of conversion are proscriptive or negative. By this I mean that my interpretation of the transformation of returning home *inscribes* it with detail and defines it affirmatively. By contrast, my interpretations of the transformations of hybridity and conversion work by *proscribing* their limits and calling attention (negatively) to what is *not* possible for these types of transformation. The reason for the difference in approach relates to the overall aim of this project, which is to explain, epistemologically, how one can be strengthened in belief in the interreligious encounter. Being transformed in the commitment to one's home tradition follows from being strengthened in one's religious belief.

Because the commitment of my project is to do justice to the women of Philadelphia and to work "from the ground up," the form of transformation to which I pay particular attention is that of being recommitted to one's home tradition. To provide the explanatory philosophical model for "returning home," I utilize Paul Ricoeur's theory of interpretation, particularly the concept of "second naiveté," in connection with the virtue of steadfastness to explain this form of transformation. While "returning home" is one outcome (and the outcome the women of Philadelphia best represent), it certainly will not be the case that every person who engages in interreligious dialogue will be strengthened in her beliefs or "return home" to her home tradition.

For this reason, I explore other kinds of transformation but do so by way of pointing out the limits of these forms of transformation. Specifically, I juxtapose my view of transformation of hybridity and the transformation of conversion with a proposal developed by Perry Schmidt-Leukel in *Transformation by Integration: How Inter-faith Encounter Changes Christianity* (2009). Schmidt-Leukel's contention is that if religious people appreciate what they find in other religious traditions, they should integrate elements from those other religious traditions into their own. While Schmidt-Leukel appreciates the depth and texture of dialogue's transformative possibilities, his proposal rests on an over-individualistic account of religious faith that cannot account for the communal nature of belief formation required by the VDP model. His position provides a foil for my own and, as such, enables me to identify the limits of these alternative forms of transformation. The chapter concludes with a reflection on the way the Christian community, at large, can interpret these forms of transformation, given current predominant Catholic and Protestants views of interreligious encounter represented in documents discussed in the first part of the chapter.

The Christian Community and Views of Interreligious Dialogue

Four basic questions guide my examination of statements from the Roman Catholic Church and the World Council of Churches: What is the function of interreligious dialogue for the church and in the world? What are the theological grounds the church offers for its understanding of dialogue's function? What role should interreligious dialogue play in the lives of Christians? What are the outcomes of interreligious dialogue imagined by the church? By answering each of these questions for both the Catholic and Protestant sets of statements, this section adumbrates a broad view of the Christian community's outlook on interreligious dialogue.

Christian Views of Interreligious Dialogue and Forms of Transformation

Throughout these sections, I call attention to relevant differences between the Roman Catholic and World Council of Churches statements in terms of authority, intention, and scope. It should also be noted that while this section aims to "take the pulse," so to speak, of the Christian church's view of interreligious dialogue, I draw on institutional sources to accomplish this. These sources may not accurately represent the views of Christians in general. Furthermore, "the Christian view of dialogue" is neither monolithic nor static and it would be misleading to portray it as such. However, these groups of documents provide clearly articulated and relevant resources for considering how the Christian community, at large, handles religious diversity and interreligious dialogue.[1]

The Roman Catholic Church and Dialogue's "Deepening" Capabilities

In May 1991, The Pontifical Council for Interreligious Dialogue (PCID), formerly called the Secretariat for Non-Christians, issued *Dialogue and Proclamation*. *Dialogue and Proclamation* (henceforth *DP*) followed closely on the heels of Pope John Paul II's encyclical *Redemptoris Missio* (December 1990), which addresses the continuing role of mission for the Church. *DP* states at the outset that its starting point is the Second Vatican Council's statement *Nostra Aetate* (October 1965), which discusses the relationship between the Church and other religious traditions.[2] I analyze

---

1. Statements on religious diversity made by the Roman Catholic Church and World Council of Churches provide important resources for assessing the Christian view, broadly, of interreligious dialogue. While there are innumerable Christian communities throughout the world (and history) that develop consequential theological positions on diversity, I have chosen these two particular groups because of their scope and reach. Examining documents from the Roman Catholic Church and World Council of Churches allows me to assess both mainline Catholic and Protestant positions and, at the same time, perspectives that, because of their respective member communities, have a global consciousness and significance. While evangelical Christians are a Christian group whose global presence and significance matches that of the Roman Catholic Church and World Council of Churches, their characteristically decentralized nature does not lend itself to providing parallel textual resources for the kind of study in which I am engaged.

2. For the purposes of this discussion, I take *Dialogue and Proclamation* to be a paradigmatic explication of the Conciliar document *Nostra Aetate* that articulates the Church's understanding of interreligious dialogue. Other significant documents from the magisterial tradition are relevant for this topic are as follows. Second Vatican Council, *Ad Gentes* (1965); Congregation for the Doctrine of Faith, *Dominus Iesus* (2000); International Theological Commission, "Christianity and the World

Virtue in Dialogue

DP through the frame of the four questions noted in the introduction to this section. The purpose of this analysis is to call attention to a prominent Catholic understanding of interreligious dialogue as an avenue of transformation both for individual believers as well as for religious traditions (including the Christian tradition).

As its title suggests, the goal of *Dialogue and Proclamation* is to discuss the basic purpose of interreligious dialogue and proclamation from the perspective of the Roman Catholic Church, and to address the relationship between these two activities. *DP* states that the purpose of proclamation is both to teach and to evangelize non-Christians (§87) and that it is an activity in "response to the human aspiration for salvation" (§67). Proclamation is soteriologically motivated and soteriologically oriented. Evangelization, as defined in *DP*, aims "to transform human culture and cultures with the power of the Gospel" (§75). While dialogue is an integral part of evangelization, *DP* states forthrightly that the Roman Catholic Church remains committed to dialogue regardless of the outcome (§53). Thus, while dialogue is important irrespective of the outcome and therefore does not actively aim at catechesis of the Christian message to others, it is still a constituent part of the Church's *evangelizing* mission. For these reasons, the concept of dialogue is at once complementary to and in tension with the concept of proclamation.

In interreligious dialogue, Christian participants act as witnesses and sharers of "Gospel values" (§9). However, this does not mean that Christians should enter dialogue with the intention of preaching the Christian gospel for the purposes of conversion. Rather, all participants in dialogue, regardless of religious tradition, enter interreligious dialogue in response to the particular divine call to which they are attuned (§84). In other words, Christians witness gospel values while Muslims represent values of the Qur'an through word and action while Hindus share their convictions about the *dharmic* path.

Theologically, Christian participation in interreligious dialogue extends God's initiative to dialogue with all humankind. Jesus Christ's ministry and the work of the Holy Spirit are foundations of this dialogic initiative. The pneumatological component of *DP*'s theological warrant is crucial here. Interreligious dialogue demands recognizing the Christological and Spirit-ordained aspects of the beliefs and practices of other

---

Religions," 149–66; Second Vatican Council, *Dignitatis Humanae* (1965); Second Vatican Council, *Gaudium et Spes* (1965); Second Vatican Council, *Lumen Gentium* (1964); Second Vatican Council, *Nostra Aetate* (1965); John Paul II, *Redemptor Hominis* (1979); John Paul II, *Redemptoris Missio* (1990).

religious persons. On one hand, the Council for Interreligious Dialogue commends dialogue because it is through interacting with religious others in an interreligious conversation that Christians can recognize the "the inchoate reality" of the "Kingdom of Christ" in religious others (§35). *DP* seems to be saying that dialogue has theological value because it opens Christians up to the presence of Christian grace in all places, even the hearts of non-Christians.

On the other hand, and perhaps more significantly, *DP* also draws attention to the notion that the Kingdom of Christ is inchoate in the hearts of *all* people, including Christians themselves: "In the last analysis truth is not a thing we possess, but a person [Christ] by whom we must allow ourselves to be possessed" (§49). Thus, the theological warrant for interreligious dialogue is as much about witnessing the presence of Christ's Kingdom in the hearts of others as it is about seeking a more complete presence—creating a more developed Kingdom—in Christian hearts.

DP lays out four forms of interreligious dialogue in which Christians engage. These include the dialogue of life, the dialogue of action, the dialogue of theological exchange, and the dialogue of religious experiences. The *dialogue of life* occurs in the quotidian, neighborly interactions we have with people in our communities. The *dialogue of action* involves diverse religious people working together toward a common goal and having a shared commitment to fight against injustice. In the *dialogue of exchange*, scholarly specialists seek to deepen their understanding of their respective religious heritages, and to appreciate each other's spiritual values. And, finally, in the *dialogue of religious experience*, people share their spiritual experiences, meditations, and prayers with each other.

DP emphasizes the idea that all Christians can and should engage in a variety of these dialogue forms. Specifically, *DP* notes that interreligious dialogue should not be seen as a "luxury activity" or "reserved for specialists" alone (§43). While interreligious dialogue is important—even necessary—for "integral development, social justice and human liberation," (§44) it is good not only for these outward social ends. In all forms of dialogue, *DP* notes that there must be "mutual acceptance of differences, or even of contradictions" and "respect for the free decision of persons taken according to the dictates of their conscience" (§41). *DP* also emphasizes the fact that Christians must be willing both to question the content of others' beliefs as well have the content of their own beliefs questioned (§32). Because the kind of interreligious dialogue recommended by the PCID non-defensively maintains the expectation that Christian beliefs will be challenged and cultivates a spirit genuine exchange, it must also address the possibilities of the realistic outcomes of dialogue.

According to *DP*, the Roman Catholic Church is not invested in interreligious dialogue only for the benefits it produces for persons in their daily lives and for the social ramifications, but also for the theological implications of dialogue (§38). *DP* notes three interrelated implications. First, Christians may be "purified" in their commitments as Christians (§49) by reminding them of the ways in which their beliefs have become moribund or distorted. Secondly, Christians may be converted to the faith of another tradition. *DP* implicitly acknowledges that the theological significance of dialogue does not always cut in favor of Christian beliefs. Dialogue demands, *DP* states, the willingness to "engage together in commitment to the truth and the readiness to allow oneself to be transformed by the encounter" (§47). It is possible that the transformation to which dialogue participants open themselves is the transformation of conversion.[3] Some may read this transformation as conversion away from explicit commitment to a Christian community. Christians and non-Christians alike open themselves to this possibility, if they engage in dialogue in the way prescribed by *DP*.

Finally *DP* encourages an attitude of deference to God's will in interreligious dialogue (§84). It also encourages participants in "prayerful discernment and theological reflection" on the ontological and soteriological significance of religious diversity (§78).[4] Christians should reflect on and pray over the fact that non-Christians find "spiritual nourishment" outside of Christianity and they are asked to rest in this mystery. *DP*'s final word on the outcome of interreligious dialogue is, simply, that, "Far from weakening their own faith, true dialogue will deepen it" (§50). *DP* reveals a bold willingness to see interreligious dialogue as in the service of faith formation—irrespective of religious tradition—rather than to its detriment.

---

3. While *DP* acknowledges the possibility of Christian conversion to another religious tradition, it does not welcome or advocate for this form of conversion.

4. *DP* suggests that dialogue presumes a certain understanding of God (i.e., God exists; the world is theistically governed). My own conception of dialogue does not demand that participants have any presuppositions about God. Rather, my understanding of dialogue presupposes only that it (dialogue) involves discussing religious beliefs (which may involve presuppositions about God) and the virtuous doxastic practices by which those beliefs are formed.

Christian Views of Interreligious Dialogue and Forms of Transformation

The World Council of Churches and Dialogue as a "Common Adventure"

The World Council of Churches (WCC) is a global fellowship of nearly three hundred and fifty Christian churches and denominations including member churches from the Anglican, Baptist, Methodist, Lutheran, Orthodox, and Reformed traditions as well as independent Christian communities. While the WCC neither includes nor itself acts as a governing body for the Christian ecumenical movement, it regularly convenes and produces documents and theological statements that are significant, although not necessarily authoritative, for its member churches. For the purpose of this chapter, I examine documents produced from WCC meetings and committee work to represent another (Protestant) mainstream Christian understanding of the significance of interreligious dialogue for Christians. The aim of my examination of the WCC documents—like my aim in examining *DP*—is to contribute toward the goal of "taking the pulse" of Christian churches on the issue of interreligious dialogue, but not to argue that all Christians would agree with the content of these documents.

That stated, there are three significant caveats to note. First, there is not a strict parallel between *DP* and the WCC documents or, more importantly, between the WCC itself and the Roman Catholic magisterial tradition. Some of the WCC documents explicitly note that they do not represent the official views of the WCC. As I have said, my analysis of them is not meant to be authoritative, but rather observational in nature. Secondly, these documents focus on both interreligious dialogue and religious pluralism. Because there is more literature in the area of religious pluralism (rather than interreligious dialogue), I extrapolate from these general statements on the grounds that interreligious dialogue is an important aspect of religious pluralism. However, I acknowledge that it is possible to separate these issues (religious pluralism and interreligious dialogue) along theoretical and practical lines. Thirdly, it is necessary to note that some documents represent the official positions of the WCC while others are preparatory material or the product of theologically innovative projects. Given this, the documents may be weighted according to their nature.

Although the WCC did not begin meeting as a formal association until after World War II, Christian leaders from across the globe voted the WCC into being in 1937 and 1938. The collective decision to establish the

Virtue in Dialogue

WCC grew out of the ecumenical movement, which is commonly viewed as beginning with a meeting of international missionaries in Edinburgh, Scotland in 1910. In 1928, the missionaries convened in Jerusalem and by its 1938 meeting in Tambaram, India, the issue of Christianity's relationship to other faith traditions was a central topic of discussion. Since its very inception, then, the question of non-Christian religious traditions has been at the heart of the WCC's concerns. In 1971, the WCC founded the Sub-Unit on Dialogue with People of Living Faiths and Ideologies. After extensive (and contentious) discussion about the relationship among Christianity, mission, and non-Christian religious others during the 1975 meeting in Nairobi, Kenya, the WCC articulated the need to "clarify further the nature, purpose, and limits of interfaith dialogue."[5]

This history, along with statements from the WCC documents themselves, point to the idea that interreligious dialogue is a *necessary* means by which Christians relate to the world. That is, the WCC shows an awareness of the deep and unavoidable reality of interreligious encounter, both historically and today. The WCC documents identify key facts about the status of the Christian church and religious identity in a globalized, technologically driven world. The WCC recognizes that that today's communities are "more complex than they once were,"[6] and that while Christianity is in decline in many of its traditional geographic strongholds, it is a "dynamic force" in many new places.[7] Accompanying this simultaneous decline and resurgence of Christianity and the reality of increasing cross-religious interaction, the WCC notes the emergence of "new forms of religious commitment" wherein people "separate personal faith from institutional belonging."[8] Through these comments, the WCC isolates two significant phenomena. First, the geographic center of Christianity has shifted from Europe and the West to the global South and the Eastern hemisphere. Secondly, the symbolic "center" of religious belonging has shifted from being located in homogenous cultures and religious institutions to diverse cultures and a more diffuse notion of religious membership. In acknowledgement of these unique contemporary circumstances,

---

5. *Dictionary of the Ecumenical Movement*, s.v. "Dialogue, Interfaith," online: http://www.oikoumene.org/en/resources/documents/wcc-programmes/inter religious-dialogue-and-cooperation/interreligious-trust-and-respect/ecumenical-dictionary-interfaith-dialogue.html.

6. WCC, *Guidelines*, §I, 5.

7. WCC, *Religious Plurality*, §7.

8. Ibid., §6.

the WCC affirms that interreligious dialogue is embedded in the everyday lives of all people.

Two WCC sources, the *Baar Statement on Theological Perspectives on Plurality* (1990) and *Religious Plurality and Christian Self-Understanding* (2006), offer indications of the theological grounds for interreligious dialogue. The *Baar Statement* is the work of the WCC's Sub-Unit on Dialogue with People of Living Faiths and it represents the officially adopted position of the WCC. *Religious Plurality and Christian Self-Understanding* (henceforth *Religious Plurality*), by contrast, is a document written by twenty scholars affiliated with the WCC in preparation for the WCC's ninth assembly with the goal of highlighting key issues and offering suggestions for future directions for the WCC with regard to religious pluralism.

The *Baar Statement* provides a general theological warrant for religious pluralism that is focused on God and creation. Because "God's glory penetrates the whole of creation,"[9] Christians must "unequivocally" affirm that God is present in the "life and traditions of peoples of living faiths."[10] The *Baar Statement* goes on to state that it is "inconceivable" to confine God's salvific activity to any particular earthly or human institution (i.e., time period, place, religious tradition, culture).[11] This theological warrant for religious pluralism gives way to a positive estimation of interreligious dialogue; that is, God is present in all people and one way that Christians can affirm this presence is through dialogue.[12]

---

9. WCC, *Baar Statement*, §II.
10. Ibid., §IV.
11. Ibid., §II.
12. The WCC offers a very practical strategy for preparing Christians for interreligious encounter. In 1986, the WCC developed a study guide titled *My Neighbor's Faith and Mine: Theological Discoveries through Interfaith Dialogue* intended, primarily, for church groups. The study guide's instructions encourage the groups who intend to use the study to include clergy and lay, men and women, and, in particular, people with different theological perspectives. The instructions do not recommend that groups necessarily be interreligious (including people of different religious traditions), but do emphasize the importance of being ecumenical (including Christians of different stripes). The instructions go on to state that if the group is interreligious, group members should decide collectively ahead of time how the group will handle interreligious conflict. This, combined with the fact that the instructions stress the importance of ecumenism, suggests that *My Neighbor's Faith in Mine* is aimed primarily at preparing Christians for encountering religious others, rather than providing a guide for the actual encounter. The curriculum is divided into eight sections. Each section includes scriptural readings, poems, pictures, or case studies that are meant to provide jumping off points for discussion.

Virtue in Dialogue

Religious Plurality proposes a Trinitarian theological warrant for religious diversity. Rather than calling attention to only God's role as is the case with the *Baar Statement*, the document *Religious Plurality* calls attention also to Christ and the Holy Spirit. *Religious Plurality* "hopes" and "expects" that the "economy" of the Holy Spirit relates to all of creation, including non-Christian people.[13] The role of Christ is even more relevant when it comes specifically to interreligious dialogue. *Religious Plurality* states, "The mystery of the incarnation is God's deepest identification with our human condition, showing the unconditional grace of God that accepted humankind in its otherness and estrangement."[14] If Christians are to learn from the incarnation, this translates practically into "explor[ing] more fully the reality of other religious traditions and our own identity as Christians in a religiously plural world."[15] More specifically, the mystery of the incarnation and the examples of Jesus Christ call Christians to the virtue of hospitality and commands Christians to recognize intellectual limitations in grasping this mystery.[16]

While Christians ought to recognize their limitations with regard to comprehending the incarnation, they should engage in interreligious dialogue "without diluting their faith or compromising their commitment to the Triune God."[17] The WCC *Guidelines on Dialogue with People of Living Faiths and Ideologies* (henceforth *Guidelines*) defines interreligious dialogue as "a true encounter between those spiritual insights and experience which are only found at the deepest levels of human life."[18] Precisely because the WCC sees dialogue as not *just* a process of comparison or an opportunity to draw similarities between one's own and others' religions, Christians should not dilute their faith or compromise this commitment. To do so would be to devalue the very nature of dialogue imagined by the WCC.

On a communal level, interreligious dialogue challenges the Christian community "to develop a spiritual climate and a theological approach that contributes to creative and positive relationships among the religious traditions of the world."[19] On an individual level, interreligious dialogue

---

13. WCC, *Religious Plurality*, §32.
14. Ibid., §28.
15. Ibid., §11.
16. Ibid., §29, §45.
17. WCC, *Guidelines*, Introduction.
18. Ibid., § II, 22.
19. WCC, *Religious Plurality*, §8.

Christian Views of Interreligious Dialogue and Forms of Transformation

challenges Christians to better live out their witness to Christ and to more fully practice their Christian virtues. The WCC documents intimate that just as the example of Jesus Christ *demands* hospitality and humility in how Christians dialogue with religious others, interreligious dialogue also contributes toward *nurturing* these types of attitudes. *Guidelines* states, for example, that in interreligious dialogue, Christians learn to listen to others which, in turn, connects with the commandment to not bear false witness against one's neighbors.[20] In another instance, *Guidelines* note that Christians should not enter dialogue in the spirit of "triumphalism or condescension" but instead "humility."[21]

In a plenary address to a WCC meeting on Christian identity and religious pluralism, Archbishop of Canterbury Rowan Williams eloquently describes the way he envisions Christian engagement with religious plurality. These remarks are consistent with the WCC's expectations for Christian participation in interreligious dialogue, as outlined in *Guidelines*. Williams holds that it is loyalty and service to Christ that makes one a Christian. In turn, Christians are, like Jesus Christ, "enabled to intimacy" with God.[22] "To be a Christian," he states, "is not to lay claim to absolute knowledge, but to lay claim to the perspective [shown to us by Christ]."[23] Interreligious dialogue is not an occasion for Christians to proselytize non-Christians. Rather, dialogue serves to remind Christians of their particular witness to Jesus Christ and unique relationship with God, both brought about by Christian identity.

The group of scholars who crafted *Religious Plurality* expresses a need to "move beyond" theology that "confines salvation to the explicit personal commitment to Jesus Christ."[24] Again, while *Religious Plurality* does not represent the official position of the WCC, it is possible to see this position as congruous with the very foundations of the WCC. For, in its roots, the WCC creates a place for constructing a theological response to plurality and continues to carve out this place. At the WCC Central Committee meeting in Addis Ababa, Ethiopia in 1971, the WCC officially defined interreligious dialogue as "a common adventure" of all Christian churches. As *The Baar Statement* makes clear, the adventure of dialogue brings the question of the relationship between the mystery of the Triune

20. WCC, *Guidelines*, § III.
21. WCC, *Guidelines*, §I, 14.
22. Williams, *Address*.
23. Ibid.
24. WCC, *Baar Statement*, §III.

God and religious diversity to the fore of all Christian minds.[25] And, as more recent work of the WCC states, dialogue enables Christians to "fresh understandings, new questions, and better expressions" of Christian faith and commitment.[26]

Although the WCC takes a generally positive view of interreligious dialogue, there are also places where the WCC documents, like *DP*, offer an earnest acknowledgement of the challenges interreligious dialogue can pose back to Christians and the Christian church. The guidelines for dialogue outlined by the WCC commend the adventure of dialogue but also advise Christian participants to be "watchful and wide awake for God" and to consider to the extent to which syncretism (presumably engendered by dialogue) may be a risk of dialogue.[27] Skepticism toward dialogue is not entirely absent from the WCC's understanding.

At various places throughout the WCC documents, the authors make an effort to connect interreligious dialogue to examples from encounters with the other from the bible (citing, for example, Jesus' conversation with the Samaritan woman at the well) as well as to the ecumenical movement. *Religious Plurality*, for example, notes, "The biblical narrative and experiences in the ecumenical ministry show that such mutual transformation is at the heart of authentic Christian witness."[28] In other words, the WCC admits a realistic expectation for *all* forms of transformation that are possible through interreligious dialogue. Perhaps because the WCC movement is an ecumenical movement and fundamentally predisposed to talking across religious communal borders (albeit Christian borders), the WCC displays an acute awareness of the possibility of *real* "mutual transformation." *Religious Plurality* calls dialogue a "two way street" and states that Christians must be prepared to receive just as they are prepared to give.[29]

In the adventure of dialogue, Christians are called "to risk, to trust, and to be vulnerable."[30] While it can be enriching, a number of problems may arise including syncretism (as already noted), inauthenticity to the Christian message, and inauthenticity to the message of other religious traditions. Just as it is dangerous to compromise the Christian message,

25. Ibid.
26. Ibid., §V.
27. WCC, *Guidelines*, §II, 24.
28. WCC, *Religious Plurality*, §43.
29. WCC, *Baar Statement*, §V.
30. WCC, *Guidelines*, §III.

Guidelines warns also against misinterpreting other religious traditions and not encountering other religious people on their own terms.[31]

Comparing VDPs and the Transformative Nature of Interreligious Dialogue

Religious diversity makes us confront—head on—the fact that religious others do not believe our beliefs and do not engage in religious practices in the way we do. Interreligious dialogue heightens and intensifies this reality. Epistemically, as Griffiths argues, we become aware of the fact that our beliefs, which hold up in our own communities, would not necessarily hold up in others. If the Christian church, at large, understands interreligious dialogue to be transformative for both Christian believers and the Christian tradition, as my reading of *DP* and the WCC documents proposes, why and how is interreligious dialogue transformative and what exactly does transformation entail?

Comparing virtuous doxastic practices and the beliefs that are formed out of them is, in a sense, a part of the conceptual structure of virtue. Nussbaum notes that Aristotle's starting point for offering a theory of the virtues is to identify "certain spheres of human experience within which it appears that all human beings must make choices one way or another, given certain general features of the human form of life." By discussing virtues in this way, Aristotle not only makes a claim about human nature (namely, that what it is to be human is to be capable of acquiring virtues; this was discussed in chapter 5), but he also sets virtues up for comparison both within and across cultures.[32] Because I root my theory of virtue in Aristotle's theory of virtue, I import this option for comparison from Aristotle as well.

Comparison is not only a part of the conceptual structure of virtue, it is also the linchpin of the VDP theory of *ultima facie* justification. When religious people, like the women of Philadelphia, engage with each other through interreligious dialogue they necessarily and naturally make comparisons. Through the concepts of analogy as well as primary and secondary theories, Yearley provided theoretical resources for defining and defending this comparative process. Yearley cautioned against two competing impulses. On one hand, we must avoid the temptation to make idols of the other people with whom we are comparing. As Nussbaum

---

31. WCC, *Guidelines*, §II, 25–27.
32. Nussbaum, "Review: Comparing Virtues," 352–53.

summarizes it, idolatry involves "recreating [others] in our own image, refusing to see their differences from ourselves, making our world homogenous and safe again by erasure." On the other hand, we must avoid the temptation to see others as "alien and incomparable [and] in terms of difference and otherness alone."[33] Comparison carries an ethic of neither domesticating nor making alien religious others. When we do comparison well we move toward the possibility of *ultima facie* justification.

There is, however, no *ultima facie* justification without *prima facie* justification. The way that believers are justified in their religious beliefs is by having those beliefs justified first within the context of the religious community that were the condition for the possibility of their belief formation. Only after *prima facie* justification can believers move toward *ultima facie* justification. In interreligious dialogue, we compare our beliefs with those of others. Recall three fundamental components of the VDP theory: Comparison inheres in the concept of virtue. Virtue inheres in the notion of epistemic justification. *Ultima facie* justification is the end state of dialogue. To achieve this level of justification, a person's circle of participation, or the circle within which she learns and tests her beliefs, must widen. This widening inevitably leads to transformation.

What does transformation look like? In the remainder of this chapter, I examine three forms of religious transformation: the transformation of returning to one's religious tradition, the transformation of religious hybridity, and the transformation of religious conversion. While each of these forms of transformation may have validity (epistemologically and theologically), I am concerned principally with the transformation of returning to one's home tradition and for that reason, discuss it first and with greatest attention to detail.

Steadfastness and the Transformation of Returning Home

Ricoeur's basic argument is that in the process of becoming philosophically mature and realizing the historical and contextual circumstances that give rise to the religious symbols that are central to our religious lives, these symbols lose their power. However, through the interpretative process, it is possible to develop a "second naiveté" toward them, and, in so doing, the symbols are reinvested with power and meaning. I have developed an epistemological theory that I believe best explains how it is

33. Ibid., 347.

theoretically possible for belief to strengthened, rather than suspended or weakened, in the encounter with the religious other. Interreligious dialogue functions as a corollary to Ricoeur's understanding of interpretation: through dialogue it is possible for our religious beliefs, attitudes, and convictions to be transformed. By practicing the virtue of steadfastness, we are able to return to our tradition and see and experience it anew and, in the transformation of returning home, the original power and meaning of our traditions become known to us.

Ricoeur's Movement of Interpretation

Ricoeur begins with the premise that given critical awareness and philosophically sophisticated modes of thinking, people lose the ability to be captivated by symbols. Symbols and stories that were formative for our moral and religious lives are divested of meaning because we have lost our naiveté toward them.[34] The witches and wolves of Grimm's fairy tales do not frighten us because we recognize them as figures that exist to convey a larger message or principle. We do not dream about trekking through *Never Never Land* and imagine how we feel there because the place is no longer real to us. Rather than raw embrace, we contextualize and critically evaluate symbols and myths. And yet, Ricoeur thinks that there is something missing.

According to Ricoeur, when we are critical toward a symbol, we may *understand* its meaning, but we cannot think imaginatively from it. The goal of Ricoeur's interpretative theory is to move beyond merely understanding a symbol's meaning. The hermeneutical space to which Ricoeur pushes—the place beyond critical understanding—mimics, in character, our original relationship with the symbol or story. Ricoeur calls this second naiveté. When we achieve second naiveté toward a symbol we re-gain our sense of childlike wonderment about it and we are seized again by its power. Yet, we are not amnestic about our critical reflection on the symbol.[35] It precisely through this movement from immediacy to critical distance and back again to immediacy that Ricoeur thinks we are able to develop a creative response to the symbol.[36]

---

34. To have naiveté toward a symbol is to relate to it immediately—literally, without mediation.

35. Ricoeur writes, "This second naiveté aims to be the postcritical equivalent of the precritical hierophany" (Ricoeur, *The Symbolism of Evil*, 352).

36. Ricoeur intends his interpretative theory to be a way between two impasses.

We enter into interpretation not to rest at the critical stage of reflection, but rather because we want to return to the kind of immediacy we felt toward the symbol that we interpret. Symbols best express their power and meaning when we have an immediate relationship to them. However, because cognitive and philosophical maturity entails taking a critical perspective toward our guiding symbols and myths, these symbols and myths will lose their power as we reflect upon them. It is the task of hermeneutics to recapture the power of symbols. Interpretation is fruitful when it brings us back to place we began. "In short," Ricoeur writes, "it is by *interpreting* that we can *hear* again."[37]

The arc or trajectory of interpretation, as Ricoeur describes it, begins with "living in a symbol" and ends with "thinking from a symbol."[38] He states, "Thought here has a kind of movement of emergence, then replunging."[39] But why emerge if only to replunge? Why not remain at the level of living in the symbol if the way that we come to think from the symbol (the goal of interpretation) is in fact a certain way of living in it? Because of our cognitive or philosophical state, remaining in an immediate relationship with the symbols—continuing to live in a symbol—is not a choice. If we are to find meaning in our religious symbols, we are obliged to move through the process of interpretation.

Losing First Naiveté in Dialogue

For circumstantial reasons—namely that diversity is internal to our life worlds, it is inevitable that we will lose first naiveté toward our religious tradition and its virtuous doxastic practices. Interreligious dialogue makes the awareness of religious diversity explicit. In dialogue, we lose our original naiveté and our unmediated commitment to our own tradition (and

---

The push beyond critical reflection to second naiveté, Ricoeur hopes, will give rise to "a creative interpretation of meaning, faithful to the impulsion, to the gift of meaning from the symbol [the first impasse], and faithful also to the philosopher's oath to seek understanding [the second impasse]" (ibid., 348).

37. Ricoeur, *The Symbolism of Evil*, 351.

38. Ricoeur writes, "... modern hermeneutics entertains the project of a revivification of philosophy through contact with the fundamental symbols of our consciousness" (*The Conflict of Interpretation*, 297). When we begin to think critically about the myth and what it means, when we begin to see it as a myth in the sense of story, we enter into reflection. In a word, reflection is "demythologizing" (ibid., 310). According to Ricoeur, reflective philosophy is "precisely the opposite of a philosophy of the immediate" (ibid., 327).

39. Ibid., 308.

Christian Views of Interreligious Dialogue and Forms of Transformation

its virtuous doxastic practices). In inquiring of others' beliefs, we ask ourselves why and how we believe what we do. Whence does x belief come? What kinds of things do we do to support it?

Through dialogue, we recognize that we no longer have first naiveté toward our religious traditions and we develop both a critical perspective on the virtuous doxastic practices that give rise to our beliefs and a critical perspective on how we engage in these practices. We can no longer relate to it as we did before we acknowledged the presence of other religious options. In Ricoeur's language, we cannot "live" in our tradition in the way that we once had.

Gaining Second Naiveté and Returning Home

As Ricouer argues, it is from the "naive" perspective that symbols have the most power; likewise, it is from this perspective that our religious traditions convey the deepest meaning. When we encounter the religious other, we emerge from a world bound by our own religious suppositions into a world of seemingly boundless religious beliefs and practices, wherein we have the opportunity to achieve this second naiveté. The transformation of returning home, therefore, is initiated when we achieve a second naiveté toward our traditions and, from that, have transformed religious beliefs, attitudes, and convictions.

Because interreligious dialogue involves the comparison of disparate beliefs and virtuous doxastic practices, participants in dialogue are able to understand each of their communities' virtuous doxastic practices from a perspective that they previously did not have. They are able to see their own VDPs through the eyes of religious others. And from this, dialogue participants achieve a second naiveté about their practices and beliefs, and so return home—renewed—to live out their faith. The VDP approach shows how it is possible for people to be faithful to the tradition, but in such a way that transforms the way they hold to and participate in that tradition. By recognizing the limits of Christian claims and practices, and by comparing those claims and practices with other kinds of claims and practices, Christian participants in interreligious dialogue take a step toward rediscovering the beliefs, attitudes, and convictions that grow out of their VDPs. Emerging out of a world bound by the perspective of our tradition allows us to achieve second naiveté and replunge back into that tradition.

The group of religiously diverse women from Philadelphia, who have talked with each other regularly for over a decade, understand themselves to be strengthened—in their beliefs and practices, and in their identities and faith—through dialogue. They note various practical instantiations of the strength they gain through dialogue: because of dialogue, they are inspired to participate in their communities with new vigor; they find themselves exploring their traditions' histories and theologies with renewed spirits; and they engage in their daily religious rituals in a more full way. The virtue of epistemic steadfastness plays a central role in their conversations with each other and leads them to be strengthened in their religious resolve.

In chapter 6, I described the epistemic virtue of steadfastness and argued that steadfastness involves taking the proper, balanced attitude toward one's own beliefs in light of other beliefs. Chaim Potok's character Danny in *The Chosen* illuminated my understanding of steadfastness. Danny's commitment to his religious practice and community while studying Freudian psychology exemplified steadfastness. Because his studies raised fundamental challenges to the presuppositions of his religious worldview, Danny had to learn to renegotiate his relationship to his tradition in order to remain a part of it. Being genuinely open to challenges to one's background beliefs—as Danny was open to reading Freud—breaks the grip of first naiveté. Exercising steadfastness through this experience is the condition for the possibility of achieving second naiveté. The position of second naiveté leads to a transformation or re-investing, perfecting, and re-aiming our religious convictions in the communal exercise of our diverse virtuous doxastic practices. In short, steadfastness in dialogue leads to strengthened religious belief and, concomitantly, the transformation of returning home.

Beyond Returning Home

Not everyone will return home. Again, my project aims to show how it is epistemologically justifiable for the interreligious encounter to lead to the strengthening of one's religious beliefs and, following this, how it is possible for one to be transformed in one's position in her home community. Other forms of transformation brought about by dialogue are also possible. Perry Schmidt-Leukel develops a vision for the kinds of transformation encouraged by dialogue. Schmidt-Leukel functions as a foil to the transformation I imagine through the VDP epistemological model. I argue that the notion of transformative integration proposed by Schmidt-Leukel is predicated on an individually-based, subjective account of the way religious beliefs are formed and religious practices engaged. To explore this premise in full, I critically analyze the way Schmidt-Leukel constructs the interreligious encounter, and then discuss and raise questions about his expectations for the implications of integration on both the individual and communal levels. In the remaining sections of the chapter, I offer brief, creative sketches of the transformations of hybridity and of conversion and, paralleling the transformation of returning home, discuss them in relation to the cardinal virtues identified in chapter 6.

Perry Schmidt-Leukel and Transformation by Integration

Perry Schmidt-Leukel offers a theologically pluralistic vision of the transformation that is brought about through the encounter with the religious other. The transformation he envisions for Christians is the transformation of integration, which is to say the transformation of incorporating or integrating elements of other religious traditions into Christian theology, practice, and identity. Schmidt-Leukel describes two forms of transformative integration: multireligious identity and syncretism.[40] Multireligious identities are those that have been "formed and developed under the influence of several religious traditions."[41] Syncretistic processes are those that "integrate to a varying extent elements from other religious traditions."[42] Together, multireligious identity and syncretism fall into the category of what Schmidt-Leukel calls "patchwork religiosity" or "religious *bricolages*."[43]

---

40. Schmidt-Leukel discusses mutlireligious identity and syncretism separately. Although he does not define their relationship to each other—and here I run into the limits of his book as a collection of essays rather than a systematic argument—I take it that the multireligious identity and syncretism are "naturally" linked to each other and both fall under the larger category of "religious *bricolage*," a term that Schmidt-Leukel uses and I introduce later in this discussion. I also point out that Schmidt-Leukel is forthright about the prospects for his project to promote multireligious identity and syncretism. Throughout his discussion, he notes barriers to and difficulties with both integrative models. And yet, he maintains a positive outlook for the possibilities of integration: "As much as it is true that not everything can be combined, it might however be equally true that there is perhaps much more room for compatibility than we would initially assume." He states that his aim in exploring this compatibility is "to contribute to a more open-minded, less fearful and indeed constructive theological approach to [these phenomena]" (Schmidt-Leukel, *Transformation by Integration*, 65–69).

41. Ibid., 47.

42. Ibid., 67.

43. Ibid., 62.

Virtue in Dialogue

As an example of syncretism, Schmidt-Leukel describes a speech delivered to the WCC by Christian theologian Chung Hyun Kyung wherein she was accompanied by "Korean and Australian Aboriginal dancers" and invoked what she called "icons of the Holy Spirit" in the "spirits of women and men oppressed through the ages."[44] Schmidt-Leukel also references Thomas Merton's religious experiences in Polunnaruwa, Sri Lanka, which Merton writes about "in his diary entirely in terms of a Buddhist enlightenment experience," to describe mutlireligious identity.[45]

Reshaping Religious Believers and Traditions

Schmidt-Leukel's premise is that the good, the holy, and the true *ought* to be a part of any person's religious faith. He states, "I take it that, for example, a Christian who encounters the Buddha in such a way that thereby a deep and existentially relevant truth is revealed to him or her, has simply not the option to reject it."[46] Because we live in globalized societies, other religious traditions are necessarily a part of our worldview or religious consciousness. The encounter with the religious other through dialogue gives us the opportunity to reflect on the beliefs and practices of religious traditions that are not our own. If we discover deep and relevant truths in them, we are not "entitled" to reject these elements. Schmidt-Leukel states, "That which is genuinely appreciated cannot be rejected; it needs to be integrated."[47] By this logic, religious *bricolage* is the necessary outcome of genuinely appreciating other religious traditions.[48] Assuming that integra-

---

44. Ibid., 70. See Chung, "Welcome the Spirit." Schmidt-Leukel also cites the *New York Times* article that reports the event (Steinfels, "Beliefs").

45. Ibid., 50.

46. Ibid., 49.

47. Ibid., 7.

48. Appreciation is a key part of this formula. Significantly, Schmidt-Leukel does not identify appreciation as a "prerequisite of interfaith encounter," but rather sees it as something that grows out of the encounter (ibid., 40). He readily acknowledges the fact that not every person will "genuinely appreciate" what they learn from religious others. For this reason, Schmidt-Leukel proposes "toleration" and "co-operation" as fair—albeit theologically unproductive—ways of handling diversity when a person fails to appreciate other religious traditions. He writes, "But while toleration and social co-operation certainly form a basis on which religions can positively contribute to the struggle for peace, they do not address the reciprocal threat that emerges from religious superiority claims" (ibid., 27). Schmidt-Leukel presents a false alternative for the outcome of the encounter with religious others. *Either* we genuinely appreciate what we learn from them *or* we merely tolerate and perhaps co-operate with them; *either* we

Christian Views of Interreligious Dialogue and Forms of Transformation

tion is a possible outcome of encountering the religious other, Schmidt-Leukel must argue for a view of the relationship between individual believers and religious traditions such that individual believers are able to integrate elements from other traditions. He accomplishes this by positioning a person's relationship to her religious traditions as subordinate to her relationship to God. "Commitment to God," Schmidt-Leukel writes, "may find its expression in the commitment to and practical involvement with some particular religious community or institution, but it cannot be simply identified with that."[49] His premises are that a person's relationship to God cannot be "contained" by one religious tradition and, related to this, that religious traditions are not ends in themselves.

Schmidt-Leukel questions the legitimacy of Catherine Cornille's "marriage metaphor" for illuminating how a person relates to her religious tradition. Cornille compares the way one relates to her religious tradition to the way one relates to her life partner or spouse: the relationship is characterized by total commitment. Cornille writes,

> To be sure, the commitment that comes with religious belonging does not always occur with a full understanding of all religious options. But just as in a life commitment to another person, it is only in the complete surrender to the other that the full richness of belonging has a chance of fruition.[50]

For Schmidt-Leukel, Cornille misconstrues the object of a person's total commitment. A person does not form "stable, reliable and exclusive"

---

have a productive theological response that results in integration *or* we merely develop amicable relations with the religious other. In Schmidt-Leukel's construction of the interreligious encounter, there is no real place in between integrating and rejecting elements from other religious traditions. As the women of Philadelphia have demonstrated, this is not quite the case. An example recounted by one member of the Philadelphia dialogue group about her ordination into the Presbyterian Church illustrates how appreciation and steadfastness can fit together. During the Presbyterian ordination ceremony, church elders lay their hands on and bless the person who is receiving holy orders. Following custom, the church elders from the Presbyterian community lay their hands on this woman (from the Philadelphia group) during her ordination. But, by special request and approval, she also had her Muslim, Jewish, and Sikh friends lay their hands on her and offer their blessings for her ministry to the Presbyterian Church. This woman neither rejects nor fully integrates, but is steadfast in her commitment to her home tradition yet appreciative of her other religious friends.

49. Schmidt-Leukel, *Transformation by Integration*, 80.
50. Cornille, "Double Religious Belonging," 48.

relationship with a religious tradition, but rather forms that kind of relationship with God.[51]

As an alternative, Schmidt-Leukel proposes the metaphor of religious traditions as "signposts or travel guides" to characterize the relationship between believers and traditions.[52] On this view, religious traditions are not ends; rather they are means—or better, markers along the way—to the end of relating to God or transcendent reality. The way that a person utilizes "signposts" is by allowing religious traditions to inform the "directional" choices one makes on her way to God. In turn, these directional choices draw the "map" of one's religious identity. He admits that a person's route to God—both in terms of religious belief and practice—can be a circuitous and convoluted one.[53] Because faith is a matter of being subjectively guided by many religious signposts, "Patchwork religiosity, so often decried," Schmidt-Leukel writes, "[is] something that on a personal level is absolutely inevitable."[54]

Reshaping Religious Believers

The most important component of Schmidt-Leukel's transformative integration equation is the individual person. While integration is individually-driven and its center of gravity, so to speak, is the individual person, Schmidt-Leukel does not see this as an individualistic, atomistic, or a-social process. Just because a person forms her religious identity from out of personal experience, Schimdt-Leukel states, this "does in itself not imply any a-social or atomistic tendencies, but just a clearer awareness of the subjective choice of faith."[55] The very concept of integration, he argues, is a communal one because it is bound up in the recognition of what one's tradition lacks in light of what other traditions offer. "Integration, therefore, raises the issue of syncretism on the individual as well as collective level."[56] Integration has its roots in a person's individual, subjective

---

51. Schmidt-Leukel, *Transformation by Integration*, 52.

52. Ibid., 53.

53. Ibid., 65. Schmidt-Leukel discusses this in terms of the coherence of patchwork religiosity—that is, how the patches all fit together. The "circuitous route to God" is my language and not Schmidt-Leukel's. I use it to connect to his earlier metaphor of religious traditions as signposts.

54. Ibid., 58.

55. Ibid., 62.

56. Ibid., 7.

experience of being guided by the signposts of other religious traditions, but it has implications for entire religious communities.

Although it has communal implications, the axis on which Schmidt-Leukel's proposal rotates is the proposition that faith is, to use his phrase, something "unmistakably individual." What role do belief and practice play within this individualized understanding of faith formation? While it may be the case that individual believers are directed by the signposts of other religious traditions and are able to integrate elements—including beliefs, practices, and attitudes—from those traditions into their own lives of faith,[57] Schmidt-Leukel does not offer a developed theory of how individual believers *are integrated* into other religious traditions.[58]

This is problematic on the VDP model because it does not account for the critical "economic" relationships among agent, virtuous doxastic

---

57. Schmidt-Leukel references Henri Le Saux (a Benedictine monk and Hindu Sannyasi, called Abhishiktananda in the Hindu community) as one example of a Christian integrating theological ideas and religious practices from another religious tradition (ibid., 51, 15n). Cornille gives depth to the Henri La Saux example: "After failing to found an Indian Christian monastic community with Jules Monchanin, he immersed himself completely in the Hindu spiritual life and became the disciple of various Hindu gurus, the most renowned of which was Ramana Maharshi. The religious experiences that he had while immersing himself in Hinduism convinced him of the need to rethink the fundamental experiences of Christianity in Hindu terms" (Cornille, "Double Religious Belonging," 47).

58. Schmidt-Leukel anticipates criticisms like mine. He states his suspicion about these kinds of critiques: ". . . what lies behind many a theological critique of the modern endorsement of the subjective choice of faith are still exclusivist positions, which in their criticism of modern subjectivity do not really reject the necessity of subjective choice itself but rather the respective outcome of that choice" (Schmidt-Leukel, *Transformation by Integration*, 61). Schmidt-Luekel holds, in effect, that the "modernist" critiques of the subjective choice of faith are motivated by fear of syncretism. In short, contesting Schmidt-Leukel on the point of individually chosen faith is simply a cloaked way of re-entrenching exclusivism. While I concede Schmidt-Leukel's point that exclusivism may be lurking below the surface in many instances of these critiques, it is possible that in some cases—and specifically my own, critiques like these raise a genuine problem with making faith and religious identity a matter of individual subjective choice. I argue that Schmidt-Leukel's proposal overburdens individual religious believers; he makes individual persons entirely responsible for their religious faith (including their identities, beliefs, and practices) and attributes little to the role of the community in shaping a person's beliefs long before she actively chooses them. Ricoeur's theory of interpretation helps to make sense of the way that people are formed—inherently and unwittingly—by the traditions that they are a part of (specifically, Ricoeur is concerned with the fundamental symbols and myths of these traditions) and proposes interpretative tools for people to discover and understand the meaning of the traditions that shape them.

practice, and community. The VDP model holds that people form their beliefs through virtuous doxastic practices, which are learned in the context of their community; in exercising VDPs, people also contribute back to the continual development of them and to their community's cultivation of these practices. If, as Schmidt-Leukel argues, a person integrates elements from other religious traditions, this would mean that this person learns new VDPs or significantly alters the ones in which she already engages. Truly habituating oneself to new a VDP, however, requires one's participation in the community that teaches it.[59] Also, by definition, VDPs exclude the possibility that they (VDPs) can be significantly changed by one person in a short period of time. VDPs are, on the whole, rather stable. More importantly still, the agent must always "give back" to the community in which the VDP arises by contributing to the development of that VDP. It is not clear that Schmidt-Leukel's notion of integrated religious identity can hold up to these demands.

Reshaping Religious Traditions

Schmidt-Leukel does indicate something about how the transformative integration he envisions for individual persons affects religious traditions, and particularly the Christian tradition. This argument comes through in his "qualified defense" of religious *bricolage*. First, Schmidt-Leukel asserts that Christian identity has never been nor will ever be static.[60] Secondly, he states that if there is real concern for loss of identity, it can be constructively handled by being "taken seriously" and establishing "criteria" by which to evaluate syncretistic developments. The integration of any foreign element into a system of thought will necessarily require the reinterpretation of its original elements.[61] That integration requires new interpretations is not a

---

59. I have not explored systematically the function of virtuous doxastic practices for persons who have been formed by and feel at home in multiple religious traditions in a strong sense. As I have noted in various places throughout the text, I am motivated to pursue the questions of this project not only for intellectual reasons but for personal ones as well. My own standpoint, and therefore starting point, is as one who is situated in a single religious tradition. As I do not claim "double religious belonging" nor was I raised in a multifaith family, multireligious identities did not factor into my methodological approach as much as they perhaps could have. It is here that one shortcoming of this project is apparent, although I hope the final sections of this chapter (as well as my future work!) may provide some insight into how multireligious identity stands with the VDP model.

60. Schmidt-Leukel, *Transformation by Integration*, 84.

61. Ibid., 75.

reason to discourage it from happening. Thirdly, he posits that transformation by integration does not result in "loss of identity but its deepening and widening."[62] In short, religious identities and traditions necessarily change; we should embrace this fact and spend our energy developing ways to arbitrate the factors that bring about those changes.[63]

On his view, the benefits—that traditions can creatively innovate, reinterpret central beliefs, and reinvent themselves in the theological future—outweigh the drawbacks—that traditions include, for a time, elements that are inconsistent with its basic tenets. However, framing religious *bricolages* viz. religious traditions in this way—as benefits versus drawbacks—obscures issues of more pressing concern. Is it the case that just because the boundaries of religious traditions have been redrawn over time (and doctrines reformulated) they will, in the future, be redrawn according to the integrative religious adaptations of individual persons? And even if religious traditions are reformulated in accord with persons' *bricolages*, does that mean people should or *can* pick and choose virtuous doxastic practices from the religious marketplace? Are individuals' *bricolages* merely examples of religious consumerism? Perhaps most importantly, what virtues (or virtuous doxastic practices) are at play Schmidt-Leukel's proposal for transformative integration?

---

62. Ibid., 85.

63. Following Robert Schreiter, Schmidt-Leukel notes that Christianity has absorbed influences from "Hellenistic, Germanic, Celtic, and Syrian" cultural and religious traditions. However, he does not discuss these or other examples of syncretism or multireligious identity in great depth. Also following Schreiter and well as Leonardo Boff, Schmidt-Leukel briefly offers some suggestions for the criteria by which to discern whether something "fits" into the Christian tradition. Boff's primary criterion is relatively diffuse; quoting Boff, Schmidt-Leukel notes that if something can be "linked to the experience of Jesus of Nazareth [as son of God]" then it may be positively incorporated into Christian identity. Schreiter's criteria—that the development in question is coherent with the Christian tradition, has the approval of the churches, and will have a positive effect on the Christian tradition as a whole—are more rigorous than Boff's. Schmidt-Leukel expresses concern that Schreiter's first criterion is logically flawed and, as he puts it, "amounts to begging the question" (ibid., 85–89). While it is Schmidt-Leukel's intention to introduce key issues surrounding the issue of syncretism, it is difficult to imagine how his argument would practically play out since he does not develop criteria or explore examples to which hypothetical criteria could be applies.

Virtue in Dialogue

The Relationship between Believer and Tradition

Schmidt-Leukel claims that it is not a real option in our globalized world to live entirely in one, bounded religious tradition. I believe that Schmidt-Leukel is descriptively right about the situation created by religious diversity. It is impossible to go about our business, religiously speaking, without running into the "signposts" of other religious traditions. When we encounter the religious other in dialogue, we cannot go back to thinking that our creeds and liturgies are the only ones. To invoke Ricouer's language, religious diversity disrupts first naiveté. However, because Schmidt-Leukel depends upon an individually-based and subjective account of faith, the conclusions he reaches about transformation are problematic on the VDP model.

The VDP model's understanding of religious belief—and faith is connected to this—is that it is communally constituted. The VDP model holds that believers are justified if their beliefs are formed out of virtuous doxastic practices. Virtuous doxastic practices are cultivated and regulated in the context of social community. Because virtues are properties "embedded" in agents and virtuous doxastic practices are exercised by agents, the VDP theory of belief formation and justification is agent-centered. And, yet, the community is never "lost" to the agent. My objection to Schmidt-Leukel's project is thus not that it focuses on the individual person or agent. Rather my objection is that his proposal leaves out any substantial account of the way community and tradition shape the religious believer in her tradition—even without her choosing it.

Judiciousness and the Transformation of Hybridity

Schmidt-Leukel defines as multireligious identity "a unique identity that is . . . formed and developed under the influence of several religious traditions."[64] "Mutlireligious identity" may also be referred to as multiple religious belonging, double religious belonging, hybrid religious identity, or interreligious belonging. Syncretism, synthesis, and symbiosis are also words often ascribed to this state of religious belonging. For simplicity's sake, "hybridity" will be my touchstone word throughout this section. It will be helpful to state clearly what is meant by hybridity and to do so, I shall follow Hill Fletcher's definition. Hybridity, Hill Fletcher states, "refers to the mixing that brings forth new forms from previously identified

---

64. Schmidt-Leukel, *Transformation by Integration*, 47.

categories.⁶⁵ The basic premise of hybridity is that religious belonging and religious identity do not exist with clean borders or according to fixed boundaries.

While it is outside the scope of this project to explore hybridity in great depth or systematic detail, it is critical to note some of the important issues connected to the notion of hybridity. First, hybridity is argued for (and against) on historical, conceptual, and theological grounds. In an example that incorporates all three approaches, Hill Fletcher encourages the Christian community to take seriously the claims of globalization theorists, whose view of religious traditions stand in contrast to the "container" theory of culture/religious traditions. A container theory view sees religious traditions as distinct, self-enclosed groups, which have collided and conflicted throughout history. The theological effects of constructing religious traditions (and religious identity) in this way are not insignificant. If religious traditions are discreet entities, they can be categorized hierarchically. It is such hierarchies that have been used, historically, to legitimate mission and sanction colonialism. By contrast, hybridity theory in this context carries the view of the "complex dynamism" of globalization to the individual level, such that both religious traditions and religious persons are constituted by the complex, dynamic interaction of a variety of groups.⁶⁶ By embracing hybridity, Hill Fletcher claims, "Christian theological outlooks will no longer be constructed as if they were set apart from the dynamic interaction with people of other faiths."⁶⁷

Along similar lines, Paul Hedges appeals to the history of the early Christian church to question the religious boundaries in which we put stock. He writes, ". . . we have a variety of Christian identities emerging and conflicting over the ensuing centuries [of early Christianity]. Where we stand and how we define Christian orthodoxy or normalcy will depend in part upon which of these identities we follow."⁶⁸ Taking a more theo-

---

65. Hill Fletcher, "Religious Pluralism in an Era of Globalization," 394 n. 1.

66. Masuzawa, in *The Invention of World Religions*, develops an argument about the constructed condition of "world religions" as a category along similar lines, albeit with a rather different tone and method. Masuzawa traces the historical development of the concept and study of religious pluralism by rhetorically analyzing developments in the fields of philology, linguistics, and the so called "science of religion," particularly in the eighteenth and nineteenth centuries. Like Hill Fletcher, Masuzawa's interest lies in pointing out (and criticizing) the material and ideological implications that result from conventional views about what diverse religions are and how they interact.

67. Hill Fletcher, "Religious Pluralism in an Era of Globalization," 408.

68. Hedges, *Controversies in Interreligious Dialogue*, 42.

logical approach, Peter Phan explores the possibility of hybrid Christian identity by raising the question of whether it is feasible to develop a Christian theology of religions that both justifies hybridity and also maintains the uniqueness and universality of Christ.[69] Phan goes on to aver ten principles that must be a part of such a theology of religions.

While there are a number of positive appraisals of hybridity, it is a hotly contested topic among Christian theologians and within the Christian community. In the previous section, I pointed out some concerns theologians express over hybridity. Cornille, for example, claims that double religious belonging "bypasses the very purpose and dynamics of religious belonging."[70] For to belong to a religious tradition, from Cornille's perspective, is to commit oneself to certain truths that are necessarily particular and exclusive to that religious tradition. Keeping this rough sketch of arguments for and against hybridity in view, what can be said about hybrid religious identity given the virtuous doxastic practice model?

Just as I have interpreted the transformation of returning home to be connected to the virtue of steadfastness, when a person undergoes the transformation of hybridity, she specially exercises the virtue of judiciousness. Judiciousness has to do with making good judgments about the information one perceives. It demands a clear, balanced, and open perspective. The judicious participant in interreligious dialogue may be profoundly affected by her dialogue partners' personal stories and accounts of religious practice and beliefs. As a result, she may feel compelled to "find out more," to enter into deeper conversation, and even to explore the religious practices of her friends. She does not forsake her own religious presuppositions and practices as a result of what she learns, but neither does she feel she can walk away from those of her dialogue companions. She thus strikes a balance between her home religious tradition and the religious traditions she encounters through engaging with others. Her judicious stance in dialogue may be supported by a conviction that, in agreement with Hill Fletcher and Hedges, no religious community is—in its origins, present state, or future—impermeable.

As re-articulated in my discussion of Schmidt-Leukel, the virtuous doxastic practice model is deeply communal. For religious beliefs to be *prima facie* justified, they must be learned and tested in the context of a home community. Following this (because belief and practice are intimately related), it is only possible to meaningfully "belong" to a religion

69. Phan, "Multiple Religious Belonging," 499.
70. Cornille, "Double Religious Belonging," 48.

by being a part of a religious community. One limit for the transformation of hybridity on the VDP model, then, is that it must involve significant communal support. The truly judicious person does not simply integrate those elements that she happens to appreciate, as Schmidt-Leukel would have it, but forms a hybrid religious identity by meditating on the beliefs, participating in the practices, and learning from the communities of multiple religious traditions.

While the communal support stipulation of the VDP model seems to initially deny the legitimacy of hybridity on the grounds that persons are justified in their beliefs only from within the context of religious communities, in fact, this stipulation uniquely prepares religious believers for *ultima facie* justification. To repeat, for religious beliefs to be *ultima facie* justified, they must be tested in the context of an interreligious community. Because the highest level of belief justification comes about by engaging with people *outside* of one's home community, hybridity is, in a sense, written into the very notion of virtuous doxastic practices.

Prudence and the Transformation of Conversion

Conversion is a concept that is at once clear in its colloquial usage and, at the same time, indistinct and controversial in its academic or formal usage. While conversion may be routinely understood to mean switching, changing, or turning from one thing into another, the precise features of this switching, changing, and turning are obscure, particularly in the case of religious conversion. What constitutes religious conversion? Does a person convert *to* or convert *from*? What are the social pressures for and implications of conversion? How is conversion constructed as a concept? How does the conceptual discourse about conversion shape the reality of conversion? As with my discussion of hybridity, although it is outside the scope of this project to explore conversion in systematic depth, a working definition of conversion is necessary.

In a report from a joint consultation between the PCID and the Office on Interreligious Relations and Dialogue of the WCC, Christian leaders recognize while they do not have "unanimity on even the meaning of conversion," they can agree to develop a code of conduct for conversion. One primary commitment of a conversion code of conduct, the report states, is that freedom of religion is a fundamental human right. The notion of freedom of religion "connotes the freedom, without any obstruction, to practice one's own faith, freedom to propagate the teachings on one's faith to people of one's own and other faiths, and also the freedom to embrace another faith out of one's own free choice."[71] The final clause of this statement suggests a loose, yet decisive, understanding of conversion: "to embrace another faith."

If religious conversion means, in a basic sense, to embrace another faith, the question of *why* a person would do so immediately rises to the surface. (A presupposition of this section is that interreligious dialogue is a possible contributing factor to conversion.) Religious conversion, as the entry on conversion in the *Encyclopedia of Religion* notes, cannot be reduced to a "monocasual force" but rather has a "pluriform nature." Beyond the theological or spiritual reasons for conversion that the *Report from Interreligious Consultation on "Conversion—Assessing the Reality"* presume, scholars of religion point to "psychological needs, sociological factors, cultural forces, economic incentives or depravations, and/or political constraints or inducements" that influence and inspire religious conversion. My working definition of conversion here maintains that all conversions are both personal and contextual in nature.[72] Religious conversion is embracing another faith tradition (other than one's "home" tradition) and involves both personal (theological, spiritual) and contextual (social, cultural, economic, etc.) factors.

Embracing another faith tradition involves the virtue of prudence. Epistemic prudence has to do with showing due care for the information one receives. It is similar to judiciousness in that in demands a balanced and open perspective. However, prudence admits of a special quality that makes it stand out from its companion virtues: timeliness and context-sensitivity. The prudent epistemic agent processes what she learns carefully, but also with sensitivity to an end point and the context in which she forms beliefs. She neither forms beliefs too quickly, as to be a guesser, nor takes so much time in forming beliefs that she does not epistemically "act" at all, as to be a skeptic. The prudent person knows, along with William James, that no bell will toll and one must take decisive action nonetheless.

Prudence is aligned with the transformation of conversion because embracing another faith tradition involves making a commitment, for personal and contextual reasons, with timeliness and in a way that is "proportionate" to the situation. In interreligious dialogue, the prudent dialogue participant listens to her colleagues' accounts of their beliefs and watches them in their practices; she reflects on her understanding of her own beliefs and practices in view of her home tradition. Recalling

71. WCC, *Report from Interreligious Consultation*, Introduction.
72. *Encyclopedia of Religion*, 2nd ed., s.v. "Conversion."

Clooney's language, she "reads" the practices of others and then "reads" again her own. She is particularly sensitive to the "genuine option" nature of dialogue and knows that what she has heard from her dialogue partners and what she had learned about herself in the process demands a response that does justice to this level of candid sharing.

Like the steadfast dialogue participant, the prudent participant is shaken out of first naiveté by dialogue. Like the judicious dialogue participant, the prudent participant is compelled to participate in another religious community. However she, like the steadfast participant and unlike the judicious participant, embraces one tradition and learns the practices of one community. She experiences the transformation of conversion. A significant stipulation on this form of transformation, realized by placing the VDP model in conversation with Schmidt-Luekel, is that there must be a genuine exchange between community members and community in the development and exercise of virtuous doxastic practices. Conversion is not simply embracing another faith tradition, but also involves becoming an *agent* of that tradition's virtuous doxastic practices. Agency demands the responsibility of learning and exercising VDPs and, at the same time, the power and ability to influence and shape those VDPs anew.[73]

A Christian Community Transformed

Both the Catholic Church and the WCC fully expect that Christians will be changed through their encounter with the religious other. They imagine the "adventure of dialogue" to be deepening, enriching, and paving the way to a more full expression of God's kingdom on earth. They earnestly hope that such changes will be to spiritual benefit of individual persons

---

73. That creativity is absent from my exposition of forms of transformation in relation to the cardinal virtues may seem conspicuously curious. In fact, creativity is the virtue that stands behind each of these forms of transformation. Creativity involves innovation and an imagination for the consequences of one's epistemic actions. Without exercising the virtue of creativity in interreligious dialogue, participants would be unable to undergo transformation. According to my interpretation, the kind of creative transformation that a dialogue participant experiences will depend on the virtue (steadfastness, judiciousness, or prudence) that is most prominently at play in her dialogue practice. It is also vital to note at this point that my description of the individual virtues and their resultant forms of transformation as discrete from each other is rhetorically motivated. I paint the "judicious participant" and "steadfast dialogue partner" in exaggerated terms so as to draw out the most salient or qualitatively efficacious aspects of virtue in various transformations, not because they (the virtues) are in reality mutually exclusive.

and to the growth and development of the Christian community, although they recognize that this will not always be the case. While there is much positive that these Christian documents convey about interreligious dialogue, they also note realistic apprehensions about what dialogue involves and where it leads, including concerns about misunderstanding others' beliefs and practices, misrepresenting one's own, and problematical melding the two in dialogue.

Keeping the virtuous doxastic practice epistemological model in view, I wish to make three responses to the Christian community's expectations, as represented by *DP* and the WCC documents, for interreligious dialogue. These responses correlate to each of the forms of transformation. First, on the VDP model, the church's intuition that dialogue is an adventure that will lead to the deepening of *Christian* faith and, often, to the transformation of returning home must be commended. The church should be heartened by Christian participation in dialogue because it is *the most powerful* means by which Christians can perfect their virtuous doxastic practices and *the only* means by which they may move toward *ultima facie* justification.

Secondly, as both *DP* and the WCC documents make plain, entering into dialogue risks vulnerability. By promoting humility and hospitality, the church prepares Christian participants in dialogue to be sympathetic and receptive to their dialogue partners' accounts of other religious beliefs and practices. In the case that Christian participants are transformed by conversion, it is a transformation wrought in encounter with religious others. The context for conversion presupposes a broad circle of participation. A broad circle of participation means that diverse people are exercising diverse VDPs together. It may provide some measure of consolation to the church that all participants—Christians and converts alike—will simultaneously subject and have their beliefs subjected to the evaluation of multiple religious persons. In summary, the significance of the Christian community for the formation of religious beliefs—be they Christian or otherwise—will never be irrelevant.

Finally, present in *DP* and the WCC documents are hints that betray an underlying—and powerful—skepticism about dialogue: that it is fertile ground for incipient syncretism. While the exact qualities and features of syncretism are left unaddressed in *DP* and the WCC documents, I take "syncretism" to refer to the "illegitimate" combining of practices and blending of beliefs of multiple religious traditions. Hybridity is a less pejorative way of talking about this form of transformation. Anxiety about syncretism or hybridity may be interpreted as anxiety over maintaining definite communal borders. While the VDP theory calls for deep interreligious engagement in order to achieve *ultima facie* justification, "home" communities always remain a primary constituent of basic epistemic justification. Thus the VDP theory protects and honors the importance of distinctive communities.

Statements by the Roman Catholic Church and the WCC, taken collectively, show a willingness to see engaging with the religious other as an essential component of everyday life. Rather than taking an attitude of defiance or having a posture of resignation toward this reality, both *DP* and WCC documents embrace it and intend to rise to its challenges. They present sophisticated theological, Christological, soteriological, and pneumatological arguments for the existence of diversity and the justification of Christian engagement with it. They recommend ways in which Christians can, on practical levels, best enter dialogue *qua* committed Christians. The virtuous doxastic practice model offers resources for fruitful theological interpretations of the transformations that Christians undergo in dialogue in the hope that—no matter what the transformative outcome—the church will continue to support engagement with religious others as a practice that builds and strengthens the virtuous doxastic practices of the Christian community.

Bibliography

Alcoff, Linda. "Is the Feminist Critique of Reason Rational?" *Philosophic Exchange: Annual Proceedings* 26 (1996) 59–79.

Alston, William. *Epistemic Justification: Essays in the Theory of Knowledge*. Ithaca, NY: Cornell University Press, 1989.

———. *Faith, Reason, and Skepticism*. Philadelphia: Temple University Press, 1992.

———. *Perceiving God: The Epistemology of Religious Experience*. Ithaca, NY: Cornell University Press, 1991.

———. "Religious Diversity and Perceptual Knowledge of God." *Faith and Philosophy* 5/4 (1988) 433–48.

———. "Response to Critics." *Religious Studies* 30/2 (1994) 171–80.

Anderson, Pamela Sue, and Beverly Clack, editors. *Feminist Philosophy of Religion: Critical Readings*. New York: Routledge, 2004.

Annas, Julia. "The Structure of Virtue." In *Intellectual Virtue: Perspectives from Ethics and Epistemology*, edited by Michael DePaul and Linda Zagzebski, 15–33. New York: Oxford University Press, 2003.

Appiah, Kwame Anthony. *Cosmopolitanism: Ethics in a World of Strangers*. New York: Allen Lane, 2006.

Aristotle. *Aristotle: Selections*. Edited and translated by Terence Irwin and Gail Fine. Indianapolis: Hackett, 1995.

Audi, Robert. *Religious Commitment and Secular Reason*. New York: Cambridge University Press, 2000.

Austin, J. L. "Three Ways of Spilling Ink." *Philosophical Review* 75/4 (1966) 427–40.

Badhwar, Neera. "The Limited Unity of Virtue." *Nous* 30/3 (1996) 306–29.

Baehr, Jason. "Character in Epistemology." *Philosophical Studies* 128/3 (2006) 479–514.

———. "Character, Reliability and Virtue Epistemology." *The Philosophical Quarterly* 56/223 (2006) 193–212.

———. "Four Varieties of Character-Based Virtue Epistemology." *The Southern Journal of Philosophy* 46/4 (2008) 469–502.

Baldwin, Erik, and Michael Thune. "The Epistemological Limits of Experience-Based Exclusive Religious Belief." *Religious Studies* 44/4 (2008) 445–55.

Barkess, Joanna. "Painting the *Sitra Achra*: Cultural Confrontation in Chaim Potok's Asher Lev Novels." *Studies in American Jewish Literature* 17 (1998) 1–24.

Baron, Marcia. "Varieties of Ethics of Virtue." *American Philosophical Quarterly* 22/1 (1985) 47–53.

Barrett, Cyril, editor. *Wittgenstein: Lectures and Conversations on Aesthetics, Psychology, and Religious Belief*. Berkeley: University of California Press, 1966.

Basinger, David. "Hick's Religious Pluralism and 'Reformed Epistemology': A Middle Ground." *Faith and Philosophy* 5/4 (1988) 421–31.

Bonjour, Lawrence. "Internalism and Externalism." In *Oxford Handbook of Epistemology*, edited by Paul Moser, 234–62. New York: Oxford University Press, 2002.

Bibliography

Bonjour, Lawrence, and Ernest Sosa. *Epistemic Justification: Internalism vs. Externalism, Foundations vs. Virtues*. Malden, MA: Blackwell, 2003.

Braaten, Jane. *Habermas' Critical Theory of Society*. Albany: SUNY Press, 1991.

———. "Towards a Feminist Reassessment of Intellectual Virtue." *Hypatia* 5/3 (1990) 1–14.

Burkle, Howard. "Jesus Christ and Religious Pluralism." *Journal of Ecumenical Studies* 16/3 (1979) 457–71.

Cates, Diana Fritz. *Aquinas on the Emotions: A Religious Ethical Inquiry*. Washington, DC: Georgetown University Press, 2009.

———. "Toward an Ethic of Shared Selfhood." *The Annual of the Society of Christian Ethics* (1991) 249–57.

Chavkin, Laura. "A MELUS Interview: Chaim Potok." *The Journal of the Society for the Study of the Multi-Ethnic Literature of the United States* 24/2 (1999) 147–57.

Chopp, Rebecca. "Theology and the Poetics of Testimony." In *Converging on Culture: Theologians in Dialogue with Cultural Analysis and Criticism*, edited by Delwin Browne, Sheila Greeve Davaney, and Kathryn Tanner, 56–70. New York: Oxford University Press, 2001.

———. "Theorizing Feminist Theology." In *Horizons in Feminist Theology: Identity, Traditions, and Norms*, edited by Rebecca Chopp and Sheila Greene Davaney, 215–31. Minneapolis: Fortress, 1997.

Christian, William. *Meaning and Truth in Religion*. New Haven: Yale University Press, 1964.

———. *Oppositions of Religious Doctrines: A Study in the Logic of Dialogue among Religions*. New York: Macmillan, 1972.

Chung, Hyun Kyung. "Seeking the Religious Roots of Pluralism." *Journal of Ecumenical Studies* 34/3 (1997) 399–402.

———. "Welcome the Spirit; Hear Her Cries." Paper presented at World Council of Churches Assembly, Canberra, Australia, Frebruary 1991. Online: http://www.cta-usa.org/foundationdocs/foundhyunkyung.html.

Churchill, Lawrence. "Flew, Wisdom, and Polyani: The Falsification Challenge Revisited." *International Journal for Philosophy of Religion* 3/3 (1972) 185–94.

Clifford, Anne. "The Global Horizon of Religious Pluralism and Local Dialogue with the Religious Other." In *New Horizons in Theology*, edited by Terrence Tilley, 162–81. Maryknoll, NY: Orbis, 2001.

Clifford, William Kingdon. *The Ethics of Belief and Other Essays*. Amherst, NY: Prometheus, 1999.

Clooney, Francis X. "Comparative Theology: A Review of Recent Books (1989–1995)." *Theological Studies* 56/3 (1995) 521–50.

———. *Comparative Theology: Deep Learning across Religious Borders*. Malden, MA: Blackwell, 2010.

———. *Hindu God, Christian God: How Reason Helps Break Down the Boundaries between Religions*. New York: Oxford University Press, 2001.

———. "Openness and Limit in the Catholic Encounter with Other Faith Traditions." In *Examining the Catholic Intellectual Tradition*, edited by Anthony Cernera and Oliver Morgan, 103–32. Fairfield, CT: Sacred Heart University Press, 2000.

———. "The Study of Non-Christian Religions in the Post-Vatican II Roman Catholic Church." *Journal of Ecumenical Studies* 28/3 (1991) 482–94.

———. "Theology, Dialogue, and Religious Others: Some Recent Books in the Theology of Religions and Related Fields." *Religious Studies Review* 29/4 (2003) 319–26.

———. *The Truth, the Way, the Life: Christian Commentary on the Three Holy Mantras of the Srivaisnava Hindus*. Walpole, MA: Peeters, 2008.

Code, Lorraine. *Epistemic Responsibility*. Providence: Brown University Press, 1987.

———. "Experience, Knowledge, and Responsibility." In *Women, Knowledge, and Reality: Explorations in Feminist Philosophy*, edited by Ann Garry and Marilyn Pearsall, 191–221. New York: Routledge, 1989.

———. "Is the Sex of the Knower Epistemologically Significant?" *Metaphilosophy* 12/3–4 (1981) 267–76.

———. "Responsibility and the Epistemic Community: A Woman's Place." *Social Research* 50/3 (1983) 537–55.

———. "Toward a 'Responsibilist' Epistemology." *Philosophy and Phenomenological Research* 45/1 (1984) 29–50.

———. *What Can She Know? Feminist Theory and the Construction of Knowledge*. Ithaca, NY: Cornell University Press, 1991.

Congregation for the Doctrine of Faith. *Declaration "Dominus Iesus" on the Unicity and Salvific Universality of Jesus Christ and the Church* (2000). Online: http://www.vatican.va/roman_curia/congregations/cfaith/documents/rc_con_cfaith_doc_20000806_dominus-iesus_en.html.

———. *Letter to the Bishops of the Catholic Church on Some Aspects of Christian Meditation* (1989). Online: http://www.vatican.va/roman_curia/congregations/cfaith/documents/rc_con_cfaith_doc_19891015_meditazione-cristiana_en.html.

Cooper, Neil. "The Intellectual Virtues." *Philosophy* 69/270 (1994) 459–69.

Cornille, Catherine. "Double Religious Belonging: Aspects and Questions." *Buddhist Christian Studies* 23 (2003) 43–49.

———. *The Im-Possibility of Interreligious Dialogue*. New York: Herder & Herder, 2008.

———, editor. *Many Mansions? Multiple Religious Belonging and Christian Identity*. Maryknoll, NY: Orbis, 2002.

Davis, Stephen T. "Theology, Verification, and Falsification." *International Journal for Philosophy of Religion* 6/1 (1975) 23–39.

D'Costa, Gavin. *Christianity and the World Religions: Disputed Questions in the Theology of Religions*. Malden, MA: Blackwell, 2009.

DiNoia, J. A. *The Diversity of Religions: A Christian Perspective*. Washington, DC: Catholic University of America Press, 1992.

Doris, John. "Persons, Situations, and Virtue Ethics." *Nous* 32/4 (1998) 504–30.

Driver, Julia. *Uneasy Virtue*. New York: Cambridge University Press, 2007.

———. "The Virtues of Ignorance." *The Journal of Philosophy* 86/7 (1989) 373–84.

Duffy, Stephen. "A Theology of the Religions and/or a Comparative Theology?" *Horizons* 26/1 (1999) 105–15.

Dunne, John S. *The Way of All the Earth: Experiments in Truth and Religion*. New York: Macmillan, 1972.

Dupuis, Jacques. *Christianity and the Religions: From Confrontation to Dialogue*. Translated by Phillip Berryman. Maryknoll, NY: Orbis, 1970.

———. *Toward a Christian Theology of Religious Pluralism*. Maryknoll, NY: Orbis, 1997.

Bibliography

Egan, Harvey. "Centenary of Catholic Theologian Karl Rahner: Interview with Harvey Egan, S.J." By Stephen Crittenden. *The Religion Report: Radio National* (April 14, 2004). Online: http://www.abc.net.au/radionational/programs/religionreport/centenary-of-catholic-theologian-karl-rahner/3377046#transcript.

Egnell, Helene. "Dialogue for Life: Feminist Approaches to Interfaith Dialogue." In *Theology and the Religions: A Dialogue*, edited by Viggo Mortensen, 249–56. Grand Rapids: Eerdmans, 2003.

———. *Other Voices: A Study of Christian Feminist Approaches to Religious Plurality East and West.* Uppsala: Studia Missionalia Svecana, 2006.

Elliot, T. S. "Little Gidding." *Four Quartets.* New York: Harcourt, 1943.

Feldman, Richard. "Clifford's Principle and James' Options." *Social Epistemology* 20/1 (2006) 19–33.

———. "Epistemological Puzzles about Disagreement." In *Epistemology Futures*, edited by Stephen Hetherington, 216–36. New York: Oxford University Press, 2006.

———. "Reasonable Religious Disagreements." In *Philosophers without Gods: Meditations on Atheism and the Secular Life*, edited by Louise M. Anthony, 194–214. Oxford: Oxford University Press, 2007.

Fernyhough, Charles. *1000 Days of Wonder: A Scientist's Chronicle of His Daughter's Developing Mind.* New York: Penguin, 2009.

Fernyhough, Charles. Interview by Jad Abumrad. *Radio Lab*, podcast audio (May 14, 2010). Online: http://www.radiolab.org/2010/may/14/.

Flew, Anthony, and Alasdair MacIntyre, editors. *New Essays in Philosophical Theology.* New York: Macmillan, 1964.

Foot, Phillipa. *Virtues and Vices: And Other Essays in Moral Philosophy.* Berkeley: University of California Press, 1992.

Fredericks, James. "The Catholic Church and Other Religious Paths: Rejecting Nothing that Is True and Holy." *Theological Studies* 64/2 (2003) 225–54.

———. *Faith among Faiths: Christian Theology and Non-Christian Religions.* New York: Paulist, 1999.

———. "Interreligious Friendship: A New Theological Virtue." *Journal of Ecumenical Studies* 35/2 (1998) 159–74.

———. "Reading the World Religiously: Literate Christianity in a World of Many Religions." In *Theological Literacy for the Twenty-First Century*, edited by Rodney Peterson, 242–56. Grand Rapids: Eerdmans, 2002.

———. "A Universal Religious Experience? Comparative Theology as an Alternative to Theology of Religions." *Horizons* 22/1 (1995) 67–87.

Fricker, Miranda. "Epistemic Injustice and the Role for Virtue in the Politics of Knowing." *Metaphilosophy* 34/1–2 (2002) 154–73.

Gale, Richard. "The Overall Argument of Alston's *Perceiving God*." *Religious Studies* 30/2 (1994) 135–49.

Gellman, Jerome. "In Defense of Contented Religious Exclusivism." *Religious Studies* 36/4 (2000) 401–17.

Gerle, Elisabeth. "Multicultural Society: Dilemmas and the Prospects." In *Theology and the Religions: A Dialogue*, edited by Viggo Mortensen, 31–45. Grand Rapids: Eerdmans, 2003.

Greco, John. "Agent Reliablism." *Nous Supplement: Philosophical Perspectives* 13 (1999) 273–96.

———. "Catholics vs. Calvinists on Religious Knowledge." *American Catholic Philosophical Quarterly* 71/1 (1997) 13–34.
———. "A Different Sort of Contextualism." *Erkenntnis* 61/2–3 (2004) 383–400.
———. "Knowledge and Success from Ability." *Philosophical Studies* 142/1 (2009) 17–26.
———. "Knowledge as Credit for True Belief." In *Intellectual Virtue: Perspectives from Ethics and Epistemology*, edited by Michael DePaul and Linda Zagzebski, 111–34. New York: Oxford University Press, 2007.
———. "Two Kinds of Intellectual Virtue." *Philosophy and Phenomenological Research* 60/1 (2000) 179–84.
———. "Virtue and Rules in Epistemology." In *Virtue Epistemology*, edited by Abrol Fairweather and Linda Zagzebski, 117–41. New York: Oxford University Press, 2001.
———. "What's Wrong with Contextualism?" *The Philosophical Quarterly* 58/232 (2008) 416–36.
Griffiths, Paul. *Problems of Religious Diversity*. Malden, MA: Blackwell, 2001.
Grimm, S. R. "Ernest Sosa, Knowledge, and Understanding." *Philosophical Studies* 106/1–2 (2001) 171–91.
Groenhout, Ruth. "The Virtues of Care: Aristotelian Ethics and Contemporary Ethics of Care." In *Feminist Interpretations of Aristotle*, edited by Cynthia Freeland, 171–200. University Park, PA: Pennsylvania State University Press, 1998.
Gutting, Gary. *Religious Belief and Religious Skepticism*. Notre Dame, IN: University of Notre Dame Press, 1983.
Habermas, Jürgen. "Conceptions of Modernity: A Look Back at Two Traditions." In *The Postnational Constellation: Political Essays*, edited and translated by Max Pensky, 130–56. Cambridge, MA: MIT Press, 2001.
———. *Moral Consciousness and Communicative Action*. Edited and translated by Christian Lendhardt and Shierry Weber Nicholsen. Cambridge, MA: MIT Press, 1990.
Hartsock, Nancy. *The Feminist Standpoint Revisited and Other Essays*. Boulder, CO: Westview, 1999.
———. "The Feminist Standpoint: Toward a Specifically Feminist Historical Materialism." In *Money, Sex and Power: Toward a Feminist Historical Materialism*, 231–51. New York: Longman, 1983.
Hedges, Paul. *Controversies in Interreligious Dialogue and the Theology of Religions*. London: SCM, 2010.
Heim, S. Mark. "Salvations: A More Pluralistic Hypothesis." *Modern Theology* 10/4 (1994) 341–60.
———. *Salvations: Truth and Difference in Religion*. Maryknoll, NY: Orbis, 2000.
Hester, Marcus, editor. *Faith, Reason, and Skepticism: Essays by William Alston, Robert Audi, Terence Penelhum, and Richard Popkin*. Philadelphia: Temple University Press, 1992.
Hibbs, Thomas S. "Aquinas, Virtue, and Recent Epistemology." *The Review of Metaphysics* 52/3 (1999) 573–94.
Hick, John. *Disputed Questions in Theology and the Philosophy of Religion*. New Haven: Yale University Press, 1993.
———. *Faith and Knowledge: A Modern Introduction to the Problem of Religious Knowledge*. Ithaca, NY: Cornell University Press, 1957.

Bibliography

———. *An Interpretation of Religion: Human Responses to the Transcendent*. New York: Macmillian, 1989.

———. *John Hick: An Autobiography*. Oxford: Oneworld, 2003.

Hill Fletcher, Jeannine. "As Long as We Wonder: Possibilities in the Impossibility of Interreligious Dialogue." *Theological Studies* 68/3 (2007) 532–54.

———. "Feminisms: Syncretism, Symbiosis, and Synergetic Dance." *Christian Approaches to Other Faiths: An Introduction*, edited by Alan Race and Paul Hedges, 136–54. London: SCM, 2008.

———. *Monopoly on Salvation? A Feminist Approach to Religious Pluralism*. New York: Continuum, 2005.

———. "Rahner and Religious Pluralism." In *The Cambridge Companion to Karl Rahner*, edited by Declam Marmion and Mary Hines, 235–48. New York: Cambridge University Press, 2005.

———. "Religious Pluralism in an Era of Globalization." *Theological Studies* 69/2 (2008) 394–411.

———. "Shifting Identity: The Contribution of Feminist Thought to Theologies of Religious Pluralism." *Journal of Feminist Studies in Religion* 19/2 (2003) 5–24.

———. "Women's Voices in Dialogue: A Look at the Parliament of the World's Religions." *Studies in Interreligious Dialogue* 16/1 (2006) 1–22.

Horsburgh, H. J. N. "Mr. Hare on Theology and Falsification." *The Philosophical Quarterly* 6/24 (1956) 256–59.

International Theological Commission. "Christianity and the World Religions." *Origins* 27 (1997) 149–66.

Inwagen, Peter van. "Is It Wrong Everywhere, Always, and for Anyone to Believe Anything on Insufficient Evidence?" In *Faith, Freedom, and Rationality: Philosophy of Religion Today*, edited by Jeff Jordan and Daniel Howard-Snyder, 137–54. Lanham, MD: Rowan & Littlefield, 1996.

James, William. *A Pluralistic Universe: Hibbert Lectures at Manchester College on the Present Situation in Philosophy*. Lincoln: University of Nebraska Press, 1996.

———. *The Varieties of Religious Experience*. Cambridge, MA: Harvard University Press, 1985.

———. *The Will to Believe, and Other Essays in Popular Philosophy*. New York: Cosimo, 2006.

John Paul II. *Dives in Misericordia* (1980). Online: http://www.vatican.va/edocs/ENG0215/_INDEX.HTM.

———. *Dominum et Vivificantem* (1986). Online: http://www.vatican.va/edocs/ENG0142/_INDEX.HTM.

———. *Redemptor Hominis* (1979). Online: http://www.vatican.va/edocs/ENG0218/_INDEX.HTM.

———. *Redemptoris Missio* (1990). Online: http://www.vatican.va/edocs/ENG0219/_INDEX.HTM.

Katzoff, Charlotte. "Religious Luck and Religious Virtue." *Religious Studies* 40/1 (2004) 97–111.

Kaufman, Gordon. "'Evidentialism': A Theologian's Response." *Faith and Philosophy* 6/1 (1989) 35–46.

Kelly, Thomas. "The Epistemic Significance of Disagreement." In *Oxford Studies in Epistemology*, edited by John Hawthorne and Tamar Gendler Szabo, 1:167–96. Oxford: Clarendon, 2005.

Bibliography

Kendall, Daniel, and Gerald O'Collins. *In Many and Diverse Ways: In Honor of Jacques Dupuis*. Maryknoll, NY: Orbis, 2003.

King, Martin Luther Jr. "Letter from Birmingham Jail." The Martin Luther King, Jr. Research and Education Institute at Stanford University. Online: http://mlk-kpp01.stanford.edu/index.php/encyclopedia/documentsentry/annotated_letter_from_birmingham/.

King, Ursula. "Feminism: The Missing Dimension in the Dialogue of Religions." In *Pluralism and the Religions: The Theological and Political Dimensions*, edited by John D'Arcy, 40–55. New York: Continuum, 1998.

Koehl, Andrew. "Reformed Epistemology and Diversity." *Faith and Philosophy* 18/2 (2001) 168–91.

Knitter, Paul F. "Commitment to One—Openness to Others: a Challenge for Christians." *Horizons* 28/2 (2001) 255–70.

———. *Introducing Theologies of Religions*. Maryknoll, NY: Orbis, 2002.

———. *No Other Name? A Critical Survey of Christian Attitudes toward the World Religions*. American Society of Missiology Series 7. Maryknoll, NY: Orbis, 1985.

———. *One Earth, Many Religions: Multifaith Dialogue and Global Responsibility*. Maryknoll, NY: Orbis, 1995.

Knitter, Paul, and John Hick, editors. *The Myth of Christian Uniqueness: Toward a Pluralistic Theology of Religions*. Maryknoll, NY: Orbis, 1987.

Lackey, Jennifer. "Knowledge and Credit." *Philosophical Studies* 142/1 (2009): 27–42.

———. "Why We Don't Deserve Credit for Everything We Know." *Synthese* 158/3 (2007) 345–61.

Lindbeck, George. *The Nature of Doctrine: Religion and Theology in a Postliberal Age*. Louisville: Westminster John Knox, 1984.

Lohre, Kathryn. "Women's Interfaith Initiatives in the United States Post 9/11." Paper presented at "World Religions after 9/11: A Global Congress," Montreal, Québec, September 11–15, 2006.

Lonergan, Bernard. *Insight: A Study of Human Understanding*. Vol. 3 of *Collected Works of Bernard Lonergan*. Toronto: University of Toronto Press, 1992.

MacIntyre, Alasdair. *After Virtue*. 1st ed. Notre Dame, IN: University of Notre Dame Press, 1981.

Marovitz, Sanford. "Freedom, Faith, and Fanaticism: Cultural Conflict in the Novels of Chaim Potok." *Studies in American Jewish Literature* 5 (1982) 129–40.

Masuzawa, Tomoko. *The Invention of World Religions: Or How European Universalism Was Preserved in the Language of Pluralism*. Chicago: University of Chicago Press, 2005.

McCarthy, Gerald, editor. *The Ethics of Belief Debate*. AAR Academic. Atlanta: Scholars, 1986.

McCarthy, Kate. "Women's Experience as a Hermeneutical Key to a Christian Theology of Religion." *Studies in Interreligious Dialogue* 6/2 (1996) 163–73.

McClendon, James W. *Biography as Theology: How Life Stories Can Remake Theology*. 1974. Reprint, Eugene, OR: Wipf & Stock, 2002.

McDowell, John. "The Role of *Eudamonia* in Aristotle's Ethics." In *Essays on Aristotle's Ethics*, edited by Amelie Rorty, 359–76. Berkeley: University of California Press, 1992.

McKim, Robert. "The Hiddenness of God." *Religious Studies* 26/1 (1990) 141–61.

Bibliography

———. *Religious Ambiguity and Religious Diversity*. New York: Oxford University Press, 2001.

———. "Theism and Proper Basicality." *International Journal for Philosophy of Religion* 26/1 (1989) 29–56.

McKinnon, Alastair. *Falsification and Belief*. Atascador, CA: Ridgeview, 1979.

Meeker, Kevin. "Pluralism, Exclusivism, and the Theoretical Virtues." *Religious Studies* 42/2 (2006) 193–206.

Misak, C. J. *Verificationism: Its History and Prospects*. New York: Routledge, 1995.

Montmarquet, James. "Epistemic Virtue." *Mind* 96/384 (1987) 482–97.

———. "Epistemic Virtue, Religious Experience, and Belief." *Faith and Philosophy* 22/4 (2005) 469–81.

———. "'Pure' versus 'Practical' Epistemic Justification." *Metaphilosphy* 38/1 (2007) 71–87.

Narayan, Uma. "The Project of Feminist Epistemology: Perspectives from a Nonwestern Feminist." In *Gender/Body/Knowledge*, edited by Alison Jagger and Susan R. Bordo, 256–70. Piscataway, NJ: Rutgers University Press, 1989.

Nathanson, Stephen. "Nonevidential Reasons for Belief: A Jamesian View." *Philosophy and Phenomenological Research* 42/4 (1982) 572–80.

Nelson, Lynn Hankinson. "Epistemological Communities." In *Feminist Epistemologies*, edited by Linda Alcoff and Elizabeth Potter, 121–59. New York: Routledge, 1993.

Netland, Harold. *Dissonant Voices: Religious Pluralism and the Question of Truth*. Vancouver: Regent College Publishing, 1999.

———. "Exclusivism, Tolerance, and Truth." *Missiology: An International Review* 15/2 (1987) 77–95.

Nhat Hanh, Thich. *The Miracle of Mindfulness: An Introduction to Meditation*. Boston: Beacon, 1975.

———. *Peace Is Every Step: The Path of Mindfulness in Everyday Life*. New York: Bantam, 1991.

Nussbaum, Martha. "Aristotle, Politics, and Human Capabilities: A Response to Antony, Arneson, Charlesworth, and Mulgan." *Ethics* 111/1 (2000) 102–40.

———. "Comparing Virtues." *Journal of Religious Ethics* 21/2 (1993) 345–67.

———. "Compassion: The Basic Social Emotion." *Social Philosophy and Policy* 13/1 (1996) 27–58.

———. *Cultivating Humanity: A Classic Defense of Reform in Liberal Education*. Cambridge, MA: Harvard University Press, 1998.

———. *Upheavals of Thought: The Intelligence of Emotions*. New York: Cambridge University Press, 2003.

———. *Women and Human Development: The Capabilities Approach*. New York: Cambridge University Press, 2001.

O'Connell, Maureen H. *Compassion: Loving Our Neighbor in an Age of Globalization*. Maryknoll, NY: Orbis, 2009.

O'Connor, D. J. "Some Consequences of Professor A. J. Ayer's Verification Principle." *Analysis* 10/3 (1950) 67–72.

O'Neill, Maura. *Mending a Torn World: Women in Interreligious Dialogue*. Maryknoll, NY: Orbis, 2007.

———. "A Model of the Relationship between Religions Based on Feminist Theory." In *Inter-Religious Models and Criteria*, edited by J. Kellenberger, 37–57. New York: St. Martin's, 1993.

———. *Women Speaking, Women Listening: Women in Interreligious Dialogue.* Faith Meets Faith. Maryknoll, NY: Orbis, 1990.

Oxtoby, Willard, editor. *Religious Diversity: Essays by Wilfred Cantwell Smith.* New York: Harper & Row, 1976.

Phan, Peter. "Multiple Religious Belonging: Opportunities and Challenges for Theology and Church." *Theological Studies* 64/3 (2003) 495–519.

Plantinga, Alvin. "Against Naturalism." In *Knowledge of God*, edited by Alvin Plantinga and Michael Dooley, 1–69. Malden, MA: Blackwell, 2008.

———. *Warrant and Proper Function.* New York: Oxford University Press, 1993.

———. *Warranted Christian Belief.* New York: Oxford University Press, 2000.

———. *Warrant: The Current Debate.* New York: Oxford University Press, 1993.

Plantinga, Alvin, and Nicholas Wolterstorff, editors. *Faith and Rationality: Reason and Belief in God.* Notre Dame, IN: University of Notre Dame Press, 1983.

Pontifical Council for Interreligious Dialogue. *Dialogue and Proclamation: Reflection and Orientations on Interreligious Dialogue and the Proclamation of the Gospel of Jesus Christ* (1991). Online: http://www.vatican.va/roman_curia/pontifical_councils/interelg/documents/rc_pc_interelg_doc_19051991_dialogue-and-proclamatio_en.html.

Porter, Steven. *Restoring the Foundations of Epistemic Justification: A Direct Realist and Conceptualist Theory of Foundationalism.* Lanham, MD: Lexington , 2006.

Potok, Chaim. *The Chosen.* Greenwich, CT: Fawcett, 1987.

———. "Culture Highways." *Religion and Literature* 19/2 (1987) 1–10.

———. *My Name Is Asher Lev.* New York: Anchor, 2003.

Pritchard, Duncan. "Apt Performance and Epistemic Value." *Philosophical Studies* 143/3 (2009) 407–16.

———. "Greco on Knowledge: Virtues, Contexts and Achievements." *The Philosophical Quarterly* 58/232 (2008) 437–47.

———. "Virtue Epistemology and Epistemic Luck." *Metaphilosophy* 34/1–2 (2003) 106–30.

Quinn, Philip. "Towards Thinner Theologies: Hick and Alston on Religious Diversity." *International Journal for Philosophy of Religion* 38/1–3 (1995) 145–64.

Quinn, Philip, and Kevin Meeker, editors. *The Philosophical Challenge of Religious Diversity.* New York: Oxford University Press, 2000.

Race, Alan. *Christians and Religious Pluralism: Patterns in the Christian Theology of Religions.* Maryknoll, NY: Orbis, 1982.

Rahner, Karl. *Foundations of Christian Faith: An Introduction to the Idea of Christianity.* Translated by William van Dyke. New York: Crossroad, 1984.

———. *Hearer of the Word: Laying the Foundation for a Philosophy of Religion.* Translated by Joseph Donceel. New York: Continuum, 1994.

———. *Theological Investigations.* Vol. 5, *Later Writings.* London: Darton, Longman & Todd, 1966.

———. *Theological Investigations.* Vol. 6, *Concerning Vatican Council II.* New York: Herder & Herder, 1971.

Reid, Thomas. *Essays into the Human Mind on the Principle of Common Sense.* Edited by Derek R. Brookes. Edinburgh: Edinburgh University Press, 1997.

Ricoeur, Paul. *The Conflict of Interpretations: Essays in Hermeneutics.* Edited by James M. Edie. Evanston, IL: Northwestern University Press, 1974.

———. *Symbolism of Evil.* Translated by Emerson Buchanan. Boston: Beacon, 1967.

Bibliography

Riggs, Wayne. "Reliability and the Value of Knowledge." *Philosophy and Phenomenological Research* 64/1 (2002) 79–96.

———. "Understanding Virtue and the Virtue of Understanding." In *Intellectual Virtue: Perspectives from Ethics and Epistemology*, edited by Michael DePaul and Linda Zagzebski, 203–26. Oxford: Clarendon, 2007.

———. "What Are the Chances of Being Justified?" *Monist* 81/3 (1998) 452–73.

Roberts, Robert C., and W. Jay Wood. "Proper Function, Emotion, and Virtues of the Intellect." *Faith and Philosophy* 21/1 (2004) 3–24.

Ruparell, Tinu. "The Dialogue Party: Dialogue, Hybridity, and the Reluctant Other." In *Theology and the Religions*, edited by Viggo Mortensen, 235–48. Grand Rapids: Eerdmans, 2003.

Schellenberg, J. L. "Pluralism and Probability." *Religious Studies* 33/2 (1997) 143–59.

———. "Religious Experience and Religious Diversity: A Reply to Alston." *Religious Studies* 30/2 (1994) 151–59.

Schmidt-Leukel, Perry. *Tranformation by Integration: How Inter-faith Encounter Changes Christianity*. London: SCM, 2009.

Schweig, Graham. *The Dance of Divine Love: India's Classic Sacred Love Story: The Rasa Lila of Krishna from the Bhagavata Purana*. Princeton: Princeton University Press, 2005.

Schüssler Fiorenza, Francis. *Foundational Theology: Jesus and the Church*. New York: Crossroad, 1984.

———. "Systematic Theology: Task and Methods." *Systematic Theology: Roman Catholic Perspectives*, edited by Francis Schüssler Fiorenza and John P. Galvin, 1–87. Philadelphia: Fortress, 1991.

Second Vatican Council. *Ad Gentes: Decree on the Mission Activity of the Church* (1965). Online: http://www.vatican.va/archive/hist_councils/ii_vatican_council/documents/vat-ii_decree_19651207_ad-gentes_en.html.

———. *Dei Verbum: Dogmatic Constitution on Divine Revelation* (1965). Online: http://www.vatican.va/archive/hist_councils/ii_vatican_council/documents/vat-ii_const_19651118_dei-verbum_en.html.

———. *Dignitatis Humanae: Declaration on Religious Freedom* (1965). Online: http://www.vatican.va/archive/hist_councils/ii_vatican_council/documents/vat-ii_decl_19651207_dignitatis-humanae_en.html.

———. *Gaudium et Spes: Pastoral Constitution on the Church in the Modern World* (1965). Online: http://www.vatican.va/archive/hist_councils/ii_vatican_council/documents/vat-ii_cons_19651207_gaudium-et-spes_en.html.

———. *Lumen Gentium: Dogmatic Constitution on the Church* (1964). Online: http://www.vatican.va/archive/hist_councils/ii_vatican_council/documents/vat-ii_const_19641121_lumen-gentium_en.html.

———. *Nostra Aetate: Declaration on the Relation of the Church to Non-Christians* (1965). Online: http://www.vatican.va/archive/hist_councils/ii_vatican_council/documents/vat-ii_decl_19651028_nostra-aetate_en.html.

Silver, David. "Religious Experience and the Facts of Religious Pluralism." *International Journal for Philosophy of Religion* 49/1 (2001) 1–17.

Simpson, Gary. *Critical Social Theory: Prophetic Reason, Civil Society, and Christian Imagination*. Minneapolis: Fortress, 2002.

Smith, Wilfred Cantwell. *Wilfred Cantwell Smith: A Reader*. Edited by Kenneth Cracknell. Oxford: Oneworld, 2001.

Bibliography

Solomon, David. "Virtue Ethics: Radical or Routine?" In *Intellectual Virtue: Perspectives from Ethics and Epistemology*, edited by Michael DePaul and Linda Zagzebski, 57–80. Oxford: Clarendon, 2007.

Sosa, Ernest. "How Do You Know?" *American Philosophical Quarterly* 11/2 (1974) 113–22.

———. "Knowing Full Well: The Normativity of Beliefs as Performances." *Philosophical Studies* 142/1 (2009) 5–15.

———. "The Place of Truth in Epistemology." In *Intellectual Virtue: Perspectives from Ethics and Epistemology*, edited by Michael DePaul and Linda Zagzebski, 155–79. Oxford: Clarendon, 2007.

———. "The Raft and the Pyramid: Coherence versus Foundations in the Theory of Knowledge." *Midwest Studies in Philosophy* 5/1 (1980) 3–25.

———. *A Virtue Epistemology: Apt Belief and Reflective Knowledge*. Vol 1. New York: Oxford University Press, 2007.

Speelman, G. "Interreligious Dialogue and Women: My Personal Experience." In *Feminist Perspectives in Pastoral Theology ESWTR Yearbook*, edited by Hedwig Heyer-Wilmes, Lieve Troch, and Rien Bons-Storm, 111–15. Leuven: Peeters, 1998.

Steinfels, Peter. "Beliefs." *New York Times*, March 16, 1991. Online: http://www.nytimes.com/1991/03/16/us/beliefs-385491.html.

Sullivan, Francis. *Salvation Outside the Church? Tracing the History of the Catholic Response*. New York: Paulist, 1992.

Swanton, Christine. *Virtue Ethics: A Pluralistic View*. New York: Oxford University Press, 2003.

———. *True Love: A Practice for Awakening the Heart*. Boston: Shambhala, 1997.

Tilley, Terrence W. "Christian Orthodoxy and Religious Pluralism." *Modern Theology* 2/1 (2006) 51–63.

———. "Incommensurability, Intratextuality, and Fideism." *Modern Theology* 5/2 (1989) 87–111.

———. "'Lord Help My Unbelief': Prayer without Belief." *Modern Theology* 7/3 (1991) 239–47.

———. *Postmodern Theologies: The Challenge of Religious Diversity*. Maryknoll, NY: Orbis 1995.

———. "Reformed Epistemology and Religious Fundamentalism: How Basic Are Our Basic Beliefs?" *Modern Theology* 6/3 (1990) 237–57.

———. *Religious Diversity and the American Experience: A Theological Approach*. New York: Continuum, 2007.

———. "Religious Pluralism as a Problem for 'Practical' Religious Epistemology." *Religious Studies* 30/2 (1994) 161–69.

———. *The Wisdom of Religious Commitment*. Washington, DC: Georgetown University Press, 1995.

Tillich, Paul. *Dynamics of Faith*. New York: Perennial, 1965.

Timmerman, John. "A Way of Seeing: Chaim Potok and Tradition." *The Christian Century* 101/17 (1984) 515–18.

Tracy, David. "Theological Method." In *Christian Theology: An Introduction to Its Traditions and Tasks*, edited by Peter Hodgson and Robert King, 35–60. Philadelphia: Fortress, 1985.

Vogelstein, Eric. "Religious Pluralism and Justified Christian Belief: A Reply to Silver." *International Journal for Philosophy of Religion* 55/3 (2004) 187–92.

Bibliography

Walden, Daniel. "A 'Zwischenmensch' (Between Person) Adrift in the Cultures." *Studies in American Jewish Literature* 4 (1985) 19–25.

Wallace, Mark I. *The Second Naiveté: Barth, Ricoeur, and the New Yale Theology*. Studies in American Biblical Hermeneutics 6. Macon, GA: Mercer University Press, 1995.

Weatherson, Brian. "Disagreements, Philosophical and Otherwise." Unpublished manuscript.

Wheeler, Arthur M. "'Bliks' as Assertions and as Attackable." *Philosophical Studies* 25/3 (1974) 199–205.

White, Roger. "Epistemic Permissiveness." *Philosophical Perspectives* 19/1 (2005) 445–59.

Williams, Bernard. *Ethics and the Limits of Philosophy*. Cambridge, MA: Harvard University Press, 1986.

Williams, Rowan. *Address: Plenary on Christian Identity and Religious Plurality* (2006). Online: http://www.oikoumene.org/en/press-centre/news/archbishop-of-canterbury-promise-and-risk-of-inter-religious-dialogue.

Wisdom, John. "Gods." *Proceedings of the Aristotelian Society* 45 (1945) 185–206.

Wood, Allen. "The Duty to Believe According to Evidence." *International Journal of Philosophy of Religion* 63/1–3 (2008) 7–24.

World Council of Churches. *Baar Statement: Theological Perspectives on Plurality* (1990). Online: http://www.oikoumene.org/en/resources/documents/wcc-programmes/interreligious-dialogue-and-cooperation/christian-identity-in-pluralistic-societies/baar-statement-theological-perspectives-on-plurality.

———. *Guidelines on Dialogue with People of Living Faiths and Ideologies* (1979). Online: http://www.oikoumene.org/en/resources/documents/wcc-programmes/interreligious-dialogue-and-cooperation/interreligious-trust-and-respect/guidelines-on-dialogue-with-people-of-living-faiths-and-ideologies.html.

———. *My Neighbor's Faith and Mine: Theological Discoveries through Interfaith Dialogue* (1986). Online: http://www.oikoumene.org/en/resources/documents/wcc-programmes/interreligious-dialogue-and-cooperation/christian-identity-in-pluralistic-societies/study-guide-my-neighbours-faith-and-mine/index.

———. *Religious Plurality and Christian Self-Understanding* (2006). Online: http://www.oikoumene.org/en/resources/documents/wcc-commissions/faith-and-order-commission/ix-other-study-processes/religious-plurality-and-christian-self-understanding.html.

———. *Report from Interreligious Consultation on "Conversion—Assessing the Reality"* (2006). Online: http://www.oikoumene.org/en/resources/documents/wcc-programmes/interreligious-dialogue-and-cooperation/interreligious-trust-and-respect/report-from-inter-religious-consultation-on-conversion.html.

Wright, Crispin. "The Verification Principle: Another Puncture—Another Patch." *Mind* 98/392 (1989) 611–22.

Wunder, Tyler. "Anti-Naturalism and Proper Function." *Religious Studies* 44/2 (2008) 209–24.

Yearley, Lee. *Mencius and Aquinas: Theories of Virtue and Conceptions of Courage*. Albany: SUNY Press, 1990.

———. "Recent Work on Virtue." *Religious Studies Review* 16/1 (1990) 1–10.

———. "Selves, Virtues, Odd Genres, and Alien Guides." *Journal of Religious Ethics* 25/3 (1997) 127–55.

Zagzebski, Linda. "Religious Luck." *Faith and Philosophy* 11/3 (1994) 397–412.

———. *Virtues of the Mind: An Inquiry into the Nature of Virtue and the Ethical Foundations of Knowledge.* New York: Cambridge University Press, 1996.
———, editor. *Rational Faith: Responses to Reformed Epistemology.* Notre Dame, IN: University of Notre Dame Press, 1994.

Index

Afterlife, 27
Alston, William P., x, xix, 90,
    103–12, 123, 127–35, 138,
    139, 148, 156, 158, 195, 196
"Anonymous Christian," 7, 11
Aquinas, Thomas, 194, 195, 199
Aristotle, x, 104; tradition of virtue
    theory, xix, 113, 132–36,
    138–48, 151, 160, 161, 167,
    175–77, 196, 227
Augustine, Saint, 129

*Baar Statement on Theological
    Perspectives on Plurality*, 223,
    225
Baehr, Jason, 148, 182, 190, 191
Badhwar, Neera, 176, 177
Bah'u'llah, 84
Baha'i, 63, 64, 72, 78, 108, 111, 199
Baldwin, Erik, 31, 32
Barth, Karl, 5
Bifano, Diana Theresa, 80
Blik, 49–53, 82
Braaten, Jane, 136, 148–50, 204
Buddha, 234
Buddhist, 7, 13, 33, 35
Buddhism, 19
Burkle, Howard, 10

Calvin, Jean, 100
Cates, Diana Fritz, 143
Catholic, x, 35, 195, 213, 214,
    216, 217. *See also* Roman
    Catholic Church
Cambridge Platonists, 1

Cantwell Smith, Wilfred, 8–10, 15,
    17, 18
Chopp, Rebecca, 67, 68, 79–81
The Chosen, 162, 165, 170, 232
Circle of participation, 205–11
Clifford, William Kingdon, ix, xviii,
    36–50, 52, 57, 66, 73, 97,
    112, 116, 119, 132, 144, 209
Clooney, Francis X., xx, 25, 26, 181,
    193, 197–99, 201, 207–9, 245
Code, Lorraine, 111, 116, 118, 133,
    138, 147, 159, 179
Community, xix, xx, 55, 63–69, 72,
    73, 76–78, 82–87, 112, 118,
    126–32, 137, 149–54, 158,
    162, 165–67, 172, 173, 179,
    180, 192, 195, 196, 198, 200,
    205, 206, 215–17, 231, 232,
    235, 237, 242–44, 246, 247;
    epistemic community, 87,
    88, 90, 128, 138, 156, 159,
    178; social community, 87,
    240
Comparative theory, 194, 195, 200,
    201
Conversion. *See* transformation
Cornille, Catherine, 235, 242
Cyprian, Saint, 1, 4

Davis, Stephen T., 49
D'Costa, Gavin, xviii, 1–4, 6, 8,
    23–33, 75, 78, 79
Decartes, René, 183
Desika, Vedanta, 199
DiNoia, J. A., 6

Index

Double religious belonging. *See* transformation
Doxastic practices, 103, 106–8, 111
Dialogue and Proclamation, xx, 213–15, 217–21, 226, 227, 246
Driver, Julia, 140–43, 145–47, 152
Duffy, Stephen, 24–26
Dunne, James, 78
Dupuis, Jacques, 1

Egnell, Helene, 81
Episcopalian, 35
Epistemology
  A priori, 24, 26, 44, 53, 64, 67, 74, 76, 86, 89, 90, 127, 137, 139, 178, 200
  A posteriori, 25, 44, 67, 74, 82, 89, 90, 101, 112, 118, 137, 139
  Contemporary, xviii, xix, 23, 36, 46, 57, 89, 127, 133, 176
  Credit view, 183–85
  Externalist, 45–47, 50, 55, 91–93, 99, 101
  Feminist, xvii, 87, 116, 137, 138
  Foundationalist, 38, 39, 47, 53, 55, 58, 59, 76, 91, 95, 99, 103
  Historical debate, xviii, 36
  Intellectual virtue, xix, 111, 114, 115, 119, 135, 136, 138, 144, 147–49, 152, 155, 158, 159, 161, 177, 183, 185–90
  Internalist, 45–47, 53, 55–59, 91, 92, 107, 200
  Luck, 185, 189
  Meta-level virtue, x, 175, 176
  Naturalized, ix, 52, 89–90, 101, 127, 132
  Normative method, 37, 40, 44, 55, 58, 74, 76, 80, 90, 116, 134, 137, 144, 199, 200
  Non-foundationalist, 38, 39, 43–47, 101, 107
  Non-normative method, 37, 52

"On the ground," xvii, 181, 215
Pure virtue, 111, 112, 120, 130
Range of truth, 31
Reformed, 90, 100, 101
Reliabilist, x, 91, 93, 96, 111, 119, 120, 128, 133, 134, 138
Self-reflection; self understanding, 12, 66, 69, 71, 76, 124
Eschatology, xvii, 8, 9; salvation, 10, 29, 30
Essence of the Three Holy Mysteries, 199
"Ethics of Belief" debates, 36, 37, 39, 49
Eucharist, 35, 125, 195
Extra ecclesia nulla salus, 1

Feminism, xvi, 24, 79, 87, 141, 143, 149. *See also* epistemology, feminist
Feldman, Richard, xviii, xix, 36, 53, 55–59, 61, 71, 73, 74, 76, 86–89, 91, 107, 112, 133, 179, 200, 209, 210
Flew, Anthony, xviii, 47–52, 57, 58, 82, 108, 179
Foot, Philippa, 136, 140–42, 144, 146
Flourishing, 151–53, 155, 210
Fredericks, James L., 25, 31

Gale, Richard, 103
Gender, 79–81, 116, 117; roles, 73. *See also* women's experience
Grace, 6, 18, 22, 26, 98, 219
God, 5, 13, 16, 22, 26, 27, 35, 42, 69, 77, 84, 85, 91–95, 100–103, 111, 130, 155, 166, 171, 180, 188, 195, 196, 199–201, 218, 220, 223–25, 235, 236; experience of 32; knowledge of 6, 8, 9, 123; symbolic language, 30, 31
Greco, John, 101, 102, 120–23, 126, 130, 134, 183, 189

Index

Griffiths, Paul, xvii, 2–5, 7, 12–16, 24, 26–33, 53, 54, 75, 78, 79, 94, 98, 179, 200, 227
Groenhout, Ruth, 143
Guidelines on Dialogue with People of Living Faiths and Ideologies, 224, 225, 227
Gutting, Gary, 32, 33

Habermas, Jürgen, 193, 202–6, 212
Habituation, xix
Hankinson Nelson, Lynn, 87
Hare, R. M., xvii, 48–52, 57, 58, 82, 132, 179
Hedges, Paul, 241, 242
Heim, S. Mark, 7–9, 11
Hick, John, 8–10, 15, 17, 18
Hill Fletcher, Jeannine, 62, 63, 80, 81, 240–42
Hinduism, 19, 21, 24, 35, 59, 129, 197, 218
Holy Spirit, 5, 15, 102, 218, 234
Hyun Kyung, Chung, 234

Imago Dei, 199
Interreligious dialogue
  "Bottom-up," xvi, xvii, 67
  Ethical impetus for dialogue; social flourishing, 66–69
  "Top-down," xvi, xvii, 2, 3, 11, 67
Interreligious conflict, 72, 200
Islam, 13, 19, 20, 64, 188, 204

James, William, xviii, 36, 39, 40, 42–47, 50, 51, 53, 57, 90, 107, 132, 170, 194, 209, 210
Jesus Christ, 4–6, 7, 9, 10, 13, 22, 27, 84, 168, 172, 201, 218, 224–26, 242; as Son of God, 19
Judaism, xx, 13, 33, 70, 77, 78, 83, 125, 129, 156, 162, 170; Hasidic, 162–69, 171–73

Justified True Belief (JTB), 45, 46, 119, 187, 189

Kant, Immanuel, 8, 15, 112
Katzoff, Charlotte, 188
Kaufman, Gordon, 30, 31
Knitter, Paul, 1, 4, 5, 7, 9
King, Ursula, 79, 80
Koehl, Andrew, 100
Krishna, 84

Lackey, Jennifer, 184–87
Literalism, 3, 4, 188
London Metaphysical Society, 36, 39

MacIntyre, Alasdair, xix, 48, 50–52, 142, 155–56, 158, 159, 179
Marxism, 24
McClendon, James Wm., 193, 202, 205–8, 210
McDowell, John, 152
McKim, Robert, xviii, xix, 12, 36, 53–59, 61, 62, 71, 73, 74, 76, 86, 87, 89, 91, 107, 108, 112, 133, 179, 200, 209, 214
Mencius, 194, 195
Merton, Thomas, 234
Metaphysic, x; supernatural, 101
Methodological conservatism, 33
Mitchell, Basil, 48, 51, 52, 57, 82, 132
Mohammed, 84, 155, 180, 201
Monotheism, 35
Montmarquet, James, 146, 148
Muslim, 12, 21, 35, 63, 64, 70, 78, 83, 109, 126, 180, 188, 218
My Name is Asher Lev, 162

Narayan, Uma, 81
Nussbaum, Martha, 149, 151–53, 227
Netland, Harold, xvii, 2–4, 6, 8, 9, 16–24, 27–33, 66, 75, 78, 79,

Index

179; functionalist interpretation of religion, 16, 17, 28
New Essays in Philosophical Theology, 47, 49, 51
New Testament, 4, 9
Nichomachean Ethics (NE), 139–41, 145, 160, 176
Nishitani, 7
Non-theism, 13, 101, 102
Nostra Aetate, 217

Office on Interreligious Relations and Dialogue, 243
O'Neill, Maura, 81

Phan, Peter, 242
Philadelphia women's interreligious dialogue group, x, xiii, xvi, xviii, 61–75, 82, 85–87, 90, 108, 111, 125, 126, 132, 143, 144, 150, 160–64, 191, 192, 195, 196, 199–202, 204, 205, 208, 210, 213, 215, 227, 231
Plantinga, Alvin, x, xix, 16, 38, 89–103, 109–12, 119, 120, 123, 127, 130, 133, 183
Plato, 23
The Pluralism Project, 80, 81
Pneumatology, xv, 218, 247
Pontifical Council for Interreligious Dialogue, xx, 213, 217, 219, 243
Potok, Chaim, xx, 156, 162–67, 169, 170, 173, 232
Prima facie justification, 92, 124, 125, 128, 134, 154–56, 178–80, 190, 191, 201, 202, 228
Principle of falsification, 47, 48
Principle of suspension (S-Principle), 53, 55, 73, 85
Principle of tentativity (T-principle), 53, 54, 71, 73

Protestant, x, 5, 213, 214, 216, 220, 221
Problems of Religious Diversity, 12

Quinn, Phillip, 1
Qur'an, 13, 15, 19, 155, 180, 188

Rahner, Karl, 6, 7, 11
Redemptoris Missio, 217
Reid, Thomas, 103
Relativism, xx, 17–18, 181, 182, 190, 191
Religion
Privatized, 23, 27–28, 33, 93, 98, 99, 132
Religious identity, 70, 71, 233
Religious Plurality and Christian Self-Understanding, 223, 224, 226
Revelation, 5
Ricoeur, Paul, 216, 228–31, 240
Riggs, Wayne, 178, 186, 187
Ritual, 32; Purification, 19, 20
Roberts, Robert, 95–97, 120, 130
Roman Catholic Church, xx, xxi, 5, 78, 123, 197, 214, 216–18, 220, 221, 245, 246. *See also* Catholic
Ruparell, Tinu, 80

Salient explanation, 184, 187, 189
Salvation, ix, xv, xvii, 1–10, 16, 19, 26, 28, 30, 35, 218, 223; Universal, 11, 15, 26–27
Schmidt-Leukel, Perry, xxi, 30, 216, 232–40, 243, 244
Schellenberg, J. L., 33
Schüssler Fiorenza, Francis, 212
Second Vatican Council, 5, 217
Secular reason, 23–25, 28
Sefcovic, Enid M. O., 80
Sensus divinitatis, 100–102, 127, 129, 130
Shintoism, 19, 20

Index

Sosa, Ernest, 111–13
Spiritual autobiography, 65, 67, 70, 77, 85, 192, 193
Storytelling, 79, 81, 124, 229
Summa Theologica, 199
Swanton, Christine, 142, 143, 147
Syncretism, 213, 214, 226, 233, 234, 236, 240, 246, 247

Theological-anthropological, xv
Theology
    Comparative, xx, 25, 26, 33
    Hermeneutic, 30, 31, 52, 229
"Theology and Falsification" debate, 36, 44, 45, 48–52, 82, 132
Theories of religious diversity (pluralism), ix, xvi, xvii, 2, 3, 9, 12, 52, 75; exclusivism, 3–8, 10, 14, 21–22, 26, 27, 29, 56; inclusivism, 6–8, 10, 15, 27, 29; pluralism, 7, 8, 10, 11, 15, 26, 27, 29; soteriological point of view, 9–11; belief, 9–11
Thich Nhat Hanh, 129
Thule, Michael, 31
Tilley, Terrence W., 10, 56, 107
Timmerman, John, 173
Tracy, David, 212
Transformation, 68, 71, 181, 193, 206–8, 215, 220, 233, 239; conversion, xx, xxi, 78, 216, 244; double religious belonging/hybridity, xx, xxi, 215, 216, 228, 240, 241–43, 246, 247; returning home, xx, 215, 216, 229, 231, 233
Transformation by Integration: How Inter-faith Encounter Changes Christianity, 216
Trinity, 5, 224

Ultima facie justification, 124, 127, 134, 155, 156, 179–81, 190–93, 201, 202, 204, 205, 208–12, 213, 227, 228, 243, 246, 247
Universal deontological criteria, ix
Universal truth, 10, 11, 15, 20, 137

Virtuous doxastic practice model (VDP theory), x, xix, xx, xxi, 127–39, 141–42, 144–45, 147, 148, 151–55, 160, 175–83, 187, 188, 190–99, 201, 205, 207–9, 212, 213, 215, 216, 227, 228, 231, 232, 237, 238, 240, 243, 244, 246, 247; creativity, 161, 172; four cardinal virtues of, x, xx, 156, 161, 165; judiciousness, 161, 167, 168, 242; primary theories, 195–97, 199; prudence, 161, 169, 172, 243, 244; secondary theories, 195–97, 199; steadfastness, 161, 165, 229, 232

Walden, Daniel, 163
Western philosophical tradition, 23, 139, 194
Williams, Bernard, 146
Williams, Rowan, 225
"The Will to Believe," 36, 41
Wisdom, John, 48
Wittgenstein, Ludwig, 15, 103
Women's experience, xvii, xviii, 65–73, 79, 80, 117
Wood, Jay, 95, 96, 97, 120, 130
World Council of Churches xx, xxi, 213–17, 221–25, 227, 234, 243–47

Yearly, Lee, xx, 181, 193–99, 208, 209, 227

Index

Zagzebski, Linda, x, xix, 89, 90, 111–34, 138, 139, 147, 148, 158, 162, 178, 195, 106

www.ingramcontent.com/pod-product-compliance
Lightning Source LLC
Chambersburg PA
CBHW070238230426
43664CB00014B/2342